Judicial Advocates
and Procurators

THE CATHOLIC UNIVERSITY OF AMERICA

CANON LAW STUDIES

NO. 133

Judicial Advocates and Procurators

AN HISTORICAL SYNOPSIS AND COMMENTARY

A DISSERTATION

Submitted to the Faculty of Canon Law
of the Catholic University of America
in Partial Fulfillment of theRequirements
for the Degree of Doctor of Canon Law

By

James J. Hogan, S. T. L., J. C. L.

Priest of the Diocese of Trenton

BeardBooks

Washington, D.C.

Copyright 1941 by Catholic University of America

Reprinted 2000 by Beard Books, Washington, D.C.

ISBN 1-58798-061-4

Printed in the United States of America

FOREWORD

The procedural law of the Catholic Church, as embodied in the fourth book of the Code of Canon Law, is an admirable piece of jurisprudence. Indeed, recognizing the perfection of the ecclesiastical process, eminent jurists are unanimous in paying tribute to its ability in arriving at just judgment. Of such perfection the Church is reasonably proud. Moreover, since the canonical trial is an institution of such decided importance, the Church is most anxious that this standard be maintained. Needless to say, the perfection of this procedural law will be preserved and its standards prove efficacious in proportion as human agents concerned are imbued with due appreciation of its canonical norms and faithfully apply them.

Specifically, in this connection, it may safely be said that nothing is more conducive to the smooth functioning of diocesan tribunals than the presence of thoroughly trained advocates and procurators. An attempt will be made in this study to arouse keener appreciation for, and to inspire more faithful application of the Church's law regarding these indispensable tribunal assistants. Accordingly, section one of this dissertation outlines in summary fashion the historical background and development of the ecclesiastical judicial advocate and procurator. Section two is devoted to a canonical commentary with reference to the present legislation as it affects these officials. It should be remarked, however, that Chapter IX has been designed not as a commentary upon the various phases of the canonical process, but rather with the intention of indicating practical points with which legal assistants may concern themselves at these stages.

Notwithstanding differences between the two offices, differences of origin, of development, and of function, historically they have always and everywhere been associated in law, and, in most places, in practice. The simultaneous treatment herein contained is justified by this combination characteristic of ecclesiastical law as well as of civil law.

The writer avails himself of this opportunity to express sentiments of gratitude to His Excellency, the Most Reverend William A. Griffin, D. D., Bishop of Trenton, and to His Excellency, the Most Reverend Moses E. Kiley, D. D., Archbishop of Milwaukee, for the opportunity afforded him for graduate study. In like manner, he acknowledges with sincere appreciation the helpful direction of the Faculty of the School of Canon Law of the Catholic University of America in the preparation of this study.

TABLE OF CONTENTS

CHAPTER VI

CHAPTER VII

CHAPTER VIII

CHAPTER IX

JUDICIAL ADVOCATES
AND PROCURATORS

ABBREVIATIONS

AAS — Acta Apostolicae Sedis
ASS — Acta Sanctae Sedis
Bull. Rom. — Bullarium Romanum
C. — Codex Justinianus
C. Th. — Codex Theodosianus
Coll. Lac. — Collectio Lacensis
CSEL — *Corpus Scriptorum Ecclesiasticorum Latinorum*
D — Digesta Justiniani
Fontes — Codicis Iuris Canonici Fontes
Instructio — Matrimonial Instruction, S. C. S., 15, Aug., 1936.
Mansi — *Sacrorum Conciliorum Nova et Amplissima Collectio*
MGH — *Monumenta Germaniae Historica*
MPG — Migne, *Patrologia Graeca*
MPL — Migne, *Patrologia Latina*
Normae — Normae Sacrae Romanae Rotae Tribunalis, 29 June, 1934
NOV. — Novellae Justiniani
S. C. S. — Sacred Congregation of the Sacraments

PRELIMINARY NOTIONS

Canonical literature makes frequent mention of advocates and procurators. Today, for example, the *advocatus diaboli* is an important official, while in more ancient times considerable emphasis centered upon the *advocati armati, advocati jurisdictionis,* and *advocati administrationis.* Similarly, with regard to procurators, various categories include fiscal and religious procurators, and those involved in marriage by proxy. This study is concerned with a specific type of advocate and procurator, namely, of those who are appointed *ad lites.*

For the purpose of orientation, it may be noted that an ecclesiastical trial signifies the legal discussion and settlement before an ecclesiastical tribunal of a controversy in an affair concerning which the Church has the right to judge.[1] Furthermore, since judicial advocates and procurators owe their existence and importance to the fact that they assist the *partes in causa* (*actor* and *reus*), the status of the parties should be understood. The *actor* is the person who brings an action against another. He is the plaintiff who seeks a thing or demands the vindication of a right, if it be a contentious trial, or who demands punishment for the guilty if he be the accuser in a criminal trial. The *reus,* or *pars conventa,* is one against whom an action is instituted. He is the defendant from whom, or against whom, something is sought.

As it is commonly used in everyday life, the term advocate denotes a person who has been called upon to render assistance: *ad auxilium vocatus.* In particular, the ecclesiastical judicial advocate is one, approved by competent ecclesiastical authority, who conducts a case for a client before a church tribunal. The rôle of advocate in this sense, whose civil counterpart we know as the counsellor at law, implies an exposition before the court of the arguments, whether of law or of fact, which lead to a vindication of the client's right under discussion.

Historically, many terms have been associated with this office: *patronus, orator, jurisconsultus, causidicus, togatus,* and *scholasticus,* to name a few. However, the Roman Law, and, later, the Decretal Law of the Church, always combined these varied designations under the

---

1. Can. 1552, § 1.

more general title *de postulando.* According to Ulpian's classical definition, *postulare* signified: *"Desiderium suum vel amici sui, apud eum qui iurisdictioni praeest, in iure exponere vel alterius desiderio contradicere."*[2]

Noteworthy divisions of the judicial advocates may be summarized as follows:

(a) *Voluntary* and *necessary,* depending upon the free acceptance of a client's request for legal assistance, or the compulsory assumption of a case upon court designation.

(b) *Ordinary* and *extraordinary,* according as they are approved and assigned for the office in a stable, general fashion, or only admitted for a particular case.

(c) *Public* and *private:* of these the first class is engaged in fiscal cases and in cases involving the public good of the Church, in which sense the *defensor vinculi* and *promotor iustitiae* may be regarded as public advocates, and the second class, with which we are concerned, is engaged in private cases.

In a general sense, a procurator, *pro alio curator,* is an agent. *"Procurator est qui aliena negotia mandato domini administrat."*[3] In other words, he is a person commissioned by a principal to act in the latter's name, to transact his business, and to manage his affairs when he, the principal, is unable or unwilling to attend to them personally. More particularly, the judicial procurator, *ad lites,* is a person legitimately appointed, and admitted by the ecclesiastical court, for the purpose of representing one of the principals, or parties, before that tribunal. As such, the judicial procurator is distinguished from the procurator *ad negotia,* commissioned for matters of a non-judicial nature.

Distinctions with reference to judicial procurators include the following:

(a) *General* and *special,* according as they are appointed for all cases or for a particular case.

2. D (3, 1) 2: cc. 1-3, X, *de postulando,* I, 37.
3. D (3, 3) 1.

(b) The general procurators may be deputed *cum libera* [administratione] or only *simpliciter*, depending upon whether or not they possess full power and freedom to act in any and all cases.

(c) *Principal* and *substitute:* the former are directly commissioned by one of the parties, the latter only indirectly or through the appointment made by the principal procurator.

(d) *Voluntary* and *necessary*, according as they are freely commissioned by the parties or assigned by law or by the court.

(e) *Genuine, presumed*, and *false*, depending upon the possession of a legitimate mandate, of a presumed mandate, or of no mandate at all.

(f) In *rem alienam* and in *rem suam:* the former represent another in court in a case which involves something beneficial accruing only to the principal; the latter represent another, but with benefit therefrom coming to themselves.

(g) With regard to the appointment of a plurality of procurators, they may be commissioned *simpliciter cum aliis*, or *in solidum*. In the first instance, joint action is required. In the second, individual action is permitted, with preference going to the one who inaugurates proceedings.

It has been remarked that these officials who defend the rights of others and who represent them in court are indispensable. Such a necessity becomes obvious when one considers the problems confronting the ordinary *actor* and *reus*. In every formal process a twofold responsibility devolves upon the parties. In the first place, the plaintiff must invoke the law regarding his claim and establish the facts upon which that claim is based. On the other hand, the defendant, taking exception to that contention, must petition the law in his own defense. Secondly, the parties must conform to and abide by the norms and regulations established by legitimate authority for the valid conducting of a judicial process. Needless to say, the average person cannot be expected to assume such functions in a satisfactory manner.

As a result, in order that the law may be properly invoked, and proofs presented in such a way as to demonstrate that the law corresponds to the facts, the assistance of an advocate is practically essential.

Similarly, in view of the numerous judicial acts that must be properly formulated in the interests of the parties, it becomes necessary to rely upon the aid of a procurator who, legitimately commissioned, is capable of representing the parties in this regard before the tribunal.[4]

---

4. Wernz-Vidal, *Ius Canonicum*, VI, *De Processibus* (Romae, 1928), p. 196, note 3; Roberti, *De Processibus* (2 vols., Romae, 1926), I, 324.

PART I

HISTORICAL CONSPECTUS

CHAPTER I

JUDICIAL ADVOCATES AND PROCURATORS IN ROMAN LAW

ARTICLE 1. ADVOCATES

A. *Historical Development of the Office*

It is in one of Rome's earliest institutions, that of patronage, that we discover the origin of the Roman advocate. Under the broad responsibility of general protection, the patron assumed the particular duty of representing his client in court and of defending him.

Gradually, however, the system of patronage fell into desuetude, and, as a result, it became customary for one requiring legal assistance to consult or to obtain the services of anyone available. Nevertheless, even to the last days of the Republic, one who defended another in court retained the old designation *patronus*. It was likewise during the Republican era that other titles began to be associated with this office. The term *advocatus* was employed to signify one who accompanied a litigant into court, assisting merely by counsel, *ad auxilium vocatus*. Actual defense or pleading on behalf of the client was entrusted to the *orator*.

It is noteworthy that, prior to the third century B. C., Rome possessed no legal profession as such. That fact is not surprising when it is remembered that a legal development follows the trend of a civilization. It was at this moment in history that a struggling agricultural nation began its military and commercial ascent to empire. Consequently, professional skill had not hitherto been a primary requisite in the legal adviser. Rather was success measured by the impression one could create before the magistrate *in iure* and before the judge *in iudicio*. In fact, even down through the classical period of Roman jurisprudence technical knowledge was not subject to public investigation.

Already in the fourth century B. C., a knowledge and practice of the law, so long enshrined among the *arcana* of the priestly college, began to be secularized. Its increasing communication to the world at large was proportionate to the inroads of plebeian influence. Finally, in 254 B. C., an innovation appeared with the first plebeian *pontifex maximus*, Tiberius Coruncanius. Those requiring legal advice were afforded the assistance of public consultation. Such a departure led to the rise of a new class of public men, men skilled in the law and prepared to render aid in legal matters. These advisers were known, from the first century B. C., as *iurisconsulti*.[1] At first the jurisconsult remained at home preparing briefs and advising clients with regard to proper procedure. Soon, however, like his modern counterpart, he added to his legal documents and opinions actual court defense. But whereas the patron and orator had generally appeared in criminal trials and the private trials before a jury, the jurisconsult was accustomed to appear before the tribunal of the *praetor urbanus* and the *praetor peregrinus*.

With the advent of Augustus (30 B. C.-14 A. D.) a change occurred which elevated the jurisconsults to a new and select status. Previously their opinions had not been fortified by any particular official weight. Now, on the contrary, the jurist Masurius Sabinus became the first jurisconsult authorized to exercise the privilege of *ius respondendi*, which rendered professional legal opinions authoritative. That is to say, the opinions of certain licensed lawyers were sanctioned by imperial authority, so much so that under certain conditions they exerted a binding force upon the judiciary. The select group of lawyers so privileged retained the name jurisconsult.[2]

Under the early Empire the various names *patronus, orator advocatus, iurisconsultus,* began to be used interchangeably, as they already were in the reign of Claudius, 41-54 A. D.[3]

A more general term, too, now designated this combination or office, *postulare,* a term which passed into the Church's Decretal law. According to the classical definition of Ulpian, *postulare* meant: *"Desiderium*

---

1. Pacchioni, *Corso di Diritto Romano* (3 vols., Torino, 1918), I, 63; Sherman, *Roman Law in the Modern World* (3 vols., New York, 1924), I, 39.

2. Sherman, *op. cit.*, I, 63.

3. Tacitus, *Annales*, 11, 7.

*suum vel amici sui apud eum qui iurisdictioni praeest, in iure exponere
vel alterius desiderio contradicere.*"[4]

During the imperial era the Roman advocate was looked upon as a
member of a definite order of society. His profession was now highly
organized, recognized by the State, and subject to State regulation. He
belonged to one of several colleges or corporations which by its own
peculiar statutes determined his rights and privileges, and established
sanctions regarding personal conduct and attention to duty.[5]

The Roman bar of the later Empire, dating from Constantine, was
divided into two sections. The first, a *collegium,* or corporate body,
comprised the advocates properly so called. Every city had its cor-
poration with a definite number of lawyers fixed by law and made
public. Side by side with special privileges existed a special discipline
regarding duties. The second class was constituted by supernumeraries.
They belonged to no organization, had no fixed locality, and possessed
nothing in the way of special privilege. While awaiting vacancies in
the superior order, they were permitted to practice in inferior courts.
Sons of lawyers in the higher group were given preference by law.[6]

With regard to position and privilege, none were more highly favored than the advocates defending the patrimonial interests of the
State, the *advocati fisci.* This office, originally introduced by Hadrian
(117-138), admitted members only by competitive selection.[7]

B. *Qualifications*

Roman law always maintained the principle that anyone who could
legally bring an action, or anyone who sustained a lawsuit, could be
assisted in court. While in Justinian law a party was free to conduct
his case personally or to avail himself of aid, the law of earlier imperial days still obliged the litigant desiring legal service to retain a
member of the bar. In like manner old praetorian prescriptions still

4. D (3, 1) 2; cc. 1-3, X, *de postulando,* I, 37.

5. C (2, 6) 6, 1; 6, 4; 7.

6. C (2, 7) 8; 11; 13; 17.

7. C (2, 7) 10; C (2, 8); Jolowicz, *Historical Introduction to Roman Law*
(Cambridge, 1932), 341.

enabled the court to assign adequate defense where it was deemed necessary.[8]

Moreover, although at last more than one lawyer was permitted to represent each side, another old ruling bound the court to assure adequately proportionate representation.[9]

On the other hand, not everyone could plead as an advocate. Those under eighteen years of age and also all deaf persons were entirely excluded from this rôle. It was likewise forbidden for certain people to plead for others; women, the blind, those convicted of capital crimes, calumniators, hired gladiators, and those guilty of certain *turpia*, could not act in such an office.[10] In addition, those branded with infamy were barred from pleading save for themselves and for certain others, such as for members of the family, relatives, patrons, wards, and the insane.[11] Soldiers, those afflicted with chronic infirmity, and those frequently absent on state business were not considered proper selections for the office of advocate.[12] Not only slaves, but even freedmen, although skilled, were barred from the practice of law.[13] Then again, it was but natural that a person could not fulfill the rôle of judge and advocate in the same case.[14] Finally, in Justinian law, only those professing the orthodox Christian Faith were admitted to legal practice. At the same time all clerics were restrained from occupying such positions in the civil tribunals.[15]

Since the possession of technical legal ability assumed an increasing importance, especially during the later Empire, it will be considered briefly under the general heading of legal education.

C. *Legal Training*

The first traces of legal training at Rome may be said to derive from the last years of the Republic. It was not before 100 B. C. that the

8. D (1, 16) 9, 5; D (3, 1) 1, 4.
9. C (2, 6) 7; Mackenzie, *Roman Law* (London, 1898), p. 444.
10. D (3, 1) 1, 5; 1, 6.
11. D (3, 1) 1, 8, 11.
12. D (3, 3) 54.
13. C (2, 6) 2.
14. C (2, 6) 6.
15. C (1, 4) 15; C (2, 6) 8; Nov. (123, 6).

law began to assume definitely scientific forms; and then the development was due principally to the writings of the jurist Scaevola. It is at this point that the private law school arises; namely, when the jurisconsult adds to his *officium respondendi, agendi, cavendi,* that of *docendi.* Starting with mere *auditores,* a system of simply observing the lawyer at his work, the school soon boasted a schedule of lectures and instruction. Down to the reign of Diocletian (284-305 A. D.), a period which, incidentally, embraces the golden age of Roman jurisprudence, the lawyer was free to gather such a group about himself.[16]

In the reign of Augustus (30 B. C.-14 A. D.) two great rival law schools had arisen, founded by the jurists Capito and Labeo, and named, after their respective pupils, the Sabinians and the Proculians. To the end of the second century Rome's lawyers were sharply divided into these two opposing schools.[17]

At Rome, in the time of Marcus Aurelius (161-180 A. D.), there existed many established legal schools. And it is from about this time that they are to be found spreading throughout the Empire. However, it was not until the reign of Diocletian that the State began to extend recognition and financial support to the great schools flourishing at Rome, Constantinople, Athens, Alexandria, and Caesarea in Cappadocia.[18]

Under the later Empire all arbitrary modes of teaching law disappeared with the establishment of a prescribed five year legal course. Studies, texts, order and method were all well defined.[19]

This course of study was brought to a high state of perfection under Justinian. A study of the entire *Corpus Iuris Civilis* was spread over the five year period. Legislation was enacted with regard to the discipline and government of the schools, and with regard to requirements for admission to the bar.[20]

16. 17, *Yale Law Journal,* 499, May, 1908.

17. Roby, *Introduction to the Study of Justinian's Digest* (Cambridge University Press, 1886), pp. 130-141; Karlowa, *Romische Rechtsgeschichte* (2 vols., Leipzig, 1885-1901), I, 709.

18. Muirhead, *Roman Law* (2. ed. London, 1899), p. 400; Karlowa, *Rom. Rechtsgeschichte,* I, 1022.

19. Sherman, *Roman Law in the Modern World,* I, 140.

20. Jolowicz, *Historical Introduction to Roman Law,* p. 465.

From Justinian's prefatory constitution to the Digest (*"Omnem rei publicae,"* 16 Dec., 533) it is evident that the Roman system of legal education was primarily a text book system, scientifically combining text with lectures and cases. This was the method sanctioned in the final words of the Constitution.[21]

D. *Remuneration*

In the early days of the Republic the rendering of legal assistance had been entirely gratuitous. However, with the breakdown of the system of patronage there was an increasing emphasis placed on the question of fees in the form of gifts, so much so, that exactions soon constituted a grave abuse. As a result, the *Lex Cincia,* passed in 204 B. C., prohibited the reception of fees for legal assistance.[22]

Owing to the fact that this law carried no sanction, it received scant observance. Fees continued to be demanded, granted, and accepted. Once again there was an attempt to remedy the situation as Augustus revived the old *Lex Cincia.* But once again, too, the regulation failed to achieve its desired end.[23]

The principle of an adequate *honorarium* gained admittance into Roman jurisprudence for the first time under Claudius (41-54 A. D.). This emperor, and later Nero (54-68 A. D.), enacted laws governing amounts, which remained in force to the time of Justinian.[24]

The right to remuneration, since the lawyer's services were not calculable by pecuniary standards, was of an honorary nature. And modern law has been strongly influenced by Roman enactments in this regard, designed to uphold the honor of the legal profession. Pacts, agreements, contracts, and excessive fees were frequently punished by expulsion from the profession.[25]

No greater tribute, says Sherman, has ever been paid the legal profession than the following praise bestowed upon it by Emperors Leo

---

21. "... quae omnia obtinere sancimus in omne aevum, ab omnibus tam professoribus quam legum auditoribus et librariis et ipsis et iudicibus observanda."
22. Tacitus, *Annales,* 11, 5.
23. Dionysius Cassius, 54, 185.
24. Tacitus, *Annales,* 11, 7; Suetonius, *Nero,* 17.
25. Mackenzie, *Roman Law,* p. 446; D (2, 14) 53; D (17, 1) 7; C (2, 6) 6, 5; 6, 6; 6, 2.

and Anthemius, 469 A. D.: "The lawyers who clarify the ambiguous facts of litigation, and who by the strength of their defensive skill exhibited in both criminal and civil suits rescue other persons in danger of ruin and restore their fortunes, are not less useful to the world than soldiers who serve their country and their homes on the battlefield. . . ."[26]

ARTICLE 2. PROCURATORS

A. *Historical Development of the Office*

Unlike the office of advocate, that of *procurator ad lites* was entirely unknown in ancient Greece. Even in Roman Law its development was of a much later date. During the first stage of Roman civil procedure, the period of the *legis actiones,* representation of the parties by another, whether *in iure* or *in iudicio,* was impossible. It was excluded by the accepted principle: *"Nemo alieno nomine lege agere potest."*[27] Consequently, the judicial procurator was unknown at Rome practically down to the beginning of the Christian era.

It is noteworthy that, by way of exception under certain circumstances, the principle admitted relaxation. The *Lex Hostilia,* for example, permitted representation in cases of theft which harmed one who was absent because of military service. And similarly in the cases of theft harming those who had not yet attained the age of puberty. Other instances, too, are to be found, such as controversy over one's juridical status, cases involving interests of the State, and representation of wards, minors, and the insane.[28]

Strictly considered it cannot be said that the principle of judicial representation found a prompt reception when the process assumed a new trend with the introduction of the formulary system. The very concept of the *formulae* was founded on the supposition that a litigant would undertake to pursue his own right.

Some historians trace the initial admission of legal representation to the *cognitoris datio.* This official, the *cognitor,* appears during the

26. C (2, 7) 14.
27. G. (4, 82) ; E. Costa, *Profilo Storico del Processo Civile Romano* (Rome, 1918), p. 121.
28. Inst. (4, 10).

period of the *legis actiones,* as one empowered to act *in iudicio* in certain cases, e. g., for those impeded by senility or illness from appearing. Solemnly, according to a set formula, the *cognitor* was constituted for a particular suit in the presence of the adversary. Thereafter he acted in his own name as a substitute for the person whose place he assumed. In this capacity the *cognitor* bound his principal as efficiently as if the principal himself had acted. Repetition of action in the same matter was thus rendered impossible. Prior to the *contestatio litis,* both parties were free to change the *cognitor* or to act personally. Afterward legitimate cause had to be shown.[29]

With the advent of the formulary system, the *cognitor* becomes a generally recognized judicial representative. His services are no longer restricted to specific cases.

It is likewise during the formulary period of Roman procedure that the procurator appears, that is, early in the Empire.[30] Historical indications point to the early procurator as a procurator *omnium bonorum,* a universal patrimonial administrator. In this capacity he would interest himself in all the affairs and negotiations of his principal, including actions. Gradually, however, it became customary to designate a procurator specifically *ad lites,* one not necessarily a lawyer, but one who, after the *contestatio litis,* would become *dominus litis.*

By the time of Justinian the principle of representation was definitely established. The procurator *ad lites* had become a figure of considerable importance in Roman Law. His profession was well established, recognized, and regulated by law.[31]

29. Debray, *De la représentation en justice par le cognitor* (Paris, 1892), p. 106; Roby, *Roman Private Law* (2 vols., Cambridge, 1902), II, 378, G (4, 82, 83, 97, 98).

30. Bertolini, *Appunti Didattici di Diritto Romano* (2 vols., Torino, 1914), II, 266; Buckland, W. W., *A Manual of Roman Private Law* (Cambridge, 1925), p. 405.

31. Eisele, *Cognitor und Procurator; Untersuchungen zur Geschichte der processualen Stellvertretung* (Tubingen, 1881). This work treats of the historical development of legal representation from the period of the *legis actiones* to the time of Justinian. P. Collinet, *Procedure Par Libelle* (Paris, 1932), 70 sq., 140 sq., 184 sq.; V. Scialoja, *Studi Giuridici,* I, *Diritto Romano* (Rome, 1933), p. 170 sq.

It may be pointed out that, while the *cognitor* disappeared during the Justinian period, one principal difference always served to distinguish the two offices. Whenever a *cognitor* represented a party, the judgment in the suit was enforced by and against his principal. On the contrary, a procurator had control of the suit, was responsible on an adverse judgment, and if successful had the right to sue upon the judgment.[32]

B. *The Mandatum*

Processual representation in Roman Law was based upon a contractual relationship of mandate. At first, during the formulary period in which the office of procurator arose, the granting of a mandate was not the strictly formal element of procedure such as we know it. The necessary authorization could be given even orally or by messenger, without any definite form, without, too, the opponent's presence or knowledge.[33]

In fact, a custom soon arose whereby a procurator could stand in judgment without a mandate, given certain conditions and circumstances. For example, some lawyers felt that a case assumed in good faith, with the necessary security granted, needed no mandate. And it is certain that children, parents, and relatives, when not legally impeded, could bring action for relatives without a mandate, provided it was not contrary to the wishes of the latter.[34]

Needless to say, it was inevitable that a great deal of litigation should arise with regard to challenging the fact and the validity of representation in court. Consequently, we find in the Justinian period an increasing amount of legislation concerning the mandate.

Diligent observance of the stipulations or limitations in the mandate had long been provided for by law. To such an extent was this true, that for certain acts a special mandate was required for validity.[35]

32. Roby, *Roman Private Law*, II, 380.

33. G (4, 84).

34. Bertolini, *Appunti Didattici di Diritto Romano*, II, 265; G (4, 84); D (3, 3) 40, 4; D (3, 3) 8, 1; C (2, 12) 12.

35. D (17, 1) 5; D (3, 3) 60; C (2, 12) 10.

C. *The Satisdatio*

With the admission and development in Roman jurisprudence of the principle of judicial representation, there arose a system of guarantees, whereby the principals were assured that such representation would not jeopardize just claims and defense. For example, let it be supposed that a defendant was represented by either a *cognitor* or a *procurator*. In that case the plaintiff, being mindful of the principle: *"bis de eadem re ne sit actio,"* possessed the right to demand of the defendant the *cautio iudicatum solvi*, thereby assuring execution of the sentence. Should the defendant be represented by a *cognitor*, he himself granted this *satisdatio;* whereas in the case of a procurator, the *cautio* was provided by that official.

On the other hand, when we find the plaintiff represented, it is necessary to make a distinction. If a *cognitor* brought action, it wasn't necessary to offer guarantee to the defendant. A second plea was impossible since it was considered that the plaintiff had acted in his own name. A procurator, however, did not bind his principal in this' manner, that is to say, did not render him incapable of acting a second time. As a result, the defendant, seeking assurance that the action of the procurator would be recognized as the action of his principal, could demand of the procurator the *cautio ratam rem dominum habiturum,* or the *cautio de rato*. This, of course, would not exclude the possibility of appeal, nor did it imply forfeiture when the procurator was not legitimately appointed.[36]

This security meant not a pledge or deposit of money, but a promise given in reply to a stipulation. Such stipulations were required by the courts, and were not subject to alteration without official approval. Later, with more rigid legislation regarding the mandate, came proportionate exemption and mitigation of the *cautio*.

D. *Qualifications*

It is hardly necessary to point out that everyone did not enjoy the right to appoint a processual procurator, or that not everyone was

---

36. G (4, 84), (4, 97) ; D (3, 3) 39, 1; Bertolini, *Appunti Didattici di Diritto Romano,* II, 266; Collinet, *Procedure Par Libelle,* pp. 182, 188; Buckland, *A Manual of Roman Private Law,* 406.

permitted to conduct a case in court *nomine alieno*. Roman Law here, too, listed total and partial exclusions of divers kinds. In general, anyone could appoint or be appointed unless expressly barred. Consequently, the more common prohibitions might be noted. Transgression of these legal restrictions opened the door for the *exceptio procuratoria*.[37]

Women, while they could sue for themselves, could not act for others, not even for an absent husband. An exception was made, for example, in the case of a daughter acting for defenseless, sick, and aged parents.[38]

As with advocates, here, too, the blind, infamous, and soldiers in active service were excluded. Again, in order that the case might stand on its own merits, those in authority were not admitted as procurators.[39]

With regard to the appointing of a representative, certain classes of those branded with infamy lacked capacity. Furthermore, although a woman could appoint a procurator without the authority of her guardian, a girl could not. Finally, sons and daughters yet under the *patria potestas* were restricted to those cases in which they themselves could bring action, as, for example, in cases involving injury.[40]

37. D (3, 3) 43, 1.
38. C (2, 12) 4; 18; D (3, 3) 41; Inst. (4, 4) 2.
39. C (2, 13) 1.
40. D (3, 3) 8; Roby, *Roman Private Law*, II, 326.

CHAPTER II

ADVOCATES AND PROCURATORS IN CANON LAW
FROM THE EARLY CHURCH TO GRATIAN

ARTICLE 1

PROCEDURAL BACKGROUND OF THE EARLY CHURCH
IN RELATION TO THESE OFFICIALS

The infant Church, quite naturally, had to contend with judicial difficulties of a spiritual and temporal nature among the faithful. While it is true that the Church did not lack canonical principles in these matters,[1] the very nature of this nascent, persecuted society, despite its internal freedom, rendered impossible the immediate formation of a definite, formal and complete canonical procedure. As a result it is not surprising that one finds no mention of ecclesiastical advocates and procurators in the Church of the first and second century. This absence of information, it might be remarked, is rendered all the more intelligible when it is remembered that no indication of such offices is derived from the Old Testament.[2]

In the course of time, however, there arose a very real and urgent need for the establishment and adoption of a more orderly execution

1. I Tim., V, 19; I Cor., VI, 1; V, 1; II Cor., II, 10; XIII, 10; Tertullian, *Apologeticus* (c. 197), c. 39 — *MPL*, I, 469; *Adv. Marcionem* (c. 207), Lib. V, c. 12 — *MPL*, II, 501; St. Cyprian, *Ep. 59, Ad Cornelium* (252), c. 14 — *MPL*, III, 818; *Didascalia:* this collection, dating from early in the third century, reflects the ancient norms and practice of the Eastern Church with regard to criminal and contentious trials in Lib. II, cc. 37-43, 44-45. Cf. F. X. Funk, *Didascalia et Constitutiones Apostolorum* (Paderborn, 1905).

2. This is no way implies that judicial defense was unknown. The assistance of Daniel on behalf of Susanna provides one clear illustration of that: cf. Dan. XIII. Nor is there any intention to discount the fact that many illustrious Christians of the early Church followed the legal profession: cf. "Earliest Traces of Christian Roman Advocates", a paper read by R. P. Harding before the Riccobono Seminar of Roman Law at Catholic University, Nov. 4, 1940. For an outline of the concept of advocate in the sense in which Christ, Mary, and the Saints might be called advocates, cf. Grabowski, "Adwokatura" — *Ateneum Kaplanskie*, XXXIII (1934), 252 sq.

of judgment. With peace restored to the Church, the Bishop's Forum was heavily taxed.[3] It will be recalled that, owing to the unwillingness of the Christians to bring their disputes before the civil tribunals, there arose another system of adjudication, the ecclesiastical forum. From Constantine (306-337) the *audientia episcopalis* obtained concurrent jurisdiction with the secular courts whenever both parties preferred the former. In fact, it appears that soon one party could even remove a suit to the episcopal court against the will of the other.[4] Under the Emperors Arcadius (398) and Valentinian (452), however, mutual consent was prescribed for entering the episcopal tribunal.[5] Of particular interest here is the fact that such an ecclesiastical system was officially recognized by the State from the fourth century, and that it continued to exert an ever widening influence, as is evident already in the Theodosian Code. That in turn it produced many effects upon Roman civil and criminal procedure is quite manifest in Justinian Law.[6]

Needless to say, with the resulting necessity of an *ordo judiciorum* in general arose the need for judicial advocates and procurators in particular, two officials who have always occupied important rôles in any well ordered system of procedure. Such ecclesiastical officials do appear at an early date. However, although one may trace the fact of their ancient existence and something of their development, it is impossible to discover anything considerable in the way of early canonical legislation touching the offices. That is to say, practically no regulations derive from the Church as from an original source of law, regarding, for example, rights, duties, appointment, qualifications, and removal.

In this connection, it must be remembered, as a matter of historical fact, that when the Church began to seek for procedural guidance and

3. C. Th. (16, 2) 12, 23, 39, 41, 47; Sherman, *Roman Law in the Modern World*, I, 130; Boyd, *The Ecclesiastical Edicts of the Theodosian Code* (New York: Columbia University Press, 1905), p. 87.

4. CUQ, *Institutions Juridiques des Romains* (2 vols., Paris, 1891-1902), II, 868.

5. L. Wenger, *Institutionen des Römischen Zivilprozessrechts* (München, 1925), p. 333; Muirhead, *Roman Law*, p. 357.

6. M. Roberti, "Cristianesimo e Collezione Giustinianee", *Cristianesimo e Diritto Romano* (Milano, 1935), p. 59.

to find it, as she actually began to do in early councils,[7] she found herself in a world whose civil and criminal procedure was Roman. Starting with the epistles of St. Paul, early ecclesiastical writings breathe a knowledge of Roman Law. Especially is this apparent in the works of the legally trained Tertullian and Lactantius. Consequently it is not difficult to realize how perfectly natural it was for the Church to turn to the Roman *ordo judiciarius*, as to a vast quarry, from which to draw the foundation stones of her own judicial edifice. As an illustration of this point, witness the position of Pope Gregory the Great (590-604), who did not hesitate, in the absence of canonical legislation, to adopt civil procedural laws.[8] It is clear, therefore, that supreme ecclesiastical authority did recognize in the Roman Law of procedure a subsidiary source for ecclesiastical processual law. This does much to explain the lack of early canonical norms with regard to advocates and procurators in particular. Generally taken, the existing civil requirements and prohibitions were admirably suited to the Church's purpose.

With regard to this consideration of civil influence upon ecclesiastical law in the early Church, one might justly inquire into the contribution of Germanic Law. Here, again, it is to be admitted, the Church derived certain new judicial elements.[9] In view of a constantly developing culture among the Franks in Gaul, the Anglo-Saxons in Britain, the Visigoths in Spain, and the Lombards in Italy, that was altogether to be expected. At the same time, history does not point to any notable contribution from this quarter with reference to forensic advocates and procurators. From the nature of their judicial institutions, there did

7. For example: I Council of Carthage (348), c. II — Mansi, III, 157; II Council of Carthage (390), cc. 6, 10 — Mansi, III, 870, 871; III Council of Carthage (397), cc. 7, 8, 9, 10 — Mansi, III, 881, 882; Council of Antioch (341), c. 14 — Mansi, II, 1332; Council of Chalcedon (451), cc. 3, 21 — Mansi, VII, 393, 399.

8. Lib. XIII, Epis. 45 — *MPL*, LVII, 1294; Wernz-Vidal, *Ius Canonicum*, VI, *De Processibus* (Rome, 1928), p. 5; Cicognani, *Canon Law* (The Dolphin Press: Philadelphia, 1934), pp. 47-48; Steinwenter, "Der Einfluss des Römischen Rechts auf der antiken kan. Proz." — *Atti del Congresso Internazionale di Diritto Romano* (Bologna, 1934), I, 225.

9. Moriarty, *Oaths in Ecclesiastical Courts*, Canon Law Studies, n. 110 (Washington, D. C.: Catholic University Press, 1937), p. 12.

arise the *advocatus armatus,* but this form of defender is so alien to the concept of judicial advocate that it may be disregarded for the purposes of this study.[10]

THE ADVOCATE IN THE EARLY CHURCH TO THE NINTH CENTURY

Numerous references to ecclesiastical defenders point to the existence of that office as to an already well established institution of the Eastern Church in the fifth century. Moreover, the testimony available indicates very strongly that these protectors, called Ἐκκλησιέκδικοι, were for the most part priests. For example, act 5 of the Council of Ephesus (431) speaks of Asphalius, a priest of the Antiochean Church, stationed as advocate of that Church at the imperial court.[11] At the Synod of Constantinople held in 448, presided over by St. Flavian, a certain John, priest and advocate of that city, was deputed to summon the heretic Eutyches.[12] Again, in canon 23 we find the Council of Chalcedon (451) charging the ecclesiastical advocate at Constantinople to expel from that city wandering and troublesome monks and clerics.[13] Later still, the Council of Constantinople, held in 536, mentions John and Theoctistus, priests and defenders of the Church.[14]

According to Thomassinus, these advocates had the right and duty of protecting the interests of the Church against the violations of her adversaries. As a result, under given circumstances, they would act not only in the ecclesiastical forum, but in the secular courts as well, defending the rights and possessions of the particular churches they represented and also the civil rights of ecclesiastics connected with

---

10. Ferraris, *Bibliotheca Canonica, Juridica, Moralis, Theologica, nec non Ascetica, Polemica, Rubricistica, Historica* (9 vols., Romae, 1885-1899), I, 143, n. 12; Gallade, *Dissertatio Historico-Canonica de Advocatis Ecclesiasticis,* cap. 3, 4, 5, 6 (Heidelberg, 1768), in Schmidt, *Thesaurus Juris Ecclesiastici* (7 vols., Heidelberg, Bamberg, Wirceburg, 1772-1779), V, 453-514.

11. Mansi, IV, 1322, A.

12. Mansi, VI, 698.

13. Mansi, VII, 390.

14. Mansi, VIII, 933.

that church. Obviously, a prototype is to be found in the civil advocate.[15]

At first glance, this rôle may not appear to be in harmony with already existing canonical norms prohibiting clerics from entering the civil courts. While it is true that we find the *Canones Apostolorum,* which probably date from the beginning of the fifth century, expressly forbidding only priests and deacons, the legislation of subsequent councils embraced all clerics, to say nothing of civil prescriptions regarding clerics in this matter.[16]

It is equally certain that in the Western Church of the early fifth century, especially in Africa and at Rome, the ecclesiastical advocate was a recognized institution. At the very beginning of the century the African bishops made a plea for advocates to protect the poor against the oppression of the rich. This petition was readily heeded by the Emperor Honorius (395-424).[17] Owing to the stringent discipline of the African Church regarding participation by clerics in secular trials, however, the rôle of ecclesiastical advocate in this region was restricted to lay persons.[18]

In the Roman Church the system of ecclesiastical defenders appears to have been patterned on that of the East rather than to bear a similarity with the other Western Churches. While some authors maintain that laymen only were commissioned for this office until the time of Gregory the Great (590-604), there appears to be convincing testimony that the appointment of clerical advocates originated in the Roman Church at a very early period. One indication may be found in the Acts of St. Sebastian, wherein the unknown author of the fourth century, speaking of Pope St. Caius (283-296), clearly establishes the existence of an advocate, and further insinuates by the con-

---

15. *Vetus et Nova Ecclesiae disciplina circa beneficia et beneficiarios,* Pars III, Lib. II, cap. 55. Hereafter the citation of this work is implied with mention of the author's name.

16. *Canones Apostolorum,* cc. 6, 83 — *MPG,* 137, 35 sq.; Council of Chalcedon (451), c. 3 — Mansi, VII, 393; Novellae 123, 6; cf. also Brunini, *The Clerical Obligations of Canons 139 and 142* (Washington, D. C.: Catholic University of America Press, 1937), p. 36.

17. Mansi, III, 778, 970; Mansi, IV, 331; C. Th. (16, 2) 38.

18. Cf. for example, I Council Carthage (348), c. 6 — Mansi, III, 147.

text his clerical status.[19] Similarly, under Pope Innocent I (402-417), one observes the establishment of seven advocates for the Roman Church. This institution may well have been the origin of the consistorial advocate, to be considered later.[20]

It is true that at this time laymen did occupy the office of defender in the Roman Church. But it is likewise certain, from the same evidence, that these lay advocates could become clerics.[21] That clerics still continued in this position may be demonstrated in a more positive manner from the epistles of Pope Felix III who reigned from 483 to 492.[22] Again, Pope Gelasius I (492-496), writing to the bishops of Southern Italy and Sicily, recognizes advocates among the minor clergy.[23]

In the reign of Gregory the Great, there was a decided emphasis upon the appointment of clerics to the office of ecclesiastical advocate. That such emphasis gave rise to a general custom, however, is highly questionable. Certainly during the early ninth century lay defenders are again prominent before the Church courts.

Be that as it may, Pope Gregory manifested a great interest with regard to these ecclesiastical officials, stimulating their efforts by the bestowal of honors and privileges.[24] Then, too, from the writings of this pontiff we derive detailed information respecting their functions in his day. For example, they are spoken of as protectors of the poor, of the injured, and of Church property; as agents of the Pope in enforcing discipline.[25]

In the course of time a trend appears in the Roman Church directed toward the elimination of priests from this occupation. Canon 19 of the Roman Council which was held in 826 under Pope Eugene II, and

19. Ferraris, *Bibliotheca*, I, 143.

20. Wernz-Vidal, *Ius Canonicum*, VI, *De Processibus* (Romae, 1928), p. 198.

21. Pope Zosimus, *Epist. ad Hesychium* (418) — Mansi, IV, 349.

22. *Epist. IX, ad Imp. Zenonem* — Mansi, VII, 1065; *Epist. XI, ad Monachos Urbis Const. et Bithyn* — Mansi, VII, 1068.

23. *Epist.* IX, c. 2 — Mansi, VIII, 37.

24. Lib. VII, *Epist. 17, Ad Bonifatium Defensorem* — Mansi, X, 96; Lib. IX, *Epist. 34, Ad Vitum Defensorem.* — Mansi, X, 271.

25. The 12 Books of Epistles of Pope Gregory contain a great number of letters to the defenders of various churches, which afford a picture of their duties and importance — Mansi, IX, 1029 — X, 383.

which legislated in this connection, provided the reason based on the nature of the priestly state.[26]

Turning to the Lombard and Frankish Kingdoms, one finds testimony at hand which points to a similarity with the African Church. Clerics, no doubt, could plead and defend in purely ecclesiastical trials within the Church courts. But they were restrained from acting in the civil tribunals, even in litigation involving ecclesiastical interests. At the same time Bishops were encouraged by the civil authorities to appoint conscientious protectors for the defense of their property.[27]

Following upon the legislation of Pippin in the eighth century, the same idea is seen to be carried over into the capitularies of Charlemagne and of Lothar I in the early ninth century, namely, that Bishops and Abbots should retain the services of learned and upright advocates for the protection of their interests.[28] This imperial insistence may be explained by the fact that otherwise many churches would have voluntarily relinquished such protection. It is true that, owing to vast possessions, the churches were frequently involved in property disputes and other litigation. Furthermore, since clerics could not defend in the secular courts, there was genuine need for protection. Nevertheless, the commissioning of lay ecclesiastical advocates connoted a certain dependence upon these officials who often proved themselves more solicitous for their personal interests than for those of the churches they represented. Later, indeed, instances of thoroughgoing exploitation and tyranny were not infrequent.

This consideration may shed some light on an enactment of the Synod of Mainz, held in the year 813. After decreeing, in canon 12, that clerics should bring suit and defend through advocates, and after

26. "Quia episcopi universique sacerdotes ad solam laudem Dei, bonorumque operum actionem constituuntur, debet ergo unusquisque eorum tam pro ecclesiasticis, quam etiam pro propriis actionibus, excepto publico videlicet crimine, habere advocatum, non malae famae suspectum, sed bonae opinionis, et laudabilis artis inventum; ne dum humana lucra attendunt, aeterna praemia perdant". — Mansi, XIV, 997.

27. *Leges Langobardorum*, II, 47, 8; III, 11, 1, in *Monumenta Germaniae Historica*, Leges, IV; *Scriptores Rerum Italicarum*, T. I, Pt. 2, p. 37, Law 7.

28. Capit. 34, datum Bononiae (801) — Mansi, XIII, 1609; Capit. 4, conditum Olonae (824) — Mansi, XIV, 483.

forbidding, in canon 14, clerics to fill such a role in secular tribunals, the Synod further enacts, in canon 50:

> Omnibus igitur episcopis, abbatibus, cunctoque clero omnino praecipimus, vicedominos, praepositos, advocatos, sive defensores bonos habere, non malos, non crudeles, non cupidos, non perjuros, non falsitatem amantes, sed Deum timentes, et in omnibus justitiam diligentes.[29]

ARTICLE 3

THE PROCURATOR IN THE EARLY CHURCH TO THE NINTH CENTURY

That the office of procurator necessarily existed in early Church courts may be safely assumed, not only owing to the nature of the institution, but also because of indirect testimony. In this connection the relation of Roman Law and early ecclesiastical procedure should be recalled, for scholars agree that the ecclesiastical procurator, as an institution, together with the legislation incident to it, was derived almost entirely from the civil judicial system.[30] As a result, the early centuries reveal practically nothing in the way of canonical legislation touching this point. Just as with advocates, so too here, the early Church found it unnecessary to add to already adequate legal requirements. Consequently, the indirect testimony mentioned is concerned solely with excluding clerical procurators from the secular tribunals.

The Fathers and early Councils expressly prohibited clerics not only from engaging themselves as procurators in unnecessary secular transactions, *ad negotia,* but likewise in judicial matters, *ad lites.* St. Ambrose (335-397), for example, exhorts the clergy:

> Non te implices negotiis saecularibus, quoniam Deo militas. Etenim si is qui imperatori militat, a susceptione litium, actu negotiorum forensium, venditione mercium prohibetur humanis legibus, quanto magis, qui fidei exercet militiam, ab omni usu negotiationis abstinere debet.[31]

29. Mansi, XIV, 69.

30. Lega, *Praelectiones in Textum Iuris Canonici de Iudiciis Ecclesiasticis. De Iudiciis Ecclesiasticis Civilibus,* Lib. I, vol. I (Romae, 1896), 131, note 1.

31. *De Officiis,* Lib. I, cap. 36 — *MPL,* 78. Likewise St. Augustine, *De Opere Monachorum.,* cap. 15 — *Corpus Scriptorum Ecclesiasticorum Latinorum.,* XLI, 556; and St. Jerome, *Epist. 52, Ad Nepotianum,* cap. 16 — *CSEL,* LIV, 439.

The mind of the Church, in like manner, appears in canon 15 of the III Council of Carthage, held in 398:

> Placuit ut episcopi et presbyteri, et diaconi, vel clerici non sint conductores, neque procuratores, neque ullo turpi vel inhonesto negotio victum quaerant. Quia respicere debent scriptum esse: 'Nemo militans Deo, implicat se negotiis saecularibus.'[32]

In addition, it is possible to trace a series of particular councils from the fifth to the eighth century, especially in France and Germany, which restrain clerics from secular occupations. Such legislation may be interpreted as embracing the question of ecclesiastical procurators in civil courts.[33]

Perhaps this attitude seems contrary to a very early decree. In canon 84 of the Arabic version sometimes attributed to the Council of Nice (325), the appointment of procurators is urged to assist the poor and needy. And in pointing out qualifications and duties, the canon speaks of aid to the imprisoned in such terms as to imply the rendering of actual judicial assistance.[34] However, this canon serves but to demonstrate that the Church's attitude was not absolute. In other words, norms preventing clerics from representing in the secular courts had for their foundation the pastoral consideration and the avoidance of avarice and ambition. With that in mind, one realizes that cases could and did arise, which, of their very nature, would permit, and even demand, relaxation of an absolute prohibition. It is not surprising, therefore, to find both of these considerations very well embodied in canon 3 of the Council of Chalcedon, held in 451.[35]

Again in canon 16 of the Council of Verno, held in 755, and in canon 14 of the Council of Mainz, celebrated in 813, one discovers identical legislation. Clerics are to refrain from the rôle of procurator in secular disputes, save where their presence is required by the public

---

32. Mansi, III, 883; III, 147; II Tim.II, 4; Nov. 123, 6.
33. Thomassinus, Pars III, Lib. III, cap. 18.
34. Mansi, II, 1010.
35. "Decrevit ... concilium, nullum deinceps, non episcopum, non clericum, vel monachum, aut possessiones conducere, aut negotiis saecularibus se immiscere, praeter pupillorum, si forte leges imponant inexcusabilem curam, aut civitatis episcopus ecclesiasticarum rerum sollicitudinem habere praecipiat, aut orphanorum et viduarum, earum quae sine ulla defensione sunt ..." — Mansi, VII, 373.

good of the Church or other charitable cause; and then, only with permission from ecclesiastical authority.[36]

It might be remarked that during this period the Roman regulations pertaining to the *mandatum* of the procurator remained in force. Pope Gregory the Great in the year 602 demanded a legitimate commission prior to admitting the judicial procurator.[37]

ARTICLE 4

APPOINTMENT, DUTIES, AND REMUNERATION OF ADVOCATES AND PROCURATORS IN THE EARLY MIDDLE AGES

Not infrequently circumstances compelled particular churches to request legal assistance from the civil power. In this manner particular customs arose in divers places whereby the secular prince assumed the right to appoint ecclesiastical advocates and procurators. From the time of Charlemagne (†814), however, this custom gradually disappeared. It has been noted that the Emperors, particularly Charlemagne and Lothar (†855), strongly urged the bishops to retain qualified defenders. Their decrees to this effect, together with conciliar legislation of the period, clearly show that the bishops enjoyed perfect freedom in commissioning their judicial officials.[38] This, of course, has special significance with regard to those clerics or laymen who would represent or defend the Church in the civil courts.

Incidentally, it is noteworthy that this testimony points to a system of election as the means of acquiring these positions. At times the election centered about officials proposed by the civil ruler. Furthermore, one discovers numerous instances, dating from the Carlovingian period, of these offices' inhering in certain families for generations as

36. Mansi, XII, 583; XIV, 69.

37. *Compilatio* I, 1, 29, *de procuratoribus.*

38. Capit. 34, datum Bononiae (801) — Mansi, XIII, 1069; Capit. 4, conditum Olonae (824) — Mansi, XIV, 483; Synod of Mainz (813), c. 12 — Mansi, XIV, 69; II Council of Rheims (813), c. 24 — Mansi, XIV, 79; Ferraris, *Bibliotheca*, "Advocati Ecclesiarum", n. 21; Thomassinus, Pars III, Lib. II, cap. 55, n. 1; Grabowski, "Adwokatura" — *Ateneum Kaplanskie*, XXXIII (1934), 256.

hereditary rights. Especially was this true of advocates, for many nobles were proud to possess such a noble and honorable dignity.[39]

One consideration suffices to afford a picture of the functions of Church advocates and procurators in ecclesiastical courts at this period. The bishop's court, from the sixth century on up until the twelfth, when it attained the zenith of its power, was not of mediocre importance. Its jurisdiction extended to a wide variety of cases, for example, to crimes against Faith, such as heresy, superstition, and sorcery; to crimes against public order, in which the spiritual and civil power joined hands, such as arson, pillaging, perjury and rape. Matrimonial cases and the execution of last testaments implied a mass of court activity. Similarly, there was a vast amount of litigation involving infringement of Church goods and property. Again, a prominent place is held by the long list of differences between bishops and their diocesan Chapters. In addition, there was an ever more firmly established *privilegium fori*. And finally, it must be remembered that frequently a bishop was a feudal lord exercising all justice in his domain, and that it was not rare for a prince to grant a bishop the power to administer all justice in a given territory, with no interference from the public tribunals.[40] Undoubtedly, tribunals of such a nature provided a vast field of endeavor for advocates and procurators.

With regard to the sustenance of these officials of the ecclesiastical court certain rights and privileges were established together with more or less definite norms of remuneration. In return for services revenues were usually provided by the church, diocese, or monastery represented. Such provision sometimes took the form of a benefice. Frequently, too, secular princes would bestow annual grants upon advocates of the Church. At the same time, both ecclesiastical courts and secular tribunals, as under Charlemagne, formulated rules governing fees from clients. Thomassinus relates that Angilramnus, Bishop of Metz (†791), designated precise amounts for his advocate in a particular case — limits

39. Cf. Grabowski, *ibid.*, pp. 255-258.

40. Hincmar of Rheims (†822), in Thomassinus, Pars III, Lib. II, cap. 55, no. 2; Fournier, *Les Officialités au Moyen Age* (Paris, 1880), Introd., pp. xiii-xiv. Cf. Pollock-Maitland, *History of the English Law* (2 vols., Cambridge: University Press, 1895), I, 88-114.

with which, further, he should be content.[41] And Pope Eugene II (824-827) sanctioned conciliar decrees with regard to observance of legal fees by adding severe ecclesiastical penalties for non-observance.[42]

ARTICLE 5

ADVOCATES AND PROCURATORS FROM THE NINTH CENTURY
TO GRATIAN

Testimony available for this period indicates a dearth of legislation with regard to judicial advocates and procurators in Church courts. There remains, however, the continued emphasis on the restriction prohibiting participation in civil tribunals on the part of these clerical officials.[43] In fact, the Council of Rheims (1131) levelled a particularly strong denunciation against certain religious who, to the detriment of their pastoral duties, persisted in pursuing secular occupations for gain, including the rendering of court assistance.[44]

Again, however, this prohibition must be viewed in the light of a decree of Pope Gelasius II (1118-1119), who permitted such defense and representation when Church interests were involved, or when charity demanded, as in cases of orphans and defenseless widows.[45]

During this period of the tenth and eleventh centuries one finds the developing collections of law granting an increasingly prominent position to procedural canons. In none of these, however, does one discover a complete, systematized treatise *de iudiciis*. Consequently, it is not surprising that here again little material appears touching upon advocates and procurators specifically. What fragmentary laws there are derive mainly from the Roman laws dealing with capacity, or restate the Church's position respecting prohibition on clerics from serving in civil tribunals. Among such collections should be noted

41. Thomassinus, Pars III, Lib. II, cap. 55, no. 3; Ferraris, *Bibliotheca*, "Advocati Ecclesiarum", nn. 32, 33.

42. Mansi, XIV, 415.

43. Council of London (1102), c. 8 — Mansi, XX, 1151; Council of Clermont (1130), c. 5 — Mansi, XXI, 438; II C. Lat. (1139), c. 9 — Mansi, XXI, 528.

44. C. 6 — Mansi, XXI, 459.

45. Cc. 1, 2, D. LXXXVII.

particularly those of Burchard, Bishop of Worms (†1025),[46] of Anselm, Bishop of Lucca (†1086),[47] of Cardinal Deusdedit, compiled about 1083-1087,[48] and of Ivo, Bishop of Chartres (†c. 1116).[49]

In order to substantiate the views expressed, one might consider for example the collection of Anselm. Owing to its relative thoroughness and logical ordering, this collection has been considered of great importance. As the title of Book III indicates, it contains quite a gathering of material relative to the parties, to witnesses, and to judges; but with regard to procurators and advocates, references are decidedly limited. There are several citations of letters to Church Defenders on the part of Gregory the Great, particularly of those in which he bestows honors and privileges upon them. No one is to be judged who has not been afforded adequate opportunity to defend himself. Moreover, an advocate was permitted no other interest in a trial, such as filling the rôle of judge or witness. Again, one branded with infamy could not assume the position of judicial procurator. And whenever criminal cases were concerned, neither party could avail himself of such a representative.[50]

In like manner this position is supported by the evidence of the collection of Cardinal Deusdedit. Throughout this work, particularly in the latter portion of Book IV, appear many procedural references. Again, however, there is a dearth of material touching the officials under consideration. Together with citations of numerous letters from Gregory the Great to various ecclesiastical advocates, one in particular is included which speaks of the seven defenders of the Roman Church

46. Burchard, in Book I of his *Liber Decretorum*, written about 1012. Cf. *MPL*, CXL, 549 sq.

47. Anselm, in Book III of his collection, written about 1083, proposes an *ordo accusandi, testificandi, judicandi*. Cf. F. Thaner, *Anselmi Collectio Canonum una cum Collectione Minore*, Fasciculus I et II (Oeniponte: Librariae Academicae Wagnerianae, 1906, 1915). Fas. I contains Bk. III.

48. V. W. Von Glanvell, *Die Kanonessammlung der Kardinals Deusdedit;* I, *Die Kanonessammlung selbst* (Paderborn, 1905).

49. Ivo compiled his *Decretum* and *Panormia* about 1090-1095; consult, e. g., *Pan.* Bk. IV, cap. 19, 56, 78 — *MPL*, CLXI, 1186, 1194, 1199; *Decretum*, Pars V, cap. 161, 248; Pars VI, cap. 331 — *MPL*, CLXI, 376, 399, 512.

50. Lib. III, capitula 7, 47, 72, 89, 100, 101.

and of their peculiar privileges,[51] while another outlines the Pontiff's instructions and counsels to such an official.[52] The author further includes manifestations of the Church's regard for the poor in this connection. He cites chapter 75 of the Council of Carthage, held in 419, requesting the establishment of *advocati pauperum,*[53] and also the position of Gregory the Great in this matter.[54] In addition, the Cardinal repeats the law of the Frankish Kings to the effect that priests and bishops should have advocates. The essential character of the mandate for procurators, as outlined by Gregory the Great, is re-emphasized, as is the prohibition excluding procurators from criminal trials.[55]

51. Lib. II, cap. 81.
52. Lib. III, cap. 96, 98.
53. Lib. IV, cap. 24.
54. Lib. III, cap. 73.
55. Lib. IV, cap. 296; lib. II, cap. 68; lib. IV, cap. 362.

CHAPTER III

CANON LAW AFFECTING ADVOCATES AND PROCURATORS FROM GRATIAN TO THE COUNCIL OF TRENT

ARTICLE 1

THE DECREE OF GRATIAN AND THE *Compilationes Antiquae*

Ecclesiastical judgments form the subject matter for most of the second part of the *Decretum,* compiled by Gratian approximately in the year 1150. Unfortunately, these procedural canons were not systematically ordered. However, there is a wealth of legislation which, when properly coördinated, affords a rather complete picture of the *ordo judiciarius* as it existed in his day.[1]

The legislation affecting advocates and procurators in particular, as embodied in the *Decretum,* does not manifest anything in the nature of an advanced legal development. What norms there are Gratian has drawn both from ecclesiastical and from civil sources. For example, legislation of the Council of Rome, held in 826, is repeated, to the effect that bishops and priests should be represented in trials, excluding criminal cases, and that no party in a criminal trial could avail himself of a procurator's aid.[2] In addition Gratian revived an ancient decree forbidding monks to leave the monastery for the assumption of judicial offices, save in cases benefiting the monastery and when permission had been granted.[3] In like manner his inclusion of Pope Gelasius' (1118-19) legislation has already been pointed out, the decree, namely, allowing clerics to enter the civil courts under certain conditions.[4]

With reference to civil law sources Gratian felt justified in reproducing portions of the Digest's title *de postulando,* concerned principally with qualifications for the office.[5] Here again we have an in-

---

1. Wernz, *Ius Decretalium* (6 vols., Romae, 1889-1904), V, 8.
2. Council of Rome (826), c. 19 — Mansi, XIV, 997; c. 3, C. V. q. 3.
3. Council of Tarragona (516), c. 11 — Mansi, VIII, 543; c. 35, C. XVI, q. 1.
4. Cc. 1, 2, D. LXXXVII.
5. D (3, 1), will be found in cc. 1, 2, C III, q. 7; so, too C (1, 4) 15 and C (2, 6) 8 in c. 7, D I, *de poenit.*

dication, just as later with the Decretalists, and even with modern authors, of the manner in which the Church looked upon the Roman *edictum prohibitorium* as a guide in this matter. Its stipulations, based so thoroughly upon the rational and equitable foundation of the natural law, were naturally made the Church's in so far as this was possible.

It may be noted at this point that the five *compilationes antiquae,* which appeared approximately between the years 1187-1227, exerted a considerable influence upon the more scientific ordering of the Church's procedural canons. Of particular interest here is the fact that the first of these collectiones, the *Breviarium extravagantium* of Bernard of Pavia (c. 1187-1191), reintroduced the old Roman title *de postulando* and *de procuratoribus.* However, notwithstanding the presence of these titles even in the four subsequent collections, there is nothing noteworthy, nothing additional that would serve to indicate a further legal development with regard to these offices. Nevertheless many principles are re-emphasized in the vast number of decretal letters of the Popes from Gratian's time to the reign of Honorius III (1216-1227), not to mention the III and IV General Lateran Councils, 1179 and 1215.

Bernard of Pavia in his private yet widely used collection cited but a single law under each of the titles mentioned. With reference to advocates he incorporated a law of the III General Lateran Council restraining clerics from the rôle of advocate before the secular tribunals save in the circumstances already considered. Subsequently this legislation of the Council was embodied in the collection of Gregory IX.[6]

The sole reference under his title *de procuratoribus* recalls a letter of Pope Gregory the Great (590-604) concerning the commissioning of a procurator in a particular case. Its importance here derives from the fact of its insistence upon the legally formulated mandate.[7]

Similarly, John of Wales in his private collection, consisting principally of decretal letters issued from the time of the first compilation to 1210, found it possible to restrict his matter under these titles. With regard to advocates a single letter is cited, that of Celestine III (1191-

---

6. C. 12 — Mansi, XXII, 225; Compil. I, lib. I, tit. 28, *de postulando;* c. 1, X, *de postulando,* I, 37.

7. Compil. I, lib. I, tit. 29, *de procuratoribus.*

1198) to the judges at Benevento, again restricting clerics in the same manner as just noted.[8]

Under the title *de procuratoribus* are included three letters. In the first, that of Alexander III (1159-1181), the principle was stressed that one cannot be compelled to designate a procurator in a grave cause. In the second, Clement III (1187-1191), distinguishing between the *criminaliter agendum* and the *non criminaliter agendum* in matrimonial cases, prohibited the parties from availing themselves of procurators in the first instance, and, while permitting their aid in the second, clearly indicated his preference for the personal conducting of such a case even here. The third letter manifested a decision of the same Pope in a private controversy, to the effect that continued judicial activity of a legitimately removed procurator in no way jeopardizes the interests of the former principal.[9]

The third compilation was promulgated as the first authentic collection of law by the Bull *"Devotioni Vestrae"* in 1210. Its compiler, Peter of Benevento, cited the solution of another particular controversy involving continued action by a legitimately dismissed procurator. Innocent III (1198-1216) decreed that an *exceptio falsi procuratoris* could be lodged not only before the sentence but also after, and, if sustained, would render the judgment null and void.[10]

A more interesting decision is contained in a letter of the same Pontiff solving the question of whether or not a person could sue through a procurator for separation because of adultery. If, for example, a husband sought from the court merely a separation from an adulterous wife he could, if it was necessary, and in so far as this was possible, act through a representative. Such a case, while involving a crime, was not a *judicium criminaliter actum,* as it would have been had he sought her punishment.[11]

In the fourth compilation, ascribed by some to Alan of England and by others to Tancred, the juridic value of which is a source of controversy, there is also a letter of Pope Innocent III involving a private controversy. The Holy Father vindicated the right of the

---

8. Compil. II, lib. I, tit. 17, *de officio advocatorum.*
9. Compil. II, lib. I, tit. 18, cc. 1, 2, 3 *de procuratoribus.*
10. Compil. III, lib. I, tit. 22, *de procuratoribus,* c. 1.
11. Compil. III, lib. I, tit. 22, *de procuratoribus,* c. 2.

procurator to recover from his principal the money expended in the legitimate pursuance of his duty.[12]

Although the author of the fifth compilation remains unknown, this collection of decretals of Honorius III (1216-1227) was authentically promulgated (c. 1226-1227) by the Bull *"Novae causarum"*. The author cites two letters of this Pontiff defining respectively the status of the procurator previous to and subsequent upon reception of letters of removal, and providing that the tenor of the mandate was to be investigated and honored in determining the procurator's precise power.[13]

ARTICLE 2

LEGISLATION OF COUNCILS IN THE TWELFTH AND THIRTEENTH CENTURIES

Already in the pontificate of Gregory VII (1073-1085) one may discern an awakening for study and research in Roman law. Fostered principally in the great schools of Bologna, Paris, and Oxford, this renewed interest reaches its zenith in the twelfth and thirteenth centuries, a phenomenon which history has come to designate as the revival of Roman law. In many respects this renaissance amounted practically to a juridical revolution. And, needless to say, it left its impression on the procedural field of law no less than on the other branches of legal study. One pertinent result is manifested by the fact that this newfound interest and consequent activity in the courts acted as a magnet upon many clerics and religious. Decidedly superior from the viewpoint of fitness, they hastened in great numbers to occupy judicial positions, not only in ecclesiastical tribunals, but in the civil courts as well. This seems to explain a series of decrees and canons touching upon advocates and procurators which appear in the various councils of this period. Much of this legislation is reflected and systematized in the later collections of Gregory IX, Boniface VIII and Clement V.

In the first place the Church's prohibition forbidding clerics to fill these offices in secular tribunals is restated and re-emphasized. At the same time the traditional exceptions continued to obtain; namely, action

12. Compil. IV, lib. I, tit. 16, c. 1, *de procuratoribus.*
13. Compil. V, lib. I, tit. 22, *de procuratoribus,* cc. 1, 2.

and defense for one's self, for the Church or in the interests of certain charitable cases, such as for the poor, the orphans, and defenseless widows. Punishments were assigned for the violation of this law. In fact the Council of Paris (1212) decreed excommunication *ferendae sententiae* for such disregard in the event that the cleric concerned already possessed an adequate benefice.[14]

In this connection, special consideration was paid to religious. Under pain of severe punishments, including excommunication and infamy, they were expressly restrained, save in cases involving necessary interests of the community or religion; and then permission of legitimate religious superiors had to be granted.[15]

What is of more interest here is that many norms appeared governing the conducting of a case before the ecclesiastical courts. For example, advocates and procurators were forbidden to assume hopeless or desperate cases. Once undertaken, a case could not maliciously be protracted. Further prescriptions demanded diligence and fidelity in the exercise of the office, the correct handling of all documents, and due respect for the court. Punishments for violations in these matters were especially outlined in the Synod of Canterbury (1295).[16] In particular, clerics were forbidden to assist or defend certain classes of unworthy people, such as the sacrilegious, excommunicated, and usurers.[17] Furthermore, under pain of an *ipso facto* incurred excommunication, they had to abstain from trials involving the effusion of blood.[18]

---

14. Council of Paris (1212), part I, c. 6 — Mansi, XXII, 820, 821; III General Council of the Lateran (1179), c. 12 — Mansi, XXII, 225; Council of Worcester (1240), c. 42 — Mansi, XXIII, 539; Council of Avignon (1279), cap. 13 — Mansi, XXIV, 241; Council of Canterbury (1295), cap. 8 — Mansi, XXIV, 1150.

15. Council of Tours (1163), c. 8 — Mansi, XXI, 1179; Council of Paris (1212), part II, c. 19 — Mansi, XXII, 831; Council of Rouen (1214), part II, cc. 21, 22 — Mansi, XXII, 910; Council of Montpellier (1214), c. 21 — Mansi, XXII, 944; Council of Champagne (1238), cc. 12, 23 — Mansi, XXIII, 490, 493.

16. Council of Paris (1212), part I, c. 6 — Mansi, XXII, 820, 821; Council of Lambeth (1281), c. 13 — Mansi, XXIV, 413; Synod of Canterbury (1295), cap. 10, 12, 13, 15 — Mansi, XXIV, 1151, 1152.

17. Council of Cologne (1266), c. 35 — Mansi, XXIII, 1151.

18. IV General Council of the Lateran (1215) c. 18 — Mansi, XXII, 1007; Council of London (1268), c. 6 — Mansi, XXIII, 1222.

And besides, in no court, lay or ecclesiastical, could a cleric act as advocate against the Church or against any ecclesiastical person, without express permission of ecclesiastical authority.[19]

Together with the above mentioned regulations there was an increasing insistence on an oath from advocates and procurators to the effect that such norms would be observed. As a prerequisite to filling these offices they had to swear to do everything possible to obtain justice for the client, and to do nothing that would in any manner detract from the majesty and dignity of the Church's tribunal.[20]

Moreover, noting the fact that incapable persons frequently presumed to occupy these positions, thus causing untold harm and confusion, several councils required a preliminary legal training. As a rule, a three year course, at least, in canon and civil law was demanded.[21]

Then, too, there is continued evidence of the Church's consideration for the underprivileged. *Advocati pauperum* had to be available, and granted to all standing in need of their services.[22]

Finally, with reference to remuneration, advocates and procurators were to adhere to particular laws, abstaining from all immoderate demands. In some places limitations with regard to fees were well defined, and penalties established for their disregard.[23]

---

19. Council of Avignon (1279), c. 13 — Mansi, XXIV, 241.

20. Council of Melun (1216), c. 1 — Mansi, XXII, 1087; Council of Rouen (1231), c. 45 — Mansi, XXIII, 218; Council of Chateau Gontier (1231), c. 35 — Mansi, XXIII, 240; Council of London (1268), c. 27 — Mansi, XXIII, 1230; II Council of Lyons (1274), cap. 19 — Mansi, XXIV, 93; Council of Langeais (1278), c. 15 — Mansi, XXIV, 216; Synod of Liege (1287), c. 3 — Mansi, XXIV, 933; Synod of Exeter (1287), c. 34 — Mansi, XXIV, 819; Synod of Canterbury (1295), c. 3 — Mansi, XXIV, 1149.

21. Council of Tours (1236), c. 2 — Mansi, XXIII, 411; Council of Langeais (1278), c. 15 — Mansi, XXIV, 216; Council of Lambeth (1281), c. 26 — Mansi, XXIV, 420; Synod of Canterbury (1295), c. 8 — Mansi, XXIV, 1150.

22. Council of Toulouse (1229), c. 44 — Mansi, XXIII, 204; Council of Champagne (1238), c. 14 — Mansi, XXIII, 490; Synod of Canterbury (1295), cc. 14, 18 — Mansi, XXIV, 1152, 1153.

23. Council of Rheims (1148), c. 6 — Mansi, XXI, 715; Council of Paris (1212), part I, c. 6 — Mansi, XXII, 820, 821; II Council of Lyons (1274), cap. 19 — Mansi, XXIV, 93; Council of Noyon (1344), c. 17 — Mansi, XXVI, 11.

ARTICLE 3

LEGISLATION OF GREGORY IX, BONIFACE VIII, AND CLEMENT V

The Church's legislation with reference to ecclesiastical judicial advocates and procurators may be said to have culminated in the collections
of law promulgated by Gregory IX (1227-1241), Boniface VIII (1294-
1303), and Clement V (1305-1314), in 1234, 1298, and 1314-17
respectively.

A. *Advocates*

It is apparent from various sections of the Gregorian Decretals
that the Roman *edictum prohibitorium* continued to be followed, in
modified form, regarding the question of qualifications. Anyone, therefore, could defend or be defended unless he was expressly hindered.
Applications of this principle were to be found in the restrictions
placed upon women in the ecclesiastical forum save in drastic cases,[24]
upon excommunicates[25] and upon Jews.[26] It might be noted that all
the commentators of the Decretals in discussing other qualifications,
such as age and ability, simply restate substantially the Roman law.[27]

Furthermore, under pain of suspension from office, of excommunication, and of subsequent infamy, it was forbidden to defend heretics.[28]

With regard to *clerical* advocates and procurators several clear principles were restated. Only in cases involving one's own welfare, that
of the Church, of relatives, or of needy persons, such as the poor, the
orphans, and widows, could a cleric appear before a civil tribunal. This
restriction was extended also to minor clerics, provided that they possessed a benefice or some ecclesiastical means of support.[29]

---

24. C. 67, X, *de appellationibus, recusationibus et relationibus,* II, 28.

25. C. 13, X *de haereticis,* V, 7; c. 7, X, *de judiciis,* II, 1; c. 8, *de sententia
excommunicationis,* V, II, in VI.

26. Cc. 16, 18, X, *de Iudaeis,* V. 6.

27. Cf. e. g., Durandus, *Speculum Juris,* Lib. I, Part IV, n. 12.

28. Cc. 11, 13, X, *de haereticis,* V. 7.

29. Cc. 1, 3, X, *de postulando,* I, 37; Faganus, Lib. I, tit. 37, nn. 11, 12, 13;
Pirhing, *Jus Canonicum in V. Libros Decretalium* (5 vols., Dilingae, 1674-
1678), Lib. I, tit. 37, n. 10.

All clerics, up to and including deacons, were free to represent and defend in the ecclesiastical forum.[30] The following legislation of Gregory IX, however, occasioned a historic controversy. *"Cum sacerdotis sit officium nulli nocere, omnibus autem velle prodesse, nonnisi pro seipso vel Ecclesia, vel, si necessitas expostulet, pro personis coniunctis, sibi licitum est postulare."*[31] Canonists commonly looked upon this as excluding the priest even from the Church court, save in the exceptional cases mentioned.[32] Notwithstanding this generally accepted interpretation, the opposite position had early supporters, as is evident from the Glossa of Hostiensis (†1271),[33] and other proponents of great authority, for example, Pope Benedict XIV (1740-1758), to name the greatest.[34] And if one regards the practice and usage of the Church in the matter, especially in modern times, it doesn't appear that the priest has been excluded from the Church court in the cases contemplated by the above mentioned restrictive interpretation. Quite the contrary is true, a situation attested to by ecclesiastical documents.[35]

Mention has already been made in this connection of Pope Innocent III's decree in 1206 regarding monks and canons regular. Only in trials concerning the welfare of their monastery, and with legitimate permission, could they assume the rôle of advocate.[36] A more stringent decree affecting the Friars Minor appeared in the collection of Clement V. They could not occupy this office even when complying with the above conditions. More than that, even in cases involving their own temporal interests they were forbidden to assist personally those who did defend them.[37]

---

30. C. 1, X, *de postulando*, I, 37.

31. C. 3, X, *de postulando*, I, 37.

32. Schmalzgrueber, *Ius Ecclesiasticum Universum* (4 vols., Romae, 1843-1844), lib. I, tit. 37, n. 10; Reiffenstuel, *Ius Canonicum Universum* (4 vols., Romae, 1843-1844), lib. I. tit. 37, n. 18.

33. *In Primum Decretalium Librum Commentaria* (Venetiis, 1581), c. 3, *de postulando*, p. 183.

34. *De Synodo Dioecesana*, lib. XIII, c. 10, n. 12.

35. Cf., for example, S. C. de Prop. Fide, Instr. *Cum Magnopere*, 11 iunii, 1880, Art. 30 — *Fontes*, IV, 2005.

36. C. 2, X, *de postulando*, I, 37; Durandus, *Speculum Juris*, I, IV, n. 2.

37. C. 1, *de verborum significatione*, V, 11, in Clem.

Furthermore, clerics were prohibited from advocating the causes of others against the churches in which they held benefices. Violation of this understandable legislation entailed the loss of the benefice.[38]

The decretalists interpreted those prohibitions which restrained clerics from trials involving the effusion of blood as embracing both advocates and procurators. Alexander III (1159-1181), in particular, legislated on this point in the III General Council of the Lateran, 1179, and these prescriptions later were incorporated into the collection of Gregory IX.[39] Even should a cleric defend or represent the accused in such a case, he risked incurring irregularity and excommunication, since subsequent death or mutilation of the client might possibly be attributed to negligence or lack of skill on his part. Consequently, the decretalists considered that clerics should decline even this rôle.[40]

It is noteworthy, in order to avoid confusion, that in a letter of Innocent III (1198-1216) to the Bishop of Ely, the term advocate is used in a wide, improper sense, having reference to the procurator and not to the defender as we understand the office.[41]

Finally, a letter of Honorius III (1216-1227), incorporated into the Decretals of Gregory IX, indicates clearly the Church's strict concern in providing adequate assistance for those not in a position to procure proper defense.[42]

B. *Procurators*

The legislation affecting procurators in these collections is more extensive. Pope Gregory incorporated into his decretals a number of papal letters to bishops dealing largely with practical solutions in particular cases. On the other hand, Popes Boniface and Clement are concerned more with evolving the old Roman principles, adapting them to the Church's requirements.

---

38. C. 1, *de verborum significatione*, V, 11, in Clem.; Durandus, *op. cit.*, I, IV, n. 17.

39. Cc. 5, 9, X, *ne clerici vel monachi saecularibus negotiis se immisceant*, III, 50.

40. Hostiensis, lib. III, tit. 50, n. 6; Fagnanus, lib. III, tit. 50, n. 23.

41. C. 14, X, *de iudiciis*, II, 1.

42. C. 1, X, *de officio iudicis*, I, 32.

In the first place, with reference to the appointment of procurators in general, the following principle of law obtains: *"Potest quis per alium, quod potest facere per seipsum."*[43] Consequently, one was at liberty to commission a procurator, provided that he himself possessed the legal capacity to stand in judgment, save in those instances in which such freedom was restricted by law.

The most noteworthy legal restraint concerned the criminal process. Representation, the power of attorney, continued to be denied to both the *actor* and the *reus* in such trials.[44] Furthermore, at times the nature of the case, or *necessitas juris,* would empower the court to demand the actual presence of the parties. The matter of questioning in a matrimonial case, or the taking of the *juramentum de veritate dicenda,* serve as illustrations of this point.[45]

A second consideration in these collections turns upon the question of what persons could receive such a commission. In this connection it has been indicated that the legal prohibitions affecting advocates, together with the principles concerning clerics, likewise obtained for the office of procurator.

In stating the principle that anyone could fill this rôle unless expressly prohibited, Boniface VIII permitted the office to be assumed by laymen even in spiritual causes.[46] Examples of express prohibition are to be found in the age requirement of twenty-five years,[47] and in an added restriction of Clement V excluding religious even from designating or substituting a procurator though a mandate empowered them to do so.[48]

Thirdly, an essential requirement for the procurator's admittance into court was the legitimate mandate. While it appears that any form of designation and acceptance provable in court sufficed, still, owing to its

43. Reg. 68, R. J., in VI°; Hostiensis, *Summa Aurea,* lib. I, *de procuratoribus,* nn. 3, 8.

44. C. 5, X, *de procuratoribus,* I, 38; cc. 15, 16, X, *de accusationibus, inquisitionibus, et denuntiationibus,* V, 1; c. 1, *de iudiciis,* II, 1, in VI; Durandus, *op. cit.,* I, III, n. 9.

45. C. 1, *de iudiciis,* II, 1, in VI; c. 14, X, *de iudiciis,* II, 1; c. 2, *de iudiciis,* II, 1, in Clem.; c. 2, *de verborum significatione,* V, 11, in Clem.

46. C. 1, *de procuratoribus,* I, 19, in VI°.

47. C. 5, *de procuratoribus,* I, 19, in VI°.

48. C. 3, *de procuratoribus,* I, 10, in Clem.

importance, the mandate was desired in writing.[49] Nevertheless, there are instances pointing to the sufficiency of a presumed mandate in certain circumstances, such as for relatives, or when one knowingly permitted another to represent him without contradiction.[50]

On the other hand, even a broad, general mandate would not bestow upon the procurator unlimited freedom of action. Some acts, or possible acts, of a trial were deemed of such consequence to the principal that a special commission for that particular phase had to be acquired. For example, a procurator, though duly appointed in *rem alienam,* could not freely bind his principal by oath, effect a compromise, or enter into an agreement with his opponent.[51] As a matter of fact, a general mandate which expressly granted permission for all special acts did not suffice for those acts. Such a commission was regarded as too general, implying that the principal had not prudently foreseen all possible eventualities. *"In generali concessione non veniunt ea, quae, quis non esset verisimiliter in specie concessurus."*[52] If, however, a particular act requiring a special mandate was definitely mentioned, then the mandate was regarded as valid also for other special acts of equal or of lesser importance.[53]

A further consideration discussed in the Decretals centered about the effects arising from the contractual mandate. The joining of issue having taken place, the procurator became *dominus litis.*[54] This is not to be understood in the absolute sense of Roman Law. Needless to say, Canon Law with its many cases of a strictly personal nature could not permit the ancient Roman arrangement in this regard.[55] Nevertheless, after the *litis contestatio* the procurator, as *dominus litis,*

49. C. 1, 9, X, *de procuratoribus,* I, 38; c. 1, *de procuratoribus,* I, 10, in Clem.

50. C. 34, X, *de officio iudicis delegati,* I, 29.

51. C. 4, *de procuratoribus,* I, 19, in VI; c. 2, *de procuratoribus,* I, 10, in Clem.; c. 9, X, *de arbitris,* I, 43; Durandus speaks of 24 such cases: — *Speculum,* I, partic. III, *de proc.,* 1, n. 4. A special mandate was required, by implication, for a *restitutio in integrum:* — c. 7, X, *de in integrum restitutione,* I, 41; glossa in c. 4, I, 19, in VI°.

52. Reg. 81, R. J., in VI°; Durandus, *op. cit.,* I, III, n. 4.

53. C. 15, X, *de rescriptis,* I, 3; c. 2, *de procuratoribus,* I, 10, in Clem.

54. C. 1, *de procuratoribus,* I, 19 in VI°; Hostiensis, *Summa Aurea,* lib. I, *de proc.,* n. 14.

55. Reiffenstuel, Lib. I, tit. 38, n. 117.

could substitute another in his place.[56] Furthermore, as *dominus litis* he could not be removed from the office unwillingly without very reasonable cause.[57] Nor, on the other hand, could he renounce the case arbitrarily.[58]

In addition, the principal had to regard the activity of the procurator as his own. *"Qui facit per alium, est perinde, ac si faciat per seipsum."*[59] In certain circumstances, of course, the principal could disclaim responsibility. For example, he was not held accountable for the acts of a false procurator. Nor had he to answer for the conduct of a procurator whose mandate had been revoked, provided that notification of the revocation had reached the proper parties. Similarly, he was not bound by the excesses of a procurator who disregarded the limitations of his mandate.[60]

Harm to the principal arising from negligence on the part of the procurator, provided that the procurator acted within his powers, had to be borne by the principal. His freedom of choice involved that risk. However, depending upon circumstances, especially if fraud or deceit was proved, he could obtain an action of complete restitution thus regaining his pretrial status.[61]

A final point emphasized in these collections considered the relative status of several procurators commissioned by the same principal. If more than one procurator had been assigned at one and the same time, and *simpliciter,* then not any of them could proceed independently of the others. On the contrary, among several designated simultaneously, but *in solidum,* he became the actual procurator in a given case who first assumed the actual conduct of the trial.[62]

---

56. Cc. 1, 3, *de procuratoribus,* I, 19, in VI°.

57. C. 2, *de procuratoribus,* I, 19, in VI°.

58. Reg. 33, R. J., in VI°: *"Mutare consilium quis non potest in alterius detrimentum."*

59. Reg. 72, R. J., in VI°.

60. Cc. 3, 4, 13, X, *de procuratoribus,* I, 38; c. 33, X, *de rescriptis,* I, 3; Reg. 22, R. J., in VI°: *"Non debet aliquis alterius odio praegravari";* Durandus, *op. cit.,* I, III, 37.

61. C. 2, X, *de in integrum restitutione,* I, 41.

62. C. 6, *de procuratoribus,* I, 19, in VI°; Reg. 54, R. J., in VI°: *"Qui prior est tempore, potior est iure."*

Should a period of time have intervened between the appointment of procurators, then the later appointee had to be regarded as having supplanted the former.[63]

Perhaps even this brief summary of the Decretal legislation concerning advocates and procurators will indicate why subsequent centuries have witnessed practically no new legislation, but rather a series of decrees and norms serving to facilitate the practical application of these laws.[64]

ARTICLE 4

THE *Ordines Judiciarii*

A further consequence of the Roman law revival, in the processual field, is manifested by the appearance of innumerable treatises on procedural law. In particular, the period from 1170 to 1270 witnessed a gradual development of the *ordines judiciarii.* These manuals, having for their foundation the similar tracts of the old Roman legists, clearly indicate a twofold trend. On the one hand, they re-outline the wonderfully organized, formal, rigid Roman process. On the other, they exhibit a gradual tempering, modification, and simplification, derived from the canonical legislation of widely scattered councils, and, later, from the more general Decretal law.

To realize the importance of these treatises, one has but to be mindful of the fact that they occupied a position corresponding to present day commentaries on the fourth book of the Code. As a result, while they do not represent any considerable legal development, they do serve to illumine, to interpret, and to vivify the existing law. Since the practical suggestions that are so abundant in these manuals will be considered in the second part of this study, it will suffice, at this juncture, to designate some of the more prominent works that treat of judicial procurators and advocates.

Around the year 1190, appeared the anonymous *Rhetorica Ecclesiastica,* which assumed the form of a brief commentary on the processual canons of Gratian. With regard to our particular point, this work

---

63. C. 14, X, *de procuratoribus,* I, 38.
64. Wernz-Vidal, VI, *De Processibus* (Romae, 1928), p. 207.

embodies the usual principles governing the position and admission of representation and defense in court.[65]

A little later (c. 1196), Richard of England drew up a *Summa de Ordine Judiciario*. With regard to the procurator he treats briefly of the office itself, of the mandate, of the requirements for office, and of the *satisdatio*. In reference to the advocate, there is again an insistence of the requisite qualifications together with the statement of norms covering a proper conduct of the case.[66]

The outstanding work of this kind in the early thirteenth century was that of Tancred of Bologna (c. 1185-1234). His *Ordo Judiciarius*, written about 1216, was vastly superior to all preceding manuals. In a rather short section on advocates, Tancred first points out the precise nature of the office. Referring to the needed capacity for occupying the position, he cites the Roman *edictum prohibitorium* together with the traditional restraints upon clerics and religious.

He very definitely states the rôle of the court in granting gratuitous patronage. And with regard to the legal honorarium, after initially pointing to the Roman usage of regulating the fees within certain limits in accordance with the type of case, the ability of the lawyer and the standard of the court's custom, he permits agreements between client and advocate, provided that any and all pacts affecting the potential fruits and benefits accruing from the case be avoided.

He excludes procurators from the criminal process *criminaliter actus*, but in reference to matrimonial trials he waives the twenty-five years age requirement as a condition for a person's designation as procurator. Tancred further discusses the effects of this contractual relationship and the various modes of terminating the contract.[67]

Proper consideration is afforded the all important mandate of the procurator both as to form and essential content, in the *Formularium* of Martin of Fano (c. 1232),[68] and in the *Summa Minorum* of Arnulphus (c. 1250-1254), a canon of Paris.[69]

---

65. Wahrmund, *Quellen zur Geschichte des Römischkanonischen Processes im Mittelalter* (5 vols., Innsbruck, 1905-1928, Heidelberg, 1931), I, 4.

66. Wahrmund, *op. cit.*, II, 1, nn. 19-26, 33-34.

67. F. Bergman, *Pilii, Tancredi, Gratiae, Libri de Judiciorum Ordine* (Göttingen, 1842), pp. 87-316.

68. Wahrmund, *op. cit.*, I, 16, 40.

69. Wahrmund, *op. cit.*, I, 53.

Of special merit was the *Summa Aurea* of the Irish William of Drogheda (†1245), written at Oxford about 1239. This manual contains an extensive treatise on the rights and duties of advocates and procurators. In addition, it is decidedly helpful in its positing of practical questions and in its imparting of practical counsel.[70]

Again, between the years 1251 and 1270, another work useful in this connection, appeared in France. It was styled the *Curialis*. In it the various methods of commissioning the procurator are outlined, together with the powers resulting therefrom. Likewise, in it there are indicated definite examples of persons arranging their defense when cited by the court.[71]

It was at this point (c. 1263) that Bonaguida of Arezzo issued his *Summa Introductoria Super Officio Advocationis in Foro Ecclesiastico*. An advocate himself under Innocent IV, a judge, and a professor of canon law, his work naturally was extremely valuable in its practical directions and suggestions, besides affording a fine picture of the actual rôle played by the advocate in his day. The first of five parts in this *Summa* sets forth general principles touching upon qualifications and practical counsels. Part two deals with the formation of the *libellus* for different types of cases and with the drawing up of appeals. In the third and fourth parts methods are elaborated for conducting the case: formation of defense, various exceptions, interrogation of witnesses. Part five considers the formation of various petitions largely of an extra-judicial nature.[72]

Another manual of practical benefit is the *Ordo Judiciarius* of Aegidius de Fuscarariis (†1289), written at Bologna c. 1263-1266. In formulating questions for witnesses, and examples for presenting a case, together with much by way of counsel and admonition, he accomplishes admirably his avowed purpose of assisting advocates.[73]

Finally, the most celebrated treatise on processes throughout the Middle Ages issued from the pen of William Durandus (c. 1237-1296). About the year 1272 he compiled his *Speculum Judiciale*, a

70. Wahrmund, *op. cit.*, II, 2, nn. 36-86, 95 sq.

71. Wahrmund, *op. cit.*, I, 24, 25.

72. Wunderlich, *Anecdota Quae ad Processum Civile Spectant* (Göttingen, 1841), pp. 132-345.

73. Wahrmund, *op. cit.*, III, 1, nn. 19-34, 105-183 sq.

work which earned him the designation *Speculator*. Annotations on the part of renowned canonists greatly enhanced its value. Chiefly responsible in this connection were John Andrea (c. 1270-1348) and Baldus de Ubaldis (c. 1327-1400). This *Ordo* is generally regarded by canonists as embodying the canonical process of the ante-Tridentine period in its most perfect form, theoretically and practically. In Book I,[74] Durandus devotes considerable attention to judicial advocates and procurators. To an extensive commentary on the existing law he, together with other canonists, added a vast amount of practical information regarding these officials in the nature of counsels, admonitions, and methodology.

It is noteworthy that legal historians pay tribute to the manner in which the Church, by her own legislation, has enriched civil legal systems. Particularly in the field of procedural law, it is pointed out, the canonical process attained such perfection after the twelfth century that it became the model for modern civil and criminal codes. Ecclesiastical regulations governing advocates and procurators, in particular, undoubtedly left a deep impression upon the rising legal castes or professions dominated, as they were originally, by canonists and romanists.[75]

ARTICLE 5

PAPAL CONSTITUTIONS

Pope Benedict XII (1334-1342), it appears, was the first Pontiff to issue a decree affecting solely judicial advocates and procurators. In the Bull *"Decens et necessarium"*[76] he endeavored to establish a more systematic ordering of these officials in the Roman Curia, espe-

---

74. *Speculum Juris* (Venetiis, 1577), Lib. I, partic. III, pp. 201-230, partic. IV, pp. 247-283.

75. Salvioli, *Storia del Diritto Italiano* (Torino, 1930), pp. 9, 89, 735; Pertile, *Storia del Diritto Italiano* (Torino, 1902), VI, pp. 257, 270; Pollock-Maitland, *History of the English Law*, I, 114, 190-197; Holdsworth, *A History of English Law*, 9 vols. (Boston: Little, Brown & Co.), II (3 ed., 1927), pp. 311-319, 484-512.

76. Benedict XII, const. *"Decens et necessarium"*, 26 October, 1340 — *Archivium Rotale*, "Constitutiones Rotae Palatii Apostolici," fol. 13; Cerchiari, *Capellani Papae* (4 vols., Romae, 1919-1921), III, 82.

cially the seven existing consistorial advocates, at the same time outlining briefly their duties, rights, and privileges. Of particular interest
is the emphasis placed upon consideration on the part of these officials
for the cases of the poor. In fact, each advocate was to propose at
least one case in *forma pauperum* at every consistory. Furthermore,
they were forbidden to assume cases in such number as to render
adequate attention impossible. Again, before undertaking to represent
or to defend a client, they had to make a diligent examination of the
case in order to determine whether or not it could be conducted justly
and with reasonable hope of success. In this, as in other points touching upon the faithful fulfillment of one's duty, oaths were demanded.
Then, too, the courts were admonished to care that legal aid be so
distributed as to provide every litigant with skilled assistance. The
standard varied with the type of case and *instantia,* and, in general, was
moderated always by a consideration of the circumstances obtaining.
The reimbursement of the procurator was to be one-half that of the
advocate. Over and above this standard, nothing in the nature of a
gift or further agreement could be tolerated. Conscious violation of
any of these provisions entailed proportionate punishment by way of
restitution, suspension, and dismissal.

This legislation was reiterated shortly by similar practical norms
on the part of Pope Gregory XI (1370-1378).[77] In addition to prescriptions regarding the previous examination of the case, the taking
of oaths, and the measuring out of punishments for negligence or
malicious defect, this Constitution regulated in a general way the
mutual relations of advocate and procurator in the process.

Pope Martin V (1417-1431), when establishing regulations for
officials of the Roman Curia in his Bull *"In apostolicae dignitatis specula"*, was not unmindful of advocates and procurators.[78] Only those
who by diligent examination were found to be sufficiently educated,
experienced, and otherwise suitable were to be admitted to practice
before the various offices and tribunals. Sanctions were levelled against
the assumption of unjust and desperate cases, against unseemly meth-

77. Gregory XI, const. *"Quamvis a felicis memoriae"*, 1 March, 1374 —
Archivium Rotale, ibid., fol. 22; Cerchiari, *op. cit.*, III, 92.
78. Martin V, const. *"In apostolicae dignitatis specula"*, 1 Sept., 1418 —
Bull. Rom., IV, 679.

ods of defense, against the introduction of inadmissible material and forms of malicious delay, and against any species of fraudulent procedure or neglect resulting in harm to the client. Prescriptions, moreover, were outlined touching upon extrajudicial conduct in the matter of dress, conversation, company, and general deportment. Once again limitations were detailed with regard to reimbursement. And finally, this Constitution is noteworthy in that it expressly forbade priests and certain other ecclesiastical dignitaries to embrace such positions.

Again setting forth regulations for tribunal officials of the Roman Curia in his Bull *"Romani Pontificis providentia"*,[79] the same pontiff similarly touched the offices of judicial advocate and procurator. He reiterated his stand against the undertaking of unworthy cases, demanding the taking of an oath to this effect. Furthermore, in order to assure adequate assistance in these matters, the examination for candidates was insisted upon. Along with this, the principle of rendering gratuitous patronage whenever necessary was restated, and the court was empowered to compel the officials concerned to assume such cases. Moreover, under severe penalty it was forbidden to serve as advocate or procurator for opposing litigants in the same case, save in such instances as were permitted by the court.

A further reformation of the college of procurators in the Roman Curia was undertaken in the following century by Pope Leo X (1513-1521). The Constitution *"Pastoralis officii"*,[80] while reforming the offices of the Curia in general, contained also several practical regulations affecting procurators. Since these regulations do no more than restate past legislation, one realizes something of the watchfulness that must have been constantly necessary in order to ward off the tendency leading to abuse in these matters. For example, the tribunal of the Sacred Rota was admonished to insist upon the requisite examination for admitting procurators to tribunal practice. The principle of assistance to the poor was again elaborated, and it was definitely prescribed that special procurators were to be designated annually for this work. Owing to the resulting confusion and the consequent inferior defense, to say nothing of added expense and delay, numerous

---

79. Martin V, const. *"Romani Pontificis providentia"*, 1424 — *Bull. Rom.,* IV, 708.

80. Leo X, const. *"Pastoralis officii"*, 13 Dec., 1513 — *Bull. Rom.,* V, 571.

cases were not to be undertaken simultaneously. Furthermore, procurators had to refrain from anything bordering on bargaining with their clients in the matter of rewards, fruits, and remuneration. It might be remarked that this Constitution was approved by the V Lateran Council (1512-1517).

It may be noted that in the foregoing Constitutions interest was centered upon the tribunals and officials of the Roman Curia, which fact continues evident in the papal legislation of the subsequent centuries. However, it must be remembered that the Roman tribunals have always stood as models, as they do today, for those of the Catholic world. Consequently, it seems clear that prescriptions enacted for these courts and their officials are to be regarded as norms affecting others, norms to be followed everywhere when application is both possible and demanded by the nature of the regulation.

A second noteworthy aspect of these constitutions, and of the following ones, is the frequent mention of consistorial advocates. Since little attention has been paid up to this point to this particular type or class of advocate, a brief word appears necessary to avoid confusion.

Authors are not in agreement when attempting to trace the origin of this *collegium.* Some maintain that it dates back to the body of the seven defenders, *the defensores regionarii,* appointed by Innocent I (402-417) to safeguard the rights of the Roman Church. Be that as it may, the number of seven special advocates in Rome did persist. Pope Benedict XII (1334-1342) implicitly recognized the existence and distinction of these advocates as opposed to simple advocates, for he spoke of those who pleaded in consistorial cases and of those who defended before auditors.[81]

To these seven senior consistorial advocates, *numerarii* or *participantes,* Sixtus IV (1471-1484) added five juniors, *supernumerarii* or *non participantes.* To anticipate, this number was approved by Benedict

---

81. Benedict XII, const. *"Decens et necessarium",* 26 Oct., 1340 — *Archivium Rotale,* "Constitutiones Rotae Palatii Apostolici", fol. 13; Cerchiari, *op. cit.,* III, 82; O. Conti, *Origini, Fasti, e Privilegi degli Avvocati Consistoriali,* Roma, 1898; Hilling, *Procedure at the Roman Curia* (New York, 1907), p. 40; Grabowski, I, "Adwokatura," Cap. XIII, "Adwokaci Konsystorscy" — *Ateneum Kaplanskie,* XXXV (1935), 365-367.

XIV (1740-1758), and it has since been retained.[82] The latter Pontiff pointed out that this College had been highly regarded by the Popes from earliest times. Its members were men renowned for learning and virtue. Owing to their knowledge, experience, and prudence, they were selected from all other advocates, and granted the right and privilege of pleading before the Roman Pontiff and the Cardinals assembled in consistory to discuss and define the many grave cases carried to the Holy See for solution. Pope Benedict himself assigned to them a special rôle in the process and ceremony of beatification and canonization. Further, he prescribed that any supplication tendered to the Holy Father sitting in consistory, provided that it did not emanate from royalty or from a cardinal, must be presented through one of these advocates. Then, again, it was the consistorial advocate who was to petition for the pallium in secret consistory.[83]

Through the centuries, this College of Consistorial Advocates has been the recipient of numberless privileges from the Sovereign Pontiffs.[84] Today, owing to the fact that contentious cases are no longer adjudicated in consistory, the consistorial advocate defends before auditors of the ordinary curial tribunals. This fact serves to explain the terminology to be encountered in the present day regulations of these tribunals. Consistorial work for these advocates is now confined to postulating in causes of beatification and canonization, and to postulating the pallium.

It might also be pointed out that Emerix, in his *Sacrae Rotae Romanae Praxis* (tit. 35), differentiates a threefold division of procurators. The superior class was that body of procurators which constituted a college of such officials for causes *Palatii Apostolici*. A second class comprised certain procurators who, although admitted to Rotal practice, were not enrolled in the college. The third and lowest order embraced those who, belonging neither to the college nor to the Sacred Rota, exercised their office before the inferior tribunals.[85]

---

82. Benedict XIV, const. *"Inter conspicuos"*, 29 Aug., 1744 — *Bull. Ben.* XIV, I, 381-397, n. 3; Ferraris, *Bibliotheca*, "Advocati Consistoriales," nn. 1-8.

83. Benedict XIV, *ibid.*, nn. 14-18 — *Fontes*, n. 347.

84. Sixtus V, const. *"Sacri Apostolatus"*, 23 Aug., 1587 — *Bull. Rom.*, VIII, 897; Benedict XIV, const. *"Inter conspicuos"*, 29 Aug., 1744 — *Fontes*, I, 347.

85. Cerchiari, *Capellani Papae*, I, 138; Wernz-Vidal, VI, *De Processibus* (Romae, 1928), p. 207, note 65.

CHAPTER IV

CANONICAL LEGISLATION ON ADVOCATES AND PROCURATORS FROM THE COUNCIL OF TRENT TO THE CODIFICATION OF CANON LAW

ARTICLE 1

COUNCIL OF TRENT (1545-1563)

The salutary decrees of the Council of Trent did much to reform the canonical process. Particularly, a considerable contribution was effected in increasing and strengthening episcopal judicial powers, together with an elimination of many cumbersome solemnities.

However, with regard to the subject under consideration, the Council confines itself to one pertinent canon, and that in an indirect manner. In order to sustain the dignity of the episcopal state, a bishop was not to be compelled to enter court personally, except in a matter involving the possibility of his deposition or privation. Consequently, this canon seems to imply that he was to be represented in all other judicial matters by a procurator.

> .... Episcopus nisi ob causam, ex qua dependendus sive privandus veniret, etiamsi ex officio, aut per inquisitionem, seu denuntiationem, vel accusationem, sive alio quovis modo procedatur, ut personaliter compareat, nequaquam citetur, vel moneatur.[1]

ARTICLE 2

PAPAL CONSTITUTIONS

Endeavoring to stem the rising tide of heresy and schism, Paul IV (1555-1559) enacted strong measures which did not pass over the office of advocate and procurator. Should such officials presume to favor or to assist heretics or schismatics in any manner whatsoever, not only was their patronage rendered null, but they themselves *ipso facto* incurred the penalty of excommunication and infamy.[2]

---

1. Conc. Trident., sess. XIII, *de ref.*, c. 6; cf. canon 1655, § 4.
2. Paul IV, const. *"Cum ex Apostolatus"*, 15 Feb., 1559, n. 5 — *Bull. Rom.*, VI, 551.

In the following year Pope Pius IV (1559-1565), in another disciplinary constitution, touches the rôle of procurator indirectly, somewhat after the manner of the Council of Trent. Striving to restore more respect for the law of episcopal residence in the proper diocese, he established penalties for those not conforming and granted certain privileges for those heeding this law. Among such privileges was included the following. No bishop could be, or should be, cited to appear personally at the Roman Curia, prescinding from the one citing or the matter involved, without a definite commission to this effect from the hand of the Holy Father. Such immunity implied that a bishop should be cited to appear, if necessary, through a procurator.[3]

In two further constitutions of the same Pontiff are likewise embodied points of practical importance. In the first, having for its purpose the reformation of the Roman Rota, it is made clear that a juridically legitimate mandate on the part of the procurator is requisite for the validity of the canonical process.[4] The second, similarly effecting a reform of curial tribunals and offices, indicates a specific and interesting field of endeavor on the part of the advocates and procurators designated for the service of the poor. Both are to manifest a special concern for those incarcerated in the papal states. Procurators were enjoined to visit the prisons daily, to learn the case facts of new inmates, and to communicate this information to the advocates. Without special permission they could accept nothing in the nature of compensation, even from the wealthy. The advocates, too, were to visit the prisons frequently, gratuitously doing all within their power to protect the interests and rights of the imprisoned. In order to facilitate this work, they had to consult with the procurators each week, thus keeping in contact with the data regarding new prisoners. Neglect on the part of the procurators in this matter was to be denounced by the advocate concerned.[5]

3. Pius IV, const. *"De salute gregis"*, 4 Sept., 1560, n. 3 — *Bull. Rom.*, VII, 55.
4. Pius IV, const. *"In throno iustitiae"*, 27 Dec., 1561, n. 13 — *Bull. Rom.*, VII, 156.
5. Pius IV, const. *"Cum ab ipso"*, 30 June, 1562, nn. 36, 37 — *Bull. Rom.*, VII, 214.

Once again, under Paul V (1605-1621), was there a reformation of the Roman tribunals and officials, with not a few regulations affecting the college of procurators. First of all, this constitution repeated *ad verba* the prescription of Pius IV regarding the care of those imprisoned. Secondly, no procurator or advocate could presume to represent or defend, nor could he be admitted, when the case lay before a judge with whom these officials were connected by the bond of consanguinity or affinity to the second degree. In like manner no procurator or advocate, under penalty of infamy and privation of office, could assist both parties in the same case. Furthermore, they were to beware anything savoring of fraud in their association with notaries and others having custody of documents and registers. Not only had the procurator to confine himself to the stipulated remuneration, but he was prohibited as well from entering into any understanding with reference to reward in the event of success. There is repetition, too, of the law demanding successful examination in the matter of learning and personal integrity before anyone was to be admitted to Rota practice. Along with this, one procurator is to be deputed annually for the service of the poor. In addition, when a client is absent, the procurator cannot permit an adverse judgment to become a *res iudicata;* he must appeal, notify his principal, and seek at least one extension of the *fatalia.* Finally, once the procurator has undertaken a case, he must do all in his power to bring it to a successful conclusion. He is cautioned against revealing the secrets of a case to the adversary.[6]

Pope Clement XIV (1769-1774), on the occasion of confirming and renewing privileges held by auditors of Curia tribunals, lays down certain regulations for the dispensing of justice in these tribunals. Touching upon the qualifications of officials, he granted the auditors added powers with regard to the approbation and admission of Rotal advocates and procurators, together with faculties for correcting and punishing these officials for non-observance of the tribunals' rules and regulations. While the rigid law requiring examination for Rotal procurators was generally heeded, nevertheless there were instances of laxity. In this constitution the Supreme Pontiff renewed the law's

---

6. Paul V, const. *"Universi agri Dominici"*, 1 March, 1612, nn. 15-18 — *Bull. Rom.*, XII, 58.

pristine vigor, admonishing auditors to concern themselves with its universal observance.[7]

An additional point of interest with regard to advocates that should be recalled at this juncture is the position of Benedict XIV (1740-1758) on priestly participation in this office:

> Seculari autem clerico minorum ordinum, etiam beneficiato, item subdiacono, immo et sacerdoti, jus ipsum canonicum permittit, ut se advocatos in tribunalibus quidem ecclesiasticis libere exhibeant; in laicalibus vero, et coram seculari judice, si causa ibidem agitanda propriam ipsorum, vel ecclesiae, cui praesunt, aut cui adscripti sunt, vel denique miserabilium personarum rem, utilitatemque respiciat. . . . [8]

ARTICLE 3

DECREES OF THE ROMAN CONGREGATIONS

In 1601 a decision of the Sacred Congregation of Bishops and Regulars, treating of a particular case, vindicated the fundamental right of a legally unimpeded person to be represented in court by a procurator.[9]

A further response of the same Congregation in 1716 sustained the right of ecclesiastics to enter the civil courts and there, without permission of the ordinary, to conduct, personally or through others, a case involving rights of their churches, the interests of the poor, or of other defenseless persons requiring such assistance.[10]

In the instruction on matrimonial processes issued for the Austrian Empire in 1855 by Cardinal Rauscher, Archbishop of Vienna, is found a regulation re-echoing a law of Gregory IX. The parties in a matrimonial case may, of course, retain legal assistance, consulting their advisers at and before every step. However, in certain phases of the process, notably in the original questioning and in the probatory stage, declarations are to be made personally, and only such immediate information is to be inserted in the acts. It is true that this instruction

---

7. Clement XIV, const. *"Cum primum"*, 16 May, 1770 — *Archivium Rotale*, "Privilegia", Tom. II, n. 8; Cerchiari, *Capellani Papae*, III, 598.

8. Benedict XIV, *De Synodo Dioecesana*, Lib. 13, cap. 10, n. 12.

9. S. C. Ep. et Reg., *Camplen.*, 20 Nov., 1601 — *Fontes*, IV, n. 1612.

10. S. C. Ep. Reg., *Castri Maris*, 8 May, 1716 — *Fontes*, IV, n. 1832, ad I, II.

is of a private nature. Nevertheless, owing to its widespread popularity, and to the fact that commendation on the part of Roman theologians and canonists gave it a certain weight, it may justifiably be listed as of importance.[11]

The Sacred Congregation of Bishops and Regulars in 1861, rendering a decision in a private controversy, reiterated the principle of one's freedom to remove a procurator provided that all contractual obligations were duly honored.[12]

A traditional prohibition regarding clerics in judicial matters was re-emphasized by an instruction of the Holy Office in 1866. Ecclesiastics personally engaging in trials involving the effusion of blood continue to incur the punishment of irregularity. This restriction must be understood to embrace judicial advocates and procurators.[13]

In 1872 the Sacred Congregation of the Council, in settling a controversy incidental to the principal issue, indicated that a specific mandate was not required in the matter of filing an appeal to a sentence, provided that subsequently such appeal was ratified by the *dominus*. Such recognition on the part of the principal would serve as the equivalent of the mandate. And this is all the more true if the one appealing does so owing to some title of interest to himself.[14]

During the years 1878 to 1883 the Sacred Congregations issued several instructions bearing upon a particular process, namely, that to be instituted by bishops in criminal and disciplinary causes of clerics.

The procedure to be followed by the bishops of North America in such matters was outlined briefly by the Sacred Congregation for the Propagation of the Faith, July 20, 1878. In replying to certain questions raised owing to this instruction, the same Congregation made this final observation: "Every rector [one suspected or accused] is free to have with him before the Council [commission of investigation] another priest, who must be approved by the bishop, in order either simply to

11. *Instructio pro Judiciis Ecclesiasticis Imperii Austriaci Quoad Causas Matrimoniales* (1855), tit. II, n. 143 — *Analecta Juris Pontificii*, series II (1857), col. 2515; c. 14, X, *de iudiciis*, II, 1.

12. S. C. Ep. et Reg., *Anagnina*, 13 Sept., 1861 — *Fontes*, IV, n. 1981.

13. S. C. S. Off., instr. (pro Vic. Ap. ad Gallas), 20 June, 1866, ad 21 — *Fontes*, IV, n. 994.

14. S. C. C., 17 Aug., 1872 — *ASS*, VII, 393.

assist him, or to make observations, or to conduct the defense." It will be noted that, while speaking of an approved priest who may assist throughout the proceedings, the response makes no mention of a lay advocate.[15]

Pope Leo XIII on June 11, 1880, through the Sacred Congregation of Bishops and Regulars, issued an instruction to the bishops of Italy regarding a summary process in the same type of case. The accused was free to conduct his own defense, but at the same time possessed the right to avail himself of legal assistance. In so doing he could select either a priest or a layman, each requiring episcopal approbation.[16] Should the defendant refuse to exercise this right, it was left to the judgment of the ordinary to appoint an advocate *ex officio*. This official, were it deemed necessary, could be sworn to secrecy. His written defense could be submitted before the day designated for final pleading, and it appears that his final summing up was permitted to take place orally.[17]

Practically identical with this decree of 1880 was the decree *"Cum Magnopere"* of 1883, issued by the Sacred Congregation for the Propagation of the Faith for the United States. Superseding, as a result, the decree of 1878 in this regard, this instruction became the law for this country. Several practical points wherein the decree *"Cum Magnopere"* differed with the instruction of 1880 should be noted.

For example, whereas the defendant formerly was free to choose a clerical or lay advocate, here his liberty was somewhat restricted. In other words, he could select a layman only when the engagement of a competent cleric was impossible. Clearly, the nature of the case appeared to demand this preference.[18] Article 30 must not be understood to imply that the accused could be assisted only in the final

15. These documents, with English translation, may be found in S. B. Smith, *Elements of Ecclesiastical Law* (5. ed., New York, 1887), II, pp. 415-424, in Appendix.

16. S. C. Ep. et Reg., Instr. 11 June, 1880, art. 27, 30 — *Fontes,* n. 2005.

17. *Ibid.,* art. 31, 32, 35 — *Fontes,* n. 2005; cf. also *ASS* (1880), XIII, 324.

18. S. C. de Prop. Fide, instr. anno 1883, art. 30: "Qua die causa proponetur, inquisito fiet facultas defensionem suam per alium sacerdotem suo nomine peragendi. Quod si idoneum non reperiat, laicum catholicum adhibere potest. Quisque autem ex iis ab Ordinario approbandus est." — *Fontes,* VII, n. 4900.

summing-up. Rather, its wording indicates that the defendant, who may have been *assisted* throughout the trial in accordance with the general law of the Church, in this one phase may even be represented by the advocate acting as a procurator, a situation ordinarily excluded from the criminal process. This viewpoint is supported by the Third Plenary Council of Baltimore in its comment on this article.[19]

A second noteworthy divergence is apparent. In accordance with the general law and universal practice, the instruction of 1880 empowered the advocate to summarize his arguments first in writing (art. 32) and then orally before the court (art. 35). Taking cognizance of objections on the part of our bishops in this regard, the Sacred Congregation in the decree *"Cum Magnopere"* eliminated oral presentation of defense. That the advocate might be in a position to defend his client thoroughly, he was granted the right to inspect the acts of the trial and to obtain a copy of the prosecutor's summation.[20]

Pope Benedict XIV (1740-1758) made mention of indults permitting clerics otherwise deprived of sufficient income to engage themselves as advocates before the civil tribunals, even in criminal cases, provided that they acted and wrote for the defense in the latter type of case.[21] A concrete example may be found in a dispensation to this effect of the Sacred Congregation of the Council in 1883. A trained yet indigent Spanish priest, promising to uphold clerical and ecclesiastical rights, was furnished with this permission. All scandal had to be removed, and the time element was left to the judgment of the ordinary.[22] This was in accord with the teaching of Pope Benedict, who made it clear that when such a one had acquired sufficient support, the bishop should realize that exercise of the indult was to be denied. Incidentally, the same Pontiff had excluded religious from the possession of such dispensations.

---

19. *Acta et Decreta Concilii Plenarii Baltimorensis III* (1884), tit. X, cap. III, n. 315: "Reus igitur ipse comparere non tenetur, sed potest, . . ."

20. S. C. de Prop. Fide, instr. anno 1883, art. 32, 33 — *Fontes,* VII, n. 4900; *Collectanea S. C. de Prop. Fide, II,* n. 1586.

21. *De Synodo Dioecesana,* Lib. XIII, cap. 10, n. 12.

22. S. C. C., *Nullius Clunien.,* 4 Aug., 1883 — *ASS,* XVI (1883-1884), 227-230.

ARTICLE 4

LEGISLATION OF PARTICULAR COUNCILS

During the period from the Council of Trent to the codification of Canon Law it is to be expected that particular councils and synods would not contribute a great deal of definite legal import or development with regard to judicial advocates and procurators. That is not to maintain that the offices were disregarded. Quite the contrary is true. However, owing to the Decretal Law and the Papal Constitutions, the general law may be said to have been thoroughly established. Consequently, the norms discovered in these councils appear obviously as repetitions, as particular applications of the general law.

As an illustration, numberless councils concerned themselves with restraining clerics from worldly occupations according to the dictum of St. Paul: *"Nemo Deo militans, implicat se negotiis saecularibus."*[23] At times, in this connection, express mention was made of clerical advocates and procurators avoiding secular courts, except in the cases permitted according to the canons.[24]

In addition, there was manifested a continued solicitude for the poor in judicial matters. Particularly, Pope Benedict XIII (1724-1730), in the Council of Rome, 1725, exhorted all bishops to designate advocates and procurators in the diocesan curia for their service.[25] His recommendation was embodied in summary form in the acts of the Council of Fermo of the following year:

---

23. II Tim., II, 4.

24. Council of Benevento (1693), Tit. XLII, cap. II — *Collectio Lacensis,* I, 77; Synod of Naples (1699), Tit. IX, n. 12 — *Coll. Lac.,* I, 227; Council of Rome (1725), cap. XVIII, n. 10 — *Coll. Lac.,* I, 440; Council of Toulouse (1850), tit. IV, cap. IV, n. 130 — *Coll. Lac.,* IV, 1069; Council of Ravenna (1855), pars IV, cap. VI, n. 5 — *Coll. Lac.,* VI, 199; Council of Bordeaux (1859), tit. III, cap. IV, n. 2 — *Coll. Lac.,* IV, 761; Council of Esztergom (1858), tit. VI, n. 10 — *Coll. Lac.,* V, 53; Council of Urbino (1859), pars II, tit. VIII, n. 150 — *Coll. Lac.* VI, 52; Council of New Granada (1868), tit. VII, cap. I, par. 14 — *Coll. Lac.* VI, 545.

25. Council of Rome (1725), tit. VIII, cap. III — *Coll. Lac.,* I, 358; see also Council of Naples (1699), in relatione ultimo loco — *Coll. Lac.,* I, 256; Council of Fermo (1726), tit. IV, § 3 — *Coll. Lac.,* I, 593; Council of Ravenna (1855), pars IV, cap. IX, n. 5 — *Coll. Lac.,* VI, 210; Council of Urbino (1859), pars II, tit. V, n. 126 — *Coll. Lac.,* VI, 43.

Quoniam vero paternam pauperum curam gerere debemus, ubi procuratores vel advocati pauperum in curiis ecclesiasticis constituti non sunt, constituantur; et quatenus opus sit, praeter exemptiones et praerogativas, iisdem de jure vel consuetudine indultas, etiam aliquod stipendium arbitrio Episcopi ex proventibus locorum piorum assignetur.[26]

Again, conscious violation of duty, or misconduct outside the court, was to be dealt with in these officials severely. A typical prescription in this regard may be found in the Council of Urbino, 1859.[27]

Furthermore, it was not uncommon to incorporate into conciliar acts, as did the III Plenary Council of Baltimore, 1884, norms concerning advocates in matrimonial trials based upon those of the Austrian Instruction of 1855.[28]

One particular innovation is to be noted in the above mentioned Council of Baltimore. By express authorization of the Holy See the Council went a step further in interpreting article 30 of the decree *"Cum Magnopere"* of the year 1883. In the criminal and disciplinary trials of clerics, the advocate now had to be himself a cleric. A former preference thus became an obligation.[29]

ARTICLE 5

REGULATIONS OF THE ROMAN TRIBUNALS

Pope Gregory XVI (1831-1846) in his *Motu Proprio* of Nov. 10, 1834, containing the *Regolamento Legislativo e Giudiziario*, effected his long-desired reform of the legislative and judicial departments, lay and ecclesiastical, throughout the Pontifical States. With the exception of a few practical enactments regarding the appointment of procurators, the method of procedure contains little having a direct bearing upon the subject of this study.[30] However, the Holy Father

---

26. Council of Fermo (1726), tit. IV, § 3 — *Coll. Lac.*, I, 593.

27. Pars II, tit. IV, n. 129 — *Coll. Lac.*, VI, 44.

28. *Acta et Decreta Concilii Plenarii Baltimorensis III (1884)*, tit. X, cap. II, n. 307; *Coll. Lac.*, V, 1304.

29. *Acta et Decreta Concilii Plenarii Baltimorensis III*, Tit. X, cap. II, n. 302; cap. III, n. 315.

30. *Acta Gregorii Papae XVI*, IV, 299 sq., n. 541 sq.

indicated that legislation affecting these officials, as well as other related matters, would constitute the subject matter of a forthcoming decree.[31]

Such a document issued from the hand of the Cardinal Secretary of State on Dec. 17, 1834, and it has subsequently been referred to, after His Eminence, as the *Editto Gamberini*.[32] In seeking to determine the juridical value of this Edict in relation to the common law, one finds that it was generally regarded by canonists as a prudent norm to be followed.[33]

Among the prescriptions regarding advocates the following should be of particular interest. In order for one to aspire to the position of advocate, it was necessary for him to be twenty-five years of age. The candidate had to furnish documents manifesting legitimacy, citizenship, and the reception of Baptism and Confirmation. Testimony, moreover, was required with reference to good religious, political, and moral conduct. A doctorate had previously to be attained from a University of the State; and, in addition, the aspirant must have spent a novitiate of five years with a practicing advocate. Over and above these requirements all the existing regulations peculiar to the Sacred Rota were sanctioned. And, in this connection, it might be remarked that a Rotal advocate was empowered to defend in all tribunals of the State. A number of disciplinary councils, assigned in the various apellate jurisdictions, exercised a constant and quite thorough surveillance over all advocates.[34]

Notable among the provisions affecting procurators was the necessary admission and approbation of the tribunal for such an official. Likewise, the requirements of age and of specified documents corresponded to those demanded of the advocate, although, unlike the advocate, this official needed to possess only a licentiate and two years of forensic practice with an approved procurator. The norms peculiar to the Sacred Rota and the Signatura in this matter were also confirmed. Rotal procurators possessed the right to represent others in all tribunals of Rome and the State. The procurator was barred from entering a

---

31. *Ibidem,* nn. 257, 422.
32. *Acta Gregorii Papae XVI,* IV, 413 sq.
33. Lega, *De Iudiciis Ecclesiasticis Civilibus,* I, 14, note 2.
34. *Acta Gregorii Papae XVI,* IV, 413 sq., nn. 229, 236, 239-245.

case in which he would find himself related to the judge. Finally, the courts were granted the faculties to level proportionate punishments against these officials should lack of respect in word or deed, or any other violation of duty demand it.[35]

A later section of the same Edict contains a minutely detailed list of fees that might be legitimately received by the advocate and procurator. Particularly in the case of the procurator is this list exhaustive, covering practically every possible act.[36]

To the Apostolic Constitution *"Sapienti Consilio"* of Pius X, which appeared in 1908, reorganizing the Roman Curia, were appended processual norms to be observed in the tribunals of the Sacred Rota and of the Apostolic Signatura. In summarizing the prescriptions regarding advocates and procurators that are of interest here, it might be noted that they do not differ substantially from the subsequent regulations of 1934.[37]

While litigants were free to appear before the Sacred Rota in their own cases, they were likewise at liberty to select defenders and representatives, fortifying them with a written mandate.[38]

After declaring that consistorial advocates hold the position of ordinary Rotal defenders, canon 44 of the Lex Propria proceeds to point out that others may be admitted, both lay and clerical. However, certain requirements are laid down, including the doctorate in Canon Law, a novitiate of three years with an auditor or advocate of the Rota, a successful examination and the consequent reception of the Rota diploma, and the oath of office. These officials are forbidden, in canon 45, to purchase cases, to seek extraordinary fees, and to form agreements with the client regarding the outcome of the case. Such pacts are nullified and render the official liable to punishment. The appendix to these norms, furthermore, embodies a list of fees established for advocates and procurators.

---

35. *Ibidem,* IV, 413 sq. nn. 247-275.

36. *Ibidem,* IV, 413 sq. nn. 452-463; 464-526; 527-529.

37. *Normae S. R. Rotae Tribunalis,* 29 June, 1934, cap. V, art. 54 — *AAS,* XXVI (1934), 449.

38. *Lex Propria S. R. Rotae et Sign. Apostolicae,* 29 June, 1908, can. 18 — *AAS,* I (1909), 20 sq.

In the same document, among regulations set forth for all offices and tribunals in common, there is again a section affecting these officials. Procurators are forbidden to demand remuneration in excess of the standards; violation entails the obligation of restitution and other penalties. For misconduct, grave negligence, and failure to fulfill his duty faithfully, he may be punished by temporary or perpetual removal.[39]

Further norms affecting the Sacred Rota were issued in 1910. The court was enjoined to require of advocates and procurators their legitimate mandate for conducting the case, and a mandate precisely for so doing before the Rota.[40] Should serious harm befall a client owing to the negligence or fraudulent activity of a procurator, that official, though his services be gratuitous, is to be disciplined according to the tribunal's canons.[41] Additional norms regulated the admission of procurators for different types of cases, and in general terms defined their manner of conducting the suit.[42] In the event that a defendant in a criminal process lacked legal assistance, or if he personally was unequal to the task of defending himself, the court had to assign an advocate gratuitously whenever circumstances warranted it.[43] Finally, it was stipulated that a procurator in all matters dealing with oaths, had to seek a special mandate.[44]

Among the regulations established in 1912 for trials before the Signatura, there are likewise several norms affecting advocates and procurators. For example, the procurator's mandate had to be attached in proper form to the introductory *libellus*.[45] From a mechanical point of view, directions were indicated with regard to drawing up the defense.[46] Lastly, these officials practicing before the Signatura were

---

39. *Ordo Servandus in Sacris Congreg., Tribun., Officiis Romanae Curiae,* 29 June, 1908, pars I, cap. IX, nn. 13, 14 — *AAS,* I (1909), 36.

40. *Regulae Servandae in Iudiciis apud S. R. Rotae Tribunal,* 4 Aug., 1910, tit. 1, § 4, nn. 1, 2 — *AAS,* II (1910), 783 sq.

41. *Ibid.,* tit. I, par. 28, n. 3.

42. *Ibid.,* tit. I, par. 39, nn. 1, 2; par. 40, nn. 1, 2, 3, 4; par. 41, nn. 1, 2.

43. *Ibid.,* tit. I, par. 109, n. 2; par. 123, n. 2.

44. *Ibid.,* tit. I, par. 149, n. 3.

45. *Regulae Servandae in Iudiciis apud Supremum Signaturae Apostolicae Tribunal,* 6 Mar., 1912, art. 12, c. — *AAS,* IV (1912), 187 sq.

46. *Ibid.,* art. 41.

granted fees double those listed in the norms of the year 1908 for Rotal officials.[47]

That the Roman tribunals stand as models of efficiency and thoroughness for the diocesan curias of the world has already been noted. As a result, the practical importance of these regulations consists not only in the fact of Roman usage, but also in this that they really exert a wide legal influence. Assuredly, the norms here cited, for example, have definitely affected the institutions under consideration, since diocesan tribunals will not have failed to embrace similar regulations in so far as it has been necessary, possible, or feasible to do so. And the footnotes to the pertinent canons of the present legislation bear witness to the influence which these particular regulations have exerted upon the general law affecting judicial advocates and procurators as it exists today.

47. *Ibid.*, art. 60.

PART II

CANONICAL COMMENTARY

CHAPTER V

THE APPOINTMENT OF JUDICIAL ADVOCATES AND PROCURATORS

ARTICLE 1

TRIALS DEMANDING AND PERMITTING THE PRESENCE OF ADVOCATES AND PROCURATORS

CANON 1655. — § 1. In iudicio criminali reus aut a se electum aut a iudice datum semper habere debet advocatum.

It is noteworthy that whereas the rubrics of Chapter II, title IV, of the fourth book of the Code primarily indicate a treatment of procurators, canon 1655 proceeds to devote primary consideration to and emphasis upon the advocate. The rubrical arrangement finds explanation in its logical connection with Chapter I which treats of the parties involved in litigation. He who represents another in judicial proceedings according to the legal principle: *"Potest quis per alium quod potest facere per seipsum"*[1] naturally is foremost. However, from the viewpoint of necessity and importance with regard to the rendering of legal assistance the advocate must occupy the place of primary consideration.

Ordinarily one possessing legal capacity to stand in court is free to avail himself of or to forego legal assistance.[2] Nevertheless, in certain circumstances such option is denied by law. First of all, canon 1655 in paragraph one demands that the defendant in a criminal trial be defended by someone other than himself.

1. Reg. 68, R. J., in VI°.
2. Canon 1655, § 3.

By the *reus,* or defendant, is understood that person, physical or moral, who has been summoned to judgment by the court and from whom or against whom something is sought by the plaintiff.[3] The *reus* in a criminal process is commonly designated by the term *accused.*

The criminal suit of canon 1655, § 1 must be understood in the strict sense of canon 1522, § 2, n. 2.[4] In other words, the canon requires adequate defense for the accused in a criminal trial *criminaliter actum,* a trial, that is, which has for its object the demand for or declaration of punishment in view of an alleged crime. Should action be instituted against a person with a view toward effecting reparation or compensation owed by reason of a delict, such action, involving as it does merely the private good, would be regarded rather as contentious and not criminal in the strict proper sense.[5]

The accused in a strict criminal process must have an advocate. More explicitly does the canon, in paragraph two, denote the essential character of this necessary assistant when it employs the synonymous term *defensor.* In other words, the defendant must be aided by an ecclesiastical counsellor at law, a legal expert, one who will be in a position to advise him and to lay before the court the arguments, whether of law or of fact, leading to a vindication of his client's right, the right, namely, which declares that before he can be punished he must be proven legally guilty.[6]

This equitable and humane provision of the Church's procedural law suffers no exception. It is a strict legal requirement which must be honored by every ecclesiastical tribunal and in each instance of every criminal suit.[7]

---

3. Coronata, *Institutiones Iuris Canonici* (Taurini, 1933), III, 77. As Noval points out, a moral non-collegiate person could only be the defendant in a contentious process — *Commentarium Codicis Iuris Canonici,* Lib. IV, *De Processibus,* Pars I, *De Iudiciis* (Augustae Taurinorum) p. 153. Hereafter this work will be referred to as *De Iudiciis.*

4. *Obiectum iudicii sunt: ... Delicta in ordine ad poenam infligendam vel declarandam; et tunc iudicium est criminale.*

5. Canon 2210. Cf. Grabowski, "Adwokatura w Ustawodawstwie Koscielnem" — *Ateneum Kaplanskie,* XXXV (1935), 242; Noval, *De Iudiciis,* p. 175.

6. Grabowski, "Adwokatura" — *Ateneum Kaplanskie,* XXXIII (1934), 249.

7. Muñiz, *Procedimientos Eclesiásticos* (3 vols., 2 ed., Seville, 1926), III, 515.

Canon Law permits the accused to designate his own advocate. Such freedom of selection, however, is not without limitation since the lawyer must be duly qualified and must meet with the approval of the ordinary in whose tribunal the action occurs.[8] In fact, should the choice of a legal assistant happen to prove an unhappy one the situation must be remedied.[9]

In the event that some personal motive would incline the accused to refuse defense, or should the counsel selected find it impossible to undertake the rôle, then must the judge or presiding judge assume the duty of providing a lawyer even contrary to the wishes of the defendant. Needless to say, the court must designate only an approved advocate who possesses the requisite juridical qualifications, thereby guaranteeing adequate legal assistance.

This law, reflecting the age-old concern of the Church for just judgment, has been drawn practically in its present form from the *Lex Propria* of the Holy Roman Rota.[10] As such, it is a clear illustration of a point manifested throughout this dissertation, namely, that of Rotal norms given the force of universal law with the Code.[11]

It has been noted that canon 1655, § 1, admits no exception. This principle is to be maintained even in the cases involving an accused person who might be regarded as perfectly capable of defending himself.[12] As a matter of fact, even prior to the Code, in criminal and disciplinary trials involving clerics, who might be expected to possess some knowledge of ecclesiastical law and practice, the employment of legal assistance was urged and it was left to the court's discretion to

8. Canons 1657, §§ 1, 2; 1658, § 2.

9. Canons 1619, § 2; 1655, § 2.

10. *Regulae Servandae in Iudiciis apud S. R. Rotae Tribunal,* Aug. 4, 1910, Tit. I, par. 109, n. 2 — *AAS,* II (1910), 783 sq. In view of the historical examination of this question, the author is unable to agree with Augustine to the effect that the provision under discussion is a modern one discountenanced in the Decretals: cf. *A Commentary on Canon Law* (8 vols., St. Louis, 1918-1922), VII, 108.

11. It is noteworthy that footnotes to the Code, Book IV, refer one hundred and sixty-five times to Rotal regulations, thus indicating a font responsible for much of the unity to be found in Church procedure.

12. Blat, *Commentarium Textus Codicis Iuris Canonici,* Lib. IV, *De Processibus* (Romae, 1927), p. 159.

appoint adequate defense where it was deemed necessary.[13]   Granted that the accused is profoundly versed in canonical procedure, the law yet maintains that when there is question of his adequate defense, particularly in criminal proceedings, he can no longer be considered sufficiently capable. Recourse must be had to the learning of another who is in a position to view the case dispassionately and to plead it with greater precision and skill.

> CANON 1655. — § 2. Etiam in iudicio contentioso, si agatur de minoribus aut de iudicio in quo bonum publicum vertitur, iudex parti carenti defensorem ex officio attribuat, aut, si casus ferat, parti etiam habenti alium adiungat.

In paragraph two, canon 1655 proceeds to demand the presence of advocates in certain types of contentious trials for the pleading of both parties. Whereas the criminal process has for its object the punishment of delicts, the contentious or civil suit is concerned with the prosecution and the vindication of rights.[14] The legal necessity for the presence of advocates in civil trials is not universal as in the criminal process but is restricted to two sets of circumstances.

First, should the suit involve minors, either as plaintiff or defendant, advocates must be employed. As a result, the canon embraces not only all physical persons who have not yet completed their twenty-first year of age,[15] but likewise, according to the common teaching of authors, moral persons, whether collegiate or non-collegiate, who are regarded as minors in law.[16] Secondly, advocates must render legal assistance in those civil processes which concern the public good, trials, namely, in which, depending upon the outcome, the public good might notably be prejudiced. Consequently, one might cite by way of example trials dealing with the validity of matrimony, of sacred ordination and of

---

13. S. C. Ep. et Reg., Instr. 11 June, 1880, art. 30, 31 — *Fontes,* IV, n. 2005; cf. *ASS,* XIII (1880), 324; S. C. de Prop. Fide, Instr. anno 1883, art. 30, 31 — *Fontes,* VII, n. 4900.

14. Canon 1552.

15. Canon 88, § 1

16. Canon 100, § 3. Cf. Noval, *De Iudiciis,* p. 175; Blat, *De Processibus,* p. 159.

religious profession. Similarly, it is fitting that lawyers assume the rôle of defense in cases in which the promoter of justice necessarily intervenes in accordance with canon 1586.[17]

It is to be noted that in the above-mentioned types of processes the necessity of acquiring lawyers extends to both plaintiff and defendant. No distinction is contained in the law confining this recourse to the defendant as in the criminal trial.

Both parties to the suit are free to designate their advocates subject to the approval of the ordinary.[18] However, as in the criminal trial, the judge is obliged to supply legal aid to either litigant in the event that it is lacking whether through neglect, unwillingness, or any other reason. Moreover, the judge is bound to provide adequate defense. Even if the parties have availed themselves of a lawyer's assistance, should the judge deem it necessary owing to the amount of aid required or because of an advocate's incompetence, he must augment the legal aid already commissioned should the party fail to remedy the situation personally. Especially in cases involving the validity of a Sacrament and the welfare of souls must the court take precautions lest the litigants' choice of advocates jeopardize rights. In canon 1655, § 2 the court is provided with the means of eliminating or of remedying evident injustice occasioned by a negligent, incapable advocate, thus assisting the judge to fulfill an obligation laid upon him by law.[19]

Since canon 1655, § 2 affects the canonical procedure in matrimonial cases, the present parallel norms governing that process should be noted:

> ARTICULUS 43, § 1. Quamvis pars per seipsam agere et respondere possit in iudicio, expedit tamen ut habeat advocatum, vel a se electum vel a praeside datum, iuxta normas quae sequuntur.
>
> § 2. Praeses, audito iudicum collegio, potest etiam alium advocatum designare, si casus ferat, veluti in casibus negligentiae advocati a parte delecti.

---

17. Toso in *Jus Pontificium*, XVIII (1938), 84; Grabowski, "Adwokatura" — *Ateneum Kaplanskie*, XXXV (1935), 243; Blat, *op. cit.*, p. 159; Noval, *op. cit.*, p. 175. While authors consider the ordination process as one involving the public good, it will be pointed out that advocates are excluded since the procedure is not of strictly judicial nature.

18. Canon 1658, § 2.

19. Canon 1619, § 2. Cf. *S. R. Rotae Decisiones*, XX (1928), 407, n. 10.

§ 3. Si uterque coniux nullitatis declarationem petat, sufficit si alteruter advocatum constituat, nisi altera pars suum proprium constituere velit, aut praeses id opportunum duxerit.

§ 4. Pars conventa, quae matrimonii nullitatem oppugnet, constituere potest advocatum, quamvis adsit vinculi defensor qui pro vinculo certare debet, cui ipsa pars argumenta et probationes suppeditare valet.[20]

Obviously, article 43 of the 1936 Matrimonial Instruction modifies canon 1655, § 2, in two particulars. First, the Instruction merely recommends and exhorts recourse to legal assistance, admitting the possibility of personal pleading which is conditioned by the requirement of legal talent. Secondly, it is not necessary for both parties in the marriage process to commission lawyers. In the event that both husband and wife impugn the validity of their marriage, one advocate for either or both will suffice to prosecute. Should the plea of one party for a declaration of nullity be opposed by the other, still one advocate would be sufficient. Naturally the plaintiff will be assisted, whereas, owing to the office of the *defensor vinculi,* the rights of the defendant will be jealously safeguarded.

Furthermore, in this connection, article 46 of the same Instruction must be borne in mind:

ARTICULUS 46: Causa a promotore iustitiae instituta ad normam art. 35, § 1, n. 2; 38 et 39, coniux, cui ius non est accusandi matrimonium, advocatum sibi constituere potest; sed, promotore iustitiae accusationem revocante vel a lata sententia non appellante, advocati eiusdem officium cessat.[21]

As Doheny aptly remarks: "It might well have been in accord with ecclesiastical law to deprive the consort, disqualified from attacking a marriage, of the right to have an advocate. In such an event the *promotor iustitiae* would have been entrusted with the pleading of the

---

20. S. Congr. Sacr., *Instructio Servanda a Tribunalibus Dioecesanis in Pertractandis Causis de Nullitate Matrimoniorum,* 15 Aug., 1936 — *AAS, XXVIII* (1936), 313-361. Hereafter this Instruction will be referred to simply as *Instructio.*

21. S. C. Sacr., *Instructio.*

case. Happily, the Instruction has seen fit to permit an advocate even to the estopped party."[22]

Needless to say, when the promotor of justice, in accordance with article 41, § 4 of the same Instruction, revokes his accusation or refuses to appeal the case, the case ceases to exist before a tribunal, and, by that very fact, so too does the rôle of the advocate permitted automatically cease. This inability of the parties to continue and of advocates to proceed, even of advocates substituted *ex officio,* was confirmed by a subsequent response of the Sacred Congregation of the Sacraments to questions proposed by the Archbishop of Milan.[23]

It is noteworthy that in the case provided for by article 46 of the 1936 Matrimonial Instruction the party is granted the aid of *an* advocate, not the freedom to avail himself of several lawyers' assistance.[24]

In certain circumstances, then, the law demands that litigants have recourse to advocates for legal assistance. Such a requirement becomes increasingly understandable the more one considers the problems confronting the average party to a lawsuit. In every formal process he is faced with a twofold responsibility. In the first place, the plaintiff must invoke the law regarding his claim and establish the facts upon which that claim is founded, whereas the defendant, taking exception to that contention, must petition the law in his own defense. Secondly, the parties in the prosecution of their rights must conform to the norms established by legitimate authority for the valid conducting of a judicial process. A satisfactory assumption and fulfillment of such responsibility is more than can reasonably be expected of the average person. Consequently, in order that the law may be invoked properly and proofs presented in such fashion as to demonstrate that the law corresponds to the facts, the assistance of a skilled legal assistant is practically indispensable. In a word, the Church's legal system, like any other body

22. *Canonical Procedure in Matrimonial Cases* (Milwaukee: Bruce Publishing Co., 1938), p. 107, note 7.

23. These replies of May 30, 1938, together with a brief comment by Roberti, may be found in *Apollinaris,* XI (1938), 498, 500, ad V, VI. Cf. also Roberti, "De condicione processuali Promotoris Iustitiae, Defensoris Vinculi, et coniugum in causis matrimonialibus" — *Apollinaris,* XI (1938), 576-582. It may be noted that here Roberti recommends recourse to the judge in the event of arbitrary relinquishing of the case by the promoter of justice.

24. Cf. canon 1656, § 3; art. 47, § 3, S. C. S., *Instructio.*

of laws, is beyond the grasp of one who has not devoted special time and study to it.[25] If that be true of the ordinary litigant, then does the necessity spoken of in canon 1655, § 2, find added forcefulness. Historically, in nothing has the Church been more solicitous than in defending *personae miserabiles,* among whom must be numbered minors, those considered incapable of defending themselves. And in like manner does the general need for legal aid find specific application in cases involving the common good owing to the social and spiritual issues at stake.

In this connection, however, it must be noted that advocates and procurators are prohibited from engaging in an official capacity in processes other than those of a contentious or criminal character. In other words, where there is question rather of administrative procedure or of procedure that is not of a strictly judicial nature, these officials may not enter a case. This does not imply that their services must be dispensed with. On the contrary, both the interested parties and the tribunal itself may and should have recourse to these legal assistants for counsel and direction.[26]

CANON 1655. — § 3. Praeter hos casus pars libere potest advocatum et procuratorem constituere, sed potest quoque in iudicio per se ipsa agere et respondere, nisi iudex procuratoris vel advocati ministerium necessarium existimaverit.

After establishing the necessity for advocates in specific types of judicial procedure, canon 1655, § 3, proceeds to set down the general principle of freedom to appear and to plead in court personally or to be represented and defended by legal experts. With the exception of the processes outlined in canon 1655, § 1 and § 2, it is left to the parties to choose between defending themselves or availing themselves of ecclesiastical lawyers. Furthermore, they are given the option of

25. Cf. Wernz-Vidal, *Ius Canonicum,* VI, Pars 1ª, 196, note 3; Roberti, *De Processibus* (Romae, 1926), I, 324; Noval, *De Iudiciis,* p. 176; Lega-Bartoccetti, *Commentarius in Iudicia Ecclesiastica iuxta Codicem Iuris Canonici,* vol. I (Romae, 1938), 333.

26. Schmalzgrueber, *Ius Ecclesiasticum Universum,* Lib. I, tit. 37, n. 2.

conducting the trial personally or of being represented before the tribunal by a procurator, which, in most instances is to be recommended.[27]

The *procurator ad lites,* it will be recalled, is an agent commissioned by a principal to act judicially in the latter's name. Legitimately appointed by a litigant and admitted by the court, his function is to represent that party before the tribunal presenting all the bills of complaint and lodging all forms of recourse and appeal. *"Procurator est qui aliena negotia mandato domini administrat."*[28]

"Potest quis per alium quod potest facere per seipsum."[29] According to this principle of law a procurator may be commissioned by anyone legally capable of standing in judgment for any judicial process provided that no prohibition governing a particular case exists in law. The Code gives no evidence of such prohibition. As a result, one must conclude that the present legislation has sanctioned the relaxation of one prohibition which existed in Decretal Law, namely, that whereby the procurator was excluded from the criminal trial.[30] Owing to the fact that penalties existing in the present law can be executed despite the absence of a guilty party, there no longer exists the necessity of debarring a procurator for such a one in the modern criminal suit.[31] Furthermore, and this must be noted with reference to the presence of procurators in general, judicial representation by no means grants the parties total exemption from the necessity of appearing personally in court. There are times when the law itself requires principals to appear and it is always within the power of the judge to demand personal appearance when he deems it necessary.[32] Needless to say, there are certain phases of the process for which a judicial agent is thoroughly incompetent and ineligible as a substitute for a litigant. The giving of

27. Roberti, *De Processibus,* I, 327.

28. D (3, 3), 1.

29. Reg. 68, R. J., in VI°.

30. C. 5, X, *de procuratoribus,* I, 38; cc. 15, 16, X, *de accusat., inquisit., et denuntiat.,* V. 1; c. 1, *de iudiciis,* II, 1, in VI; Durandus, *Speculum Juris,* I, III, n. 9; Reiffenstuel, *Ius Canonicum Universum,* Lib. I, tit. 38, nn. 62-66

31. Cf. Lega-Bartoccetti, *Commentarius in Iudicia Ecclesiastica,* I, 342; Smith, *Elements of Ecclesiastical Law,* II, 48; Eichmann, *Das Prozessrecht des Codex Iuris Canonici* (Paderborn, 1921), p. 94.

32. Canon 1647; cf. canons 1742; 1743, § 3; 1746; art. 45, S. C. S., *Instructio.*

testimony in a matrimonial trial provides an apt illustration, for "They alone [the parties] can give adequate testimony as to their thoughts, motives, intentions, and the like."[33]

Since the present norms governing matrimonial processes were issued as recently as 1936, few authors have raised the question regarding freedom to commission a procurator when a plea for declaration of nullity has been introduced by the promoter of justice. At times, the parties lack processual capacity to challenge personally the validity of their marriage.[34] In the event that the promoter of justice impugns its validity, the parties must be summoned in order that the suit be contested.[35] May one or both of the parties authorize procurators to represent them under such circumstances? The writer agrees with Doheny who feels that such a course is entirely permissible subject to the condition of a possible adverse decision on the part of the presiding judge or tribunal.[36] This view appears to be justified since the consorts in such action must be designated *partes*, thus coming within the extension of canon 1655, § 3. Furthermore, such freedom seems to be permissible from the fact that in these cases legal assistance on the part of advocates is explicitly granted.[37]

It must be noted that the freedom which litigants enjoy of standing in court personally and of pleading their own cases is prudently conditioned by the Church's law. Should the exercise of that freedom jeopardize one's legal position in the court's opinion, aid on the part of an advocate or procurator may always be prescribed. From what has been noted regarding the necessity for these officials one realizes the wisdom of this restricting clause, and one can appreciate, too, Hilling's reason for advising tribunals not to encourage personal assumption of defense but rather the employment of legal experts in all cases.[38]

---

33. Doheny, *Canonical Procedure in Matrimonial Cases*, p. 106.

34. Art. 35-39, *Instructio*.

35. Art. 75, *Instructio*.

36. *Canonical Procedure in Matrimonial Cases*, p. 159; cf. canon 1647; art. 45, *Instructio*.

37. Art. 46, *Instructio*.

38. "Die Heranziehung der Advokaten zu den kirchlichen Prozessen" — *Archiv für katholisches Kirchenrecht*, CIII (1923), 132.

In particular, freedom to act or not through a procurator is conditioned in another sense. Just as advocates are compulsory in certain circumstances,[39] so, too, the law demands that some persons in order to stand in court at all must act through representatives, subject always to the requirement of canon 1647. For example, minors who have not yet completed their fourteenth year may plead in spiritual causes and in trials connected with spiritual causes, but only through a tutor designated by the ordinary or through a chosen procurator approved by the ordinary.[40] In like manner, when litigation arises involving a conflict of rights between a moral person and the rector or administrator concerned, the moral person must be represented in court by a procurator commissioned by the ordinary.[41] It must be noted that failure on the part of moral persons and minors to comply with the law in this regard results in the performance of invalid acts, for there is here question of the procurator supplying processual incapacity.[42] A third trial demanding representation is that engaged in by an excommunicated person who is to be shunned or tolerated after pronouncement of a condemnatory or declaratory sentence, provided he desires to introduce a suit with a view to avoiding some danger to his soul.[43] A person in these circumstances, for example, through the agency of a procurator might seek a declaration of matrimonial nullity.[44] In addition, actions involving persons whose state or condition of life renders personal appearance before a tribunal impossible, such as nuns and invalids, must be conducted through procurators.[45]

In the discussion of paragraph two of canon 1655 mention was made of the fact that the *defensor vinculi* in the matrimonial process is *ex officio* an advocate for the respondent.[46] The question here suggests itself, to what extent, if at all, may the *defensor vinculi* be regarded

39. Canon 1655, §§, 1, 2.

40. Canon 1648, § 3.

41. Canon 1649.

42. Canon 1892, n. 2. Cf. Hanssens, "De Sanctione Nullitatis in Processu Canonico" — *Apollinaris*, XI (1938), 259, n. 72.

43. Canon 1654, § 1.

44. Noval, *De Iudiciis*, p. 166; Blat, *De Processibus*, p. 155.

45. Canon 1770, § 2, n. 2; Roberti, *De Processibus*, I, 328; Coronata, *Institutiones Iuris Canonici*, III, 89.

46. Art. 43, § 4, *Instructio*.

as a procurator *ex officio* for the defendant as well? For example, should the respondent lacking a personally designated procurator fail to appear at a given session, could the *defensor* in his or her name proceed with acts peculiar to that session which lie within the province of the duly commissioned procurator? It would seem that the *defensor* must be denied such power. In the first place, he lacks the definite, special mandate which is so rigidly demanded by law that a judicial act placed in the name of another without such authorization renders the process irremediably void.[47] The nature of his position causes the *defensor* to protect the bond which a respondent desires upheld. But this coincidence of purpose is not sufficient of itself to empower him to act in the name of the defendant. Furthermore, to take a more fundamental view of the question, the *defensor* is not legally in a position to accept a mandate even if tendered to him. Very clearly he is forbidden to exercise his office in a trial in which previously he has occupied the rôle of advocate or procurator.[48] Consequently, there seems to be all the more reason to exclude the *defensor* from assuming the two rôles simultaneously. His duty, *ex professo,* is to safeguard the marriage bond. Therefore, in his capacity of public official he cannot in the same case adhere *ex officio* to one of the parties since, theoretically at least, a conflict could arise between his defense of the bond and the representing of a party whose bond he upholds.[49]

CANON 1655. — § 4. At Episcopus, si quando in causa est, aliquem constituat, qui eius personam, procuratorio nomine, gerat.

In addition to the persons already considered who must by law act through a procurator,[50] the present canon, in paragraph four, emphasizes a particular ruling affecting bishops who must likewise stand in judgment by means of a representative. Whether he enters court as plaintiff or defendant, and regardless of whether the suit be civil or

---

47. Canons 1659; 1892, n. 3.
48. Canon 1613, §§ 1, 2.
49. Cf. *S. R. Rotae Decisiones,* XXI (1923), 189, n. 13.
50. Canons 1648, § 3; 1649; 1654, § 1; 1770, § 2, n. 2.

criminal, a bishop is obliged to designate a procurator for cases affecting himself. Blat includes the cases in which the bishop would stand before a tribunal in the interests of his cathedral church or of the *mensa episcopalis.*[51] His personal appearance before a tribunal would not be invalid, yet the obligation is a grave one designed to safeguard episcopal dignity and to leave bishops unhampered in their pastoral labor.[52] For this reason the law must be understood to embrace titular bishops, and also abbots and prelates who govern autonomous independent territories.[53] Furthermore, it has reference to their appearance before all tribunals save those constituted by the Supreme Pontiff himself and the ordinary tribunals of the Holy See.[54]

This prescription of law does not exclude bishops from personal judicial intervention in defense of the rights of others.[55]

ARTICLE 2

THE NUMBER OF ADVOCATES AND PROCURATORS PERMITTED IN ECCLESIASTICAL TRIALS

CANON 1656. — § 1. Unicum quisque potest eligere procuratorem, qui nequit alium sibimet substituere, nisi expressa facultas eidem facta fuerit.

§ 2. Quod si, iusta causa suadente, plures ab eodem deputentur, hi ita constituantur, ut detur inter ipsos locus praeventioni.

§ 3. Advocati autem plures simul constitui queunt.

51. *De Processibus,* p. 161; cf. canon 1653, par. 1.

52. Coronata, *Institutiones Iuris Canonici,* III, 88; Augustine, *A Commentary on Canon Law,* VII, 109; Roberti, *De Processibus,* I, 327; Cocchi, *Commentarium in Codicem Iuris Canonici,* VII (2 ed., Taurini, 1936), 131; cf. Conc. Trid., Sess. XIII, *de ref.,* c. 6.

53. Canon 215, § 2; cf. Coronata, *Institutiones,* III, 88.

54. Cf. canon 1557, § 1, n. 3; § 2, n. 1; Vermeersch-Creusen, *Epitome Iuris Canonici,* III (5 ed., Romae, 1936), 40.

55. For example, cf. canon 1653, § 5; Roberti, *De Processibus,* I, 327.

§ 4. Utrumque munus, procuratoris et advocati, etiam in eadem causa et pro eodem cliente eadem persona exercere potest.[56]

After granting the parties in an ecclesiastical trial full liberty to avail themselves of legal assistance in the persons of advocates and procurators, and after determining the processes in which this assistance is legally compulsory, the Code establishes norms governing the numerical extent of that aid. How many procurators and advocates may a litigant commission for a given case?

Anyone possessing the legal capacity to commission a procurator can and should designate but one such judicial agent to represent his or her person. The term *"unicum"*, together with the prescription of paragraph two demanding a just cause for authorization of a plurality, clearly indicates that the law wishes this office to be in the exclusive control of a single person.[57] The juridical reason for this restriction is obvious. The procurator stands before the court in a very definite capacity, namely, representing the legal person who has commissioned him to do so. Since the principal has but one juridical personality, it is evident that he should be represented by but one agent at a time. Furthermore, owing to the inevitable confusion that would follow an attempt to act through several procurators simultaneously, practical reasons as well have dictated this regulation.[58]

Canon Law, however, recognizes certain situations in which two or more procurators might be designated by a litigant. A just cause is required, and, where the matrimonial process is in question, likewise proper authorization from the president of the tribunal.[59] The just cause, to be determined according to the prudent judgment of the judge,[60] might consist, for example, in the amount of litigation in which the party is involved, or perhaps in the mass of judicial work with which a particular agent is engaged.

---

56. Cf. art. 47, S. C. S., *Instructio.*
57. Noval, *De Iudiciis*, p. 176.
58. Cf. Doheny, *Canonical Procedure in Matrimonial Cases*, p. 108.
59. Canon 1656, § 2; Art. 47, § 2, *Instructio.*
60. Noval, *De Iudiciis*, p. 177.

Nevertheless, the prescription of paragraph one permitting but a single agent to function at a time is not modified. When the commissioning of a plurality is permitted the individual procurators must be authorized *in solidum* thus making the principle of exclusive precedence, or rule of prevention, operative.[61] This is a departure from the old law. Formerly it was possible for a principal to authorize several agents to act in his name *simpliciter cum aliis* or *in solidum*. In the first instance joint action was required. In the second individual action was permitted with actual representation assumed by the one who inaugurated proceedings.[62] The present legislation abolishes the designation of several procurators *simpliciter*. As a result, a plurality of procurators can be appointed only in such a way that the one who precedes the others by actually assuming to represent his principal excludes the others from so doing. *"Qui prior est tempore, potior est iure."*[63] Such actual precedence and resulting exclusion of others, is effected by the delivery of a legitimate citation or by the spontaneous entry of the parties into court.[64] By this clear, simple provision the Code puts an end to the numerous difficulties which inevitably arose in the old law owing to simultaneous and successive designation of procurators as well as to appointment *in solidum* and *simpliciter*, difficulties which tended to protract the process at times interminably.

An additional modification of the old law induced by canon 1656 with regard to the judicial procurator concerns the question of substitution. Formerly, after the *litis contestatio* the procurator became *dominus litis* to such an extent that he was empowered to substitute another in his place.[65] The Code, making no distinction between the period preceding the joinder of issue and following, makes it impossi-

---

61. Blat points out that this should be made clear to the several procurators commissioned in this fashion. — *De Processibus*, p. 162.

62. C. 6, *de procuratoribus*, I, 19, in VI°; Reg. 54, R. J., in VI°; cf. Reiffenstuel, *Ius Canonicum Universum*, Lib. I, tit. 38, nn. 23, 24.

63. Reg. 54, R. J., in VI°.

64. Canon 1725, n. 5. Cf. canon 1568; Noval, *De Iudiciis*, p. 177; Coronata, *Institutiones Iuris Canonici*, III, 89.

65. Cc. 1, 3, *de procuratoribus*, I, 19, in VI°. Cf. Reiffenstuel, *Ius Canonicum Universum*, Lib. I, tit. 38, n. 33; Bouix, *Tractatus de Iudiciis Ecclesiasticis*, I, 218.

ble for the procurator to place his commission in the hands of another of his own volition. In order to effect substitution the law requires that the party grant him express permission to delegate, which faculty ordinarily should be in writing after the manner of the principal mandate itself.[66] An attempt to substitute one's commission without express authorization would result in invalid representation thus exposing the process to the charge of irremediable nullity.[67]

The Code has prudently restricted this delegation of power owing to the gravity of such substitution. It would not be fitting were the procurator to be in a position to pass on as he sees fit the complete authorization and consequent responsibility which the mandate entails.[68] Augustine mentions another reason for this restriction, namely, that frequently the procurator is selected *de industria personae*, because of some personal qualification which may not be found in the substitute.[69]

It may be noted in this connection that the substitution of a procurator would not constitute a procedural act which precludes the abatement of a trial unless the parties concerned were notified.[70]

With regard to the number of advocates who may be called upon for legal aid by a party in one and the same trial, Canon Law makes no restriction.[71] In accordance with a well established principle of law, here particularized,[72] a party in an ecclesiastical trial is permitted to avail himself of any number of lawyers that may prove helpful or necessary. A plurality of advocates for the same process may be designated simultaneously or at intervals as the occasion demands.[73]

As legal experts, their duty is to employ every legal means calculated to effect a successful issue for their clients. Consequently, joint action toward that end, a practice extremely common in civil legal systems, in no way infringes upon the rights of the parties or upon the prerogatives of the tribunal. Furthermore, it is in keeping with the age-

66. Canon 1659; Noval, *De Iudiciis,* p. 176.
67. Canon 1892, n. 3; Blat, *De Processibus,* p. 162.
68. Doheny, *Canonical Procedure in Matrimonial Cases,* p. 108.
69. *A Commentary on Canon Law,* VII, 109.
70. Cf. canon 1736; Coronata, *Institutiones Iuris Canonici,* III, 167.
71. Canon 1656, § 3; art. 47, § 3, *Instructio.*
72. Reg. 20, R. J., in VI°: *Nullus pluribus uti defensionibus prohibetur.*
73. Blat, *De Processibus,* p. 162.

old desire of the Church's procedural law that a litigant be afforded every possible means of defending himself as completely and as efficaciously as possible.[74]

In paragraph four, canon 1656 retains the legal foundation for a practice that has become quite ordinary in most tribunals, including that of the Holy Roman Rota, namely, the designation of one person to fill the dual rôle of advocate and procurator in one and the same process.[75] While the offices are really distinct, it has proven an extremely practical measure to entrust the twofold responsibility of representation and defense to one person. To such an extent is that true that the Matrimonial Instruction of 1936, which clearly distinguishes the essential characteristics of each office, indicates freedom to commission a procurator distinct from the advocate.[76]

Such combining of offices in the one legal expert which, incidentally, was not unknown in Decretal Law,[77] may be permitted only with a complete observance of the Canon Law regarding qualifications requisite for each office and regarding the procurator's mandate.[78]

Doheny raises a question of interest and of considerable practical importance in this connection. Discussing article forty-four of the 1936 Matrimonial Instruction, he is of the opinion that in the event no procurator has been commissioned the parties may be considered to have entrusted his prerogatives to the advocate unless the presiding judge has decreed the designation of a procurator. The present writer questions the soundness of that view. "Ordinarily," reasons Doheny, "the parties in a matrimonial trial intend to give full powers of attorney to their advocate." That is undoubtedly the case. And he emphasizes an established principle of law in continuing: "This designation of powers of attorney should be carefully stipulated." But does the following conclusion rest on a solid legal basis? "However, should it be omitted, the *presumption* is that the advocate enjoys the power

---

74. For examples of cases tried before the S. R. Rota in which two or more advocates were engaged, cf. *AAS*, XXVIII (1936), 127, 138, 139.

75. Cf. art. 54, § 1, *Normae S. R. Rotae Tribunalis*, 29 June, 1934 — *AAS*, XXVI (1934), 449, sq. Hereafter reference will be made to these regulations as *Normae*.

76. Art. 44, §§ 1, 2, *Instructio*.

77. C. 4, *de procuratoribus*, I, 19, in VI°.

78. Canons 1657; 1659; cf. Blat, *De Processibus*, p. 163.

of both, unless the judge chooses to select a different person as attorney."[79] The provision of article 44, § 1, of the 1936 Matrimonial Instruction in no way modifies the strict requirement of law with reference to the express, written mandate. Authors are generally agreed that the Code has rendered impossible the assumption of a presumed judicial mandate.[80]

ARTICLE 3

The Qualifications of Judicial Advocates and Procurators

> **CANON 1657. — § 1. Procurator et advocatus esse debent catholici, aetate maiores, bonae famae; acatholicus non admittitur, nisi per exceptionem et ex necessitate.**

Canon Law demands that judicial procurators and advocates be endowed with certain legal qualifications. In the first place, they must be Catholics. Consequently, this first requirement excludes pagans, heretics, schismatics and apostates from the exercise of these offices in ecclesiastical courts. Moreover, in order to act in this capacity it is necessary to be a Catholic in actual communion with the Church since an excommunicated person is likewise expressly prohibited from assuming these judicial occupations.[81]

In view of the religious character which pervades the ecclesiastical process, the requirement of Catholicity is not surprising. Not only is it conducted in a religious manner,[82] but it likewise frequently involves

79. Italics are the writer's. Cf. Doheny, *Canonical Procedure in Matrimonial Cases,* p. 106.

80. Canons 1659; 1892, n. 3; cf. Noval, *De Iudiciis,* p. 180; Roberti, *De Processibus,* I, 332; Cappello, *Summa Iuris Canonici,* III (Romae, 1936), 145; Hanssens, "De Sanctione Nullitatis in Processu Canonico" — *Apollinaris,* XI (1938), 260. It doesn't appear that article 74, § 4, of the 1936 Matrimonial Instruction is to be extended to include all procuratorial power.

81. Canons 2263; 2256, n. 2; cf. Noval, *De Iudiciis,* p. 177; Muñiz, *Procedimientos Eclesiásticos,* III, 45. Those suspected of heresy in the canonical sense would also be barred: cf. canon 2315.

82. Cf. canons 1636; 1874, § 1.

litigation bearing upon important religious issues. As a result, the Church in re-emphasizing this qualification has in mind not only the lack of understanding of Church practice and procedure on the part of the average non-Catholic, but also the incongruity of finding such key positions possessed by men entertaining dogmatic prejudices with regard to the very matters under discussion.[83]

Secondly, in order to represent a client or to plead his cause in an ecclesiastical court it is necessary for the procurator or advocate to have completed his twenty-first year of age.[84] Needless to say, the responsibilities entailed in the exercise of these positions demand the presence of none but mature, experienced minds.

Again, those not enjoying good moral reputation are excluded from the office of advocate and procurator. The loss of one's good name in Canon Law, whether by legal deprivation or by common acceptance, renders that person juridically incapable of performing legitimate ecclesiastical acts, thereby closing the door to the exercise of the offices in question.[85] Furthermore, it should be noted that besides the penal sanctions which deprive a person of his reputation there are other canonical penalties which explicitly prohibit the exercise of legitimate ecclesiastical acts[86] or which declare certain persons incapable of positing them.[87] These penalties directly disqualify one from assuming the office of advocate and procurator.[88]

It is hardly necessary to point out that the law considers persons bereft of their good name and moral standing as entirely unfit to exercise the honorable profession of ecclesiastical advocate and procurator

83. Cf. c. 13, X, *de haereticis*, V, 7; c. 7, X, *de iudiciis*, II, 1; c. 8, *de sententia excommunicationis*, V, 11, in VI°; cc. 16, 18, X, *de Iudaeis*, V, 6.

84. Canon 88, § 1.

85. Cf. canons 2293; 2294; 2256, n. 2; 2291, n. 8.

86. Cf. canons 1743, § 3; 2315; 2350, § 2; 2357, § 2.

87. Cf. canons 2253; 2354, § 1; 2375; 2385.

88. Canon 2256, n. 2. It is noteworthy that the parallel article of the 1936 Matrimonial Instruction, article 48, § 1, instead of "bona fama" demands those who are "outstanding for honesty and religious character." Lega-Bartoccetti, too, point out that the absence of *infamia* required by the old law is not at all as extensive as the qualification of *bona fama* called for by the Code — *Commentarius in Iudicia Ecclesiastica*, I, 351.

which has always demanded a high standard of personal conduct. Their appearance before the court would detract decidedly from the dignity and from the majesty of the Church's tribunal.

With regard to the qualifications thus far noted, Canon Law provides for relaxation in exceptional cases. Non-Catholics may be permitted to assume the rôle of judicial advocate and procurator in certain circumstances. First of all, such admission must be dictated by necessity. In the case of the advocate it is the ordinary who will judge whether or not such necessity really exists, while in the case of the procurator, except for matrimonial trials, the decision will be referred to the judge.[89]

It is possible to conceive of circumstances in which, owing to an utter absence of qualified persons, it is impossible to observe the law requiring legal representation and defense without admitting a non-Catholic. In like manner, instances of moral necessity may arise in which prudence might suggest the employment of a non-Catholic. A striking example is proposed by Doheny, that of admitting a non-Catholic procurator for an insane party to a matrimonial process in view of the fact that the non-Catholic had already acted in that capacity before the secular court in a civil suit.[90]

Given the necessity, the non-Catholic may be admitted to practice in the ecclesiastical tribunal only and always by way of exception. In other words, such permission must be regarded clearly as a special concession in a particular case and not as a general approbation warranting subsequent exercise of the office.

Although canon 1657, § 1 provides specifically for the exceptional admission of only non-Catholics in cases of necessity, authors are agreed in maintaining that this mitigating clause extends to modify the other qualifications noted as well, provided that the persons in question are trustworthy.[91] Lega-Bartoccetti, for example, consider that the law

---

89. Noval, *De Iudiciis*, p. 178; Art. 48, § 4, *Instructio*.

90. *Canonical Procedure in Matrimonial Cases*, p. 110.

91. Lega-Bartoccetti, *Commentarius in Iudicia Ecclesiastica*, I, 338; Coronata, *Institutiones Iuris Canonici*, III, 90; Augustine, *A Commentary on Canon Law*, VII, 112.

intends to exclude such persons from being approved for the office in a stable manner, and that, consequently, it is justifiable to include minors and those laboring under the penalty of infamy.[92] However, it would appear that three restrictions must be noted. Even in a case of necessity the employment of a minor must be conditioned by the qualification regarding requisite canonical learning.[93] Furthermore, an excommunicated person after pronouncement of a declaratory or condemnatory sentence and one branded with legal infamy cannot validly posit legitimate ecclesiastical acts.[94]

It is of interest to inquire at this point whether the enumeration of what may be called moral and physical qualifications in paragraph one is exhaustive. Canon Law, it will be remembered, adopted the Roman *edictum prohibitorium* which declared that any one might assume the office unless expressly excluded.[95] Commentators agree that the present legislation retains that principle with its resulting provisions.[96] However, since the qualifications required in canon 1657 exclude practically everyone expressly barred in the old law, it will suffice at this juncture to emphasize three noteworthy facts.

First, lay persons possessing requisite qualifications are not excluded from rendering legal assistance as advocate and procurator in Church tribunals, not even in cases concerning spiritual matters.[97] This principle of Decretal Law has been retained explicitly to the present day in the Tribunal of the Holy Roman Rota.[98]

Secondly, although the Code fails to exclude women explicitly from exercising these judicial positions as did the old law, the majority

92. *Loc. cit.*

93. Canon 1657, § 2.

94. Canons 2265; 2294, § 1.

95. C. 1, *de procuratoribus*, I, 19, in VI°; cf. Pirhing, *Ius Canonicum*, I, 37, n. 10.

96. For example, cf. Lega-Bartoccetti, *ibid.*, p. 337.

97. Lega-Bartoccetti, *Commentarius in Iudicia Ecclesiastica*, I, 337, 350; Noval, *De Iudiciis*, p. 177; Blat, *De Processibus*, p. 163; Coronata, *Institutiones Iuris Canonici*, III, 90; Vermeersch-Creusen, *Epitome Iuris Canonici*, III, 42.

98. C. 1. *de procuratoribus*, I, 19, in VI°; *Normae*, art. 54, § 2.

of authors maintain that this principle of the old law, in virtue of canon 6, n. 2, should be retained save in drastic cases.[99]

Thirdly, the Code in freely admitting all secular clerics to the office of advocate and procurator in ecclesiastical courts[100] together with an absence of any restriction in canon 1657, appears to have settled the old law controversy regarding priests in particular.[101] The present legislation undoubtedly grants priests full power to plead in ecclesiastical tribunals both directly and indirectly.[102] No longer is there a question of injury to sacerdotal dignity owing to the forensic clamor which once characterized the process and which was the cause, in part at least, for restraining priests from the office. In fact, a practical argument in support of this view derives from a consideration of canonical requirements themselves, for few indeed, other than priests, will be in a position to satisfy them.[103] Furthermore, the present norms of the Holy Roman Rota make explicit reference to priests in the rôle of judicial advocate.[104]

Since this study is confined to judicial advocates and procurators in Church tribunals, there is no need for examining the canonical legis-

---

99. C. 67, X, *de appellat., recusat., et relat.*, II, 28; Roberti, *De Processibus*, I, 335; Eichmann, *Das Prozessrecht des Codex Iuris Canonici*, p. 95; Cocchi, *Commentarium in Codicem Iuris Canonici*, Lib. IV, 132; Lega-Bartoccetti, *loc. cit.*, 337, 351; Grabowski, "Adwokatura" — *Ateneum Kaplanskie*, XXXIV (1934), 150. Canonists engaged in preparing the *schemata* for the fourth book of the Code were likewise in agreement on this point — Cf. Roberti, *Codicis Iuris Canonici Schemata*, Lib. IV, *De Processibus*, p. 148. Augustine does not restrict an otherwise qualified woman — *A Commentary on Canon Law*, VII, 111; while Couly allows her to act as procurator — "Officialité: Procureurs et Avocats" — *Le Canoniste*, XLVII (1925), 505.

100. Canon 139, § 3; cf. canon 108, § 1; 1657, § 3.

101. For a general outline of this controversy consult p. 39 of this dissertation. A brief summary of the legislation involved may likewise be found in Grabowski's "Adwokatura w Unstawodawstwie Koscielnem" — *Ateneum Kaplanskie*, XXXIV (1934), 154, 155.

102. Lega-Bartoccetti, *Commentarius in Iudicia Ecclesiastica*, I, 339; Muñiz, *Procedimientos Eclesiásticos*, III, 45; Vermeersch-Creusen, *Epitome*, III, 41, 42; Blat, *De Processibus*, p. 163; Coronata, *Institutiones Iuris Canonici*, III, 90; Roberti, *De Processibus*, I, 341; Cocchi, *Commentarium in Codicem Iuris Canonici*, Lib. IV, 132; Couly in *Le Canoniste*, XLVII (1925), 505.

103. Canon 1657, § 2; art. 48, *Instructio*.

104. Art. 54, § 2, *Normae*.

lation regarding the exercise of these offices by clerics before the secular courts. The possibility of so acting in the civil tribunals and the conditions necessary have been very adequately treated in the dissertation of Doctor Brunini.[105]

In connection with canon 1657, § 1, there is a qualification peculiar to the procurator which, while not mentioned in the Code, should be considered, namely, that of residence proximate to the tribunal in which he acts. It is true that modern means of conveyance permit a wide latitude in this respect. Yet to facilitate his summoning and appearance according to the court's requirements he should not be unreasonably distant unless for special reasons the judge has granted permission.[106]

CANON 1657. — § 2. Advocatus debet praeterea esse doctor vel alioqui vere peritus, saltem in iure canonico.

Over and above the requirements of religion, age and reputation the Church demands a further and most important qualification particularly in the judicial advocate, that of adequate technical skill. The silence of the canon with reference to the procurator in this connection serves once again to bring into bold relief the distinction between the two offices. In attempting to guarantee for her tribunals lawyers steeped in canonical science the Church demands men in possession of the doctor's degree. It is true that the doctorate does not always furnish proof of unquestionable competence in matters judicial. Nevertheless, owing to the course of study which it does presuppose, it is a practical guarantee of such competence, although not such a guarantee as would deprive the ordinary of his right to seek further proof of capability.[107]

While prescribed by law, the doctorate is not of absolute necessity.[108] Nevertheless, whenever it is lacking it must be replaced by proven, recognized legal ability. In other words, an aspirant to this office

---

105. *The Clerical Obligations of Canons 139 and 142*, pp. 36-43.

106. Art. 55, *Normae;* art. 47, § 4, *Instructio.*

107. Couly, "L'Officialité: Procureurs et Avocats" — *Le Canoniste Contemporaine,* XLVII (1925), 514.

108. A doctorate at least in Canon Law is absolutely required of Rotal advocates: Art. 54, § 2, *Normae.*

must demonstrate to the satisfaction of the ordinary, for example by documents, articles, or by actual forensic practice, that he possesses not a superficial smattering or acquaintance with legal terms but a genuine grasp of those principles especially which are so necessary for the conscientious fulfillment of his duty.[109]

In demanding technical ability the Code emphasizes *"saltem in iure canonico"*. Obviously, since the canon speaks of requirements for ecclesiastical lawyers in Church tribunals, the legal training of the advocate must be based, as a minimum, upon the most important foundation, the Church's Canon Law. But clearly the clause expresses a desire for something more. The Legislator calls for ecclesiastical lawyers who likewise have acquired academic degrees in, or at least familiarized themselves with, the Roman Law, and, in' particular, with the civil law of their respective nations.[110] Numerous points of contact have always existed between the Canon Law and civil legal systems. A practical illustration is found today in the law of the Code which declares that practically all matters touching contracts will be governed by the civil contract law of the land.[111] This single example serves to show the practical impossibility of adequately studying certain parts of Canon Law if one lacks a really fine working knowledge of civil law.[112]

Furthermore, the advocate should feel it is his duty to inquire diligently into all of those branches of learning which his varied practice will point out as being of practical necessity. For example, he must keep apace with the latest findings of psychology and psychiatry, and he must be conversant with the medical and surgical concepts and terminology with which he is constantly confronted.

---

109. Fallon points out that an ordinary may lawfully appoint one lacking academic degrees, yet of proven ability, in preference to the holder of a degree whose knowledge is known to be more theoretical than practical: "Significance of the Words *'Ceteroqui periti'* in c. 1589" — *The Irish Ecclesiastical Record,* LII (1938), 510, 511.

110. Grabowski, "Adwokatura" — *Ateneum Kaplanskie,* XXXIV (1934), 164; Muñiz, *Procedimientos Eclesiásticos,* III, 45; Cocchi, *Commentarium in Codicem Iuris Canonici,* Lib. IV, 133; Blat, *De Processibus,* p. 164.

111. Canon 1529.

112. Cf. canons 1016; 1080; 1508; 1513, § 2; 1520; 1523, n. 2; 2198; 2223, § 3, n. 2.

Needless to say, the more one considers the responsibility assumed by an advocate the better one appreciates this necessary requirement of legal training. It cannot be overemphasized that the selection of a lawyer possessed of profound canonical knowledge has an incalculable bearing upon the issue of a process. A case imperfectly or incompletely presented may be lost unreasonably, even before the most honorable and best intentioned judges. Tribunals, even the most competent, find it necessary to have a clear exposition of the facts of a case and to have the principles of law involved recalled with precision, clarity and method. Judges are not infallible. And it would be unreasonable to expect a thorough appreciation on their part of varied circumstances which may easily and completely change the aspect of a case unless a fully prepared advocate sets forth the case in its true light. As a matter of fact, greater canonical skill is required by law in the lawyer than in the synodal judge.[113] The moral certitude necessary for pronouncing sentence the judge must obtain *ex actis et probatis*.[114] A far more difficult and delicate rôle is that of the advocate who must strive by his investigation of fact and law to adduce proof of sufficient cogency to warrant this certitude in the judge. In the absence of trained judges the need for skilled lawyers is all the more apparent. The advocate could then do much in lightening the judge's burden by his diligent observance of processual laws and by his stressing of principles and precise evalution of proofs.[115] It is noteworthy that one of the primary motives adduced for the recent constitution of eighteen regional matrimonial tribunals in Italy was the resulting greater opportunity for adjudication by skilled tribunal ministers.[116]

It might be noted, too, that norms more stringent than the Code in this regard govern admittance of advocates to the Tribunal of the Holy Roman Rota. Over and above the doctorate in Canon Law, one aspiring to practice before the Rota must serve a three-year period of

113. Cf. canons 1657, § 2; 1573, § 4.

114. Canon 1869.

115. Cf. Hilling, "Die Heranziehung der Advokaten zuden kirchlichen Prozessen" — *Archiv für kath. Kirchenrecht*, CIII (1923), 135.

116. Motu Proprio Pii PP. XI, "Qua Cura," Dec. 8, 1938 — *AAS*. XXX (1938), 410-413.

additional study and practice terminating with an examination before the Rotal College.[117]

The Matrimonial Instruction of 1936 in treating of the qualifications of advocates and procurators in this particular process advanced a step beyond the Code in the matter of legal training required:

> ARTICLE 48, § 2: Advocatus sit oportet praeterea doctor saltem in iure canonico et per triennium tirocinium laudabiliter exercuerit; quod valde optandum est ut fecerit apud Tribunal S. R. Rotae. ARTICLE 48, § 3: Procurator sit oportet in iure canonico saltem prolyta et per annum tirocinium, de quo in § 2, laudabiliter expleverit.

With regard to the legal training of lawyers engaged in matrimonial trials, the Instruction is decidedly more exacting than canon 1657, § 2. There is no option here with reference to the doctorate. It is absolutely prescribed. More than that, it is required that the one who intends or is intended for this rôle must devote a three-year additional period of further legal study and practice by way of apprenticeship in some well-functioning tribunal. And it is strongly urged that this advanced course be pursued at the most practical and thorough training school in the Church for this work, the *Studium* of the Holy Roman Rota.[118]

A second point wherein the Instruction differs radically with the Code consists in the demand that judicial procurators engaged in matrimonial processes possess at least a licentiate degree in Canon Law. They, too, must successfully devote an additional year to the *praxis processualis* after the manner of the advocate.

The practical necessity of such prescriptions is apparent to one who appreciates the tremendous need for accurate and timely adjudication of marriage cases in our day. And in order that this provision might be viewed in the sincere and serious light intended by the Sacred

---

117. Art. 54, § 2, *Normae.*

118. The Rotal decree of Dec. 21, 1911 outlining the nature, work and requirements of the *Studium* may be found in the *adnotationes* of Bernardini to the 1936 Instruction — *Apollinaris*, IX (1936), 537, 538. For a brief summary of past legislation relative to obligatory legal training, cf. Grabowski, "Adwokatura" — *Ateneum Kaplanskie*, XXXIV (1934), 162 sq.

Congregation, the writer recommends a re-reading of the introduction to the Instruction with particular attention devoted to the following:

> Hinc S. Sedis mens est, et hoc Rm̃i locorum Ordinarii probe noscant, ut electi iuvenes, doctorali saltem in iure canonico in hac Alma Urbe laurea decorati, praesertim apud Studium S. R. Rotae, ad processus rite conficiendos atque ad recte iudicandum erudiantur, iustitia ac veritate ducibus.[119]

A practical question suggests itself as a consequence of the rigid requirements of the Instruction. At first sight these qualifications appear to be so strictly required that an ordinary[120] cannot even in particular cases admit those not satisfying the standards of the Instruction. Such absolute necessity, however, in the sense of either meeting the qualifications or permitting the parties to remain without legal assistance cannot be admitted.

There are many dioceses in which, for the present, the requirements of the Instruction cannot be absolutely demanded, dioceses in which, owing to a lack of priests or to financial difficulty, there are few doctors and no one with Rotal experience. Such officials, it is true, might possibly be borrowed, while some places could perhaps avail themselves of Consistorial advocates and procurators. But this certainly cannot always be accomplished. On the other hand, one cannot reasonably suppose that the Sacred Congregation desired to occasion a greater evil, namely, lack of defense, in eliminating a lesser evil. Furthermore, if by way of exception in case of necessity the Instruction admits a non-Catholic, one who legally cannot possess the desired qualification, then *a fortiori* one may be admitted to the office of advocate and procurator as an exception in case of necessity who lacks full legal training provided that he otherwise meets the requirements of canon 1657.[121]

Regularly, however, the norms of the Instruction are to be complied with and a real effort made to effect a situation as prescribed. Prescinding from a consideration of whether or not these norms affect retroactively those officials who already enjoyed general approbation

---

119. Cf. art. 21, *Instructio;* canon 1380. Likewise in this vein, consult the address of the pro-Dean before the Holy Father on the occasion of the solemn inauguration of the Rotal judicial year in 1923 — *AAS*, XV (1923), 567-569.

120. Cf. art. 48, *Instructio.*

121. Art. 48, § 1, *Instructio;* canon 1406, § 1, n. 8.

prior to the Instruction, it can be stated that those not possessing the required qualifications are ineligible for enrollment in the diocesan register of advocates and procurators.[122]   However, in order that the register of approved officials be not lacking or inadequate, Ciprotti recommends that ordinaries petition the Holy See for a dispensation in this regard. Permission could be requested of the Sacred Congregation of the Sacraments that the more learned and experienced officials of the diocese be enrolled in this roster.[123]

> **CANON 1657. — § 3. Religiosus admitti potest, nisi aliud in constitutionibus caveatur, in causis tantum in quibus vertitur utilitas suae religionis, de licentia tamen Superioris.**

After detailing the qualifications required of ecclesiastical advocates and procurators in general, paragraph three of canon 1657 proceeds to restate the old law concerning the circumstances in which religious may exercise these offices in Church tribunals.[124]

In the first place, the canon refers to and includes all those who have pronounced vows, from which they have not been legitimately released, in some religious society.[125]   However, as Brunini points out, this legislation should be extended to embrace those living a common life in imitation of religious without vows.[126]

Secondly, there is question here of religious practicing in ecclesiastical tribunals beyond the confines of their religious society.[127]   Religious

---

122. *Ibidem,* art. 53, § 1. Bernardini maintains, justifiably it seems, that the law is retroactive with reference to generally approved lawyers since otherwise the law's purpose would be defeated — *Apollinaris,* IX (1936), 536. Ciprotti, writing in the *Rassegna di Morale e Diritto,* III (1937), opposes that view, arguing that the Instruction does not destroy acquired rights.

123. "De Advocatis et Procuratoribus in Causis de Nullitate Matrimonii" — *Apollinaris,* X (1937), 469.

124. C. 2, X, *de postulando,* I, 37; c. 3, *de procuratoribus,* I, 10, in Clem.; Durandus, *Speculum Juris,* I, 4, n. 2; Reiffenstuel, *Ius Canonicum Universum* Lib. I, tit. 37, n. 26.

125. Canon 488, n. 7.

126. *The Clerical Obligations of Canons 139 and 142,* p. 42.

127. Cf. canon 1658, § 4.

are permitted to exercise the rôle of advocate and procurator before diocesan courts in but one type of trial, namely, in a suit which involves the interests of their own religious society. Noval emphasizes that the *"utilitas"* must be direct. In other words, the subject matter of the litigation must pertain to one's own house, community, congregation, or Order, and not to a society of which he is not a member.[128]

Commentators of the present legislation agree that the old law with reference to Friars Minor remains unchanged. These particular religious may not act as advocate or procurator even in cases which involve the material resources of their own Order, owing to the fact that they possess nothing of their own even in common.[129] It doesn't appear, however, that they would be so excluded in criminal processes or in trials having reference to the spiritual rights which have not been renounced by religious profession.[130]

Canon Law permits religious to enter ecclesiastical courts as lawyers for the good of their respective societies subject to two conditions. First, there must be no express prohibition contained in their particular Constitutions restraining them from such judicial activity. Secondly, they must previously have obtained the permission of their legitimate religious superiors. This permission must be understood as distinct from the authorization by mandate or commission required by the court of any procurator or advocate.[131]

Canon 1657, § 3, together with canon 1658, § 4, indicates clearly that the law does not consider the office of advocate and procurator as an office incompatible with the religious state for the exercise of which a dispensation of the Holy See is necessary.[132] It should be noted, in

128. *De Iudiciis*, p. 178. Blat maintains that included is the possibility of a religious pleading a cause involving his own right — *De Processibus*, p. 165.

129. C. 1, *de verborum significatione*, V, 11, in Clem.; cf. Reiffenstuel, *Ius Canonicum Universum*, Lib. I, tit. 37, n. 26; canon 582, n. 2; Schaefer, *De Religiosis* (2 ed., Muenster, 1931), p. 323; Wernz-Vidal, *Ius Canonicum*, VI, pars I, 231; Coronata, *Institutiones Iuris Canonici*, III, 90.

130. Cf. Coronata, *loc. cit.*

131. Canons 1659; 1661.

132. Canon 626, § 1. Cf. Fallon, "Appointment of Religious to Certain Offices in the Diocesan Curia" — *The Irish Ecclesiastical Record*, LII (1938), 507-510.

fact, that the *Album Advocatorum Rotalium,* the register of those officially authorized to practice before the Holy Roman Rota, contains
the names of several religious.[133] Such approval is an indication, it
would seem, that in a case of necessity and by way of exception religious may act in any ecclesiastical court process, provided they have
permission of their superiors and in the absence of a restraining prescription in their Constitutions. This would be particularly true with
regard to men canonically qualified.[134] In the event that few duly
qualified officials are available, or owing to the presence of a religious
of outstanding canonical ability, an ordinary might petition the Holy
See for permission to enroll religious in the diocesan register of approved advocates and procurators.

ARTICLE 4

OFFICIAL APPROBATION OF JUDICIAL ADVOCATES AND PROCURATORS

CANON 1658. — § I. Quilibet pro lubitu a parte potest
eligi et deputari procurator, dummodo secundum prae-
cedentem canonem idoneus sit, quin opus sit ut Ordinarii
approbatio antecesserit.

§ 2. Advocatus autem, ut ad patrocinium
admittatur, indiget approbatione Ordinarii, quae aut ge-
neralis sit ad omnes causas aut specialis pro certa causa.

Possession of the requisite qualifications detailed in canon 1657 does
not of itself always empower one to enter the ecclesiastical courts in
the capacity of legal assistant. Apart from the question of proper
authorization to act for and in the name of the litigants, the subject
matter of the following chapter, the law at times demands official
approbation on the part of judicial authority. Canon 1658 outlines
the circumstances in which approval is necessary and indicates the
varying sources from which it derives.

---

133. Bernardini, *Leges Processuales Vigentes apud S. R. Rotae Tribunal,*
pp. 88-91.
134. Canon 1657; Art. 48, *Instructio.* Article 48, be it noted, contains no
exclusion of religious.

With regard to judicial procurators, provided that all of the requirements of canon 1657 are satisfied, anyone may be selected and commissioned freely by the parties without any necessity for previously
seeking approval of the procurator from the ordinary of the tribunal
concerned. This in no way implies that the judge cannot refuse to
admit the one who is designated should sufficient cause warrant
rejection.[135]

On the contrary, before advocates can be admitted to exercise their
office, approbation, express or tacit, must be received from the ordinary of the particular tribunal involved. This approval, therefore, does
not pertain to the judge.[136] And since it proceeds from the ordinary
of the place in which the lawyer wishes to plead, it is evident that
approbation avails only for that tribunal for which it is granted. For
example, an advocate desiring to continue a case in an appellate court
would require further approval.[137]

Canon 1658 speaks of a twofold manner of granting approbation.
First, it might be forthcoming in a general manner thereby officially
authorizing a particular lawyer to engage in any trial coming before
the tribunal. Secondly, the ordinary has it within his power to approve
an advocate for a particular case. Such approbation would cease with
the completion of duty in that process. Citing the legal principle *"Cui
licet quod est plus, licet utique quod est minus,"*[138] Blat observes
that the ordinary is perfectly free to approve advocates for all cases
of a particular nature, to which, as a result, their activity would be
confined.[139] On the other hand, for a just cause the ordinary could
exclude from a particular process even one approved in general.[140]

135. Blat, *De Processibus*, p. 165; cf. canon 1663.

136. Canon 198, § 1; cf. Coronata, *Institutiones Iuris Canonici*, III, 91, note
1. Approbation, however, need not be granted by the bishop personally. For
example, the ordinary could empower the *Officialis* once for all to grant it in his
name — Roberti, "Avvocati Rotali e Curie Minori" — *Il Monitore Ecclesiastico*,
XLVIII (1936), 55.

137. Roberti, *De Processibus*, I, 341; Coronata, *op. cit.*, III, 91.

138. Reg. 53, R. J., in VI°.

139. *De Processibus*, p. 165; cf. Grabowski, "Adwokatura" — *Ateneum Kaplanskie*, XXXV (1935), 238.

140. Cf. Roberti in *Il Monitore Ecclesiastico*, XLVIII (1936), 55.

Furthermore, approval may be granted for specific periods of time after which renewal would be required.[141]

The unrestricted freedom which a litigant enjoys in selecting a procurator, from the viewpoint of approbation, has been curtailed by the Matrimonial Instruction of 1936. In matrimonial processes the choice of this assistant must meet with the approval of the ordinary just as in the case of the advocate.[142] Too often the Church's tribunals have had to contend with unqualified officials and with the confusion and retardation resulting therefrom. Consequently, in order to eliminate unfortunate selections by the parties, and in order to make available officials in whom the parties may find a guarantee of qualification, the Instruction makes obligatory the use of none but approved procurators as well as advocates.

Since both the Code and the Instruction speak of general approbation, a question arises with regard to the most practical manner of its being granted. In order that people may be aware of approved officials in their respective districts, and in order, too, to release the ordinary from the necessity of repeatedly granting special approbation, the Instruction itself has prescribed an extremely practical solution. Bishops are to draw up and make public a list or register containing the names of advocates and procurators who have been approved for practice in their tribunals.[143] There is no reason why this roster prescribed for the matrimonial court should not be recommended and followed with regard to processes in general. In imitation of the Sacred Rota's annual publishing of the *Album Advocatorum Rotalium*,[144] ordinaries from year to year could make known the names of those approved, perhaps by the erection of a conspicuous register within the Chancery Office for priests to see. In making such a register, however, since the

141. Grabowski, *loc. cit.*, 238. Formularies of episcopal approbation for a determined case or for all cases may be found in Cappello, *Praxis Processualis,* pp. 21, 187; Labouré-Byrnes, *Procedure in the Diocesan Matrimonial Courts of First Instance,* pp. 130, 160, 161. On p. 159 of the latter work will be found a form for the application of such approbation.

142. Art. 48, § 4, *S. C. S., Instructio.*

143. Art. 53, § 1, *Instructio.*

144. Cf. Bernardini, *Leges Processuales Vigentes apud S. R. Rotae Tribunal,* pp. 88-91.

approval is now given for the *officium,* special attention must be devoted to the question of canonical requirements.[145]

It should be noted that the approbation of canon 1658 is not to be arbitrarily refused. That is, the right of a bishop to approve cannot be exercised in a manner that would destroy the right of a litigant to choose an advocate or procurator. It should be withheld only for solid reasons based upon a lack of qualifications required in Canon Law.[146]

A further consideration in connection with the necessity of episcopal approbation is based upon the fact that bishops have the right to require of those exercising judicial offices certain qualifications in addition to those prescribed by the common law.[147] Should a bishop feel justified in establishing certain regulations to be observed in his own tribunal, he should be in a position legally to insure their observance. Consequently, the fact that an advocate or procurator possessed all the qualifications of canon 1657, would not of itself necessarily make him acceptable in the bishop's estimation.

It was precisely because of this point, in fact, that an interesting question arose for solution by the Holy See in 1923, a question which, it might be added, has witnessed elaboration in the Matrimonial Instruction of 1936. Owing to a controversy arising from a bishop's particular regulation, the following *dubium* was submitted to the Supreme Tribunal of the Apostolic Signatura: *"An advocati ecclesiastici et laici, approbati ad causas ecclesiasticas defendendas apud Curiam Romanam, non exclusis advocatis consistorialibus, indigeant approbatione Ordinarii loci ut suscipiant in Curiis dioecesanis easdem causas."* The response was in the affirmative. In expounding the law involved, the Signatura recalled the legislative power of the bishop, canon 335,

145. Canon 1657; Art. 48, *Instructio.* For a brief historical summary of previous legislation with reference to the establishment of legal organizations in the Church, cf. Grabowski, "Adwokatura" — *Ateneum Kaplanskie,* XXXV (1935), 239.

146. Muñiz, *Procedimientos Eclesiásticos,* III, 45; Smith, *Elements of Ecclesiastical Law,* II, 53; Wernz-Vidal, *Ius Canonicum,* VI, pars I, 202.

147. Cf. canon 335, § 1; art. 56, § 1, *Normae;* Coronata, *Institutiones Iuris Canonici,* III, 86, 90. For particular examples, cf. Grabowski, "Adwokatura" — *Ateneum Kaplanskie,* XXXIV (1934), 161, 162.

§ 1, and pointed to the fact that in this regard it was unrestricted by the common law or by Pontifical limitation.[148]

At that time, therefore, the Church's highest Tribunal clearly vindicated the right of a bishop to establish regulations for his tribunal aside from the common law which must be observed by all without distinction. Authors have commonly supported that decision.[149]

In 1936, however, the Sacred Congregation of the Sacraments expressly declared in the Matrimonial Instruction that Consistorial and Rotal Advocates do not need this previous approval of the ordinary " . . . *cum ius habeant patrocinium exercendi in quibuslibet dioecesanis tribunalibus.*"[150] Moreover, the bishop in drawing up his register of approved advocates and procurators is required to indicate the right which these particular officials have in law of practicing before his tribunal.[151] Only for a grave cause may the bishop curtail this right, in which case recourse may be lodged with the Sacred Congregation of the Sacraments.[152]

This privilege of exemption, it appears to the writer, can be sustained only with reference to matrimonial processes. Nevertheless, since this type of trial is most frequent and most important, there is a strong indication that Consistorial and Rotal Advocates should be admitted freely in any type of case. An official attitude that would lightly exclude from an inferior court officials licensed to practice before the highest courts of the Church would indeed be strange. Because of proven exceptional talent, these officials should not only be received but eagerly sought after. At the same time, the author believes that bishops do not have to admit such lawyers in other trials without approbation since he fails to perceive that they possess the right of exemption. As a matter of fact, if the *"ius"* of article 48, § 4, refers to

148. Supremum Sign. Apost. Tribunal, "Romana Iurium", 15 Dec., 1923 — *AAS*, XVI (1924), 105-112. Cf. *Ius Pontificium*, IV (1924), 9, 10; *Periodica*, XIII (1924), 96.

149. Vermeersch-Creusen, *Epitome*, III, 42; Roberti, *De Processibus*, I, 341; Coronata, *Institutiones*, III, 90; Cocchi, *Commentarium in Codicem I. C.*, Lib. IV, 133.

150. Art. 48, § 4, *Instructio.*

151. Art. 53, § 1, *Instructio.*

152. Art. 48, § 4, *Instructio.*

a right not granted in and by the Instruction itself, but rather to a right of prior origin, the writer is unable to disclose the source of that right. The Signatura, in 1923, denied the existence of such a right seemingly in a universal sense. And in February of 1936, just prior to the Instruction, such an eminent canonist as Roberti appears unaware of such a right. Writing in *Il Monitore Ecclesiastico*[153] he asks specifically: "Should Rotal Advocates be admitted to practice before the tribunal of any diocesan curia"? His article, commendably, is in support of the affirmative opinion. But it should be noted that he was able to raise the question at all. Furthermore, his argumentation is based entirely upon the reasonableness of such a course, with no mention being made of rights involved. Torre views Article 48, § 4, as a new procedural element,[154] while Doheny speaks of it as "one of the most notable innovations of the Instruction. . . . "[155]

CANON 1658. — § 3. In iudicio coram Sanctae Sedis delegato, ipsius delegati est approbare et admittere advocatum, quo pars uti se velle ostenderit.

Whenever any type of process is conducted before a delegate of the Roman Pontiff himself, or before the delegate of a Roman Congregation or Tribunal,[156] the source of approbation for judicial advocates is to be found in the person of the delegated judge. It is he who should approve and admit, according to his discretion, the lawyers which plaintiff and defendant wish to employ.

In view of the procurator's need for approbation in matrimonial trials, it is likewise from the delegate that approval would come in this type of case.[157]

Should the delegate be constrained for any reason to appoint or to augment legal assistance, he is free to commission and to approve officials from within or without the diocese, provided that those desig-

153. XLVIII (1936), 54-56.
154. *Epitome Instructionis Matrimonialis 1936*, p. 28.
155. *Canonical Procedure in Matrimonial Cases*, p. 103.
156. Canon 7.
157. Art. 48, § 4, *Instructio*.

nated possess the necessary qualifications and provided, too, that he is not otherwise restricted in his selection by the letters of delegation.[158]

> CANON 1658. — § 4. Procurator et advocatus, in causis quae ad normam can. 1579, §§ I, 2 aguntur in religionis tribunali, eligendi sunt ex eadem religione et ante patrocinii susceptionem approbandi ab eo, qui partes iudicis in causa agit; in causis vero quae ad normam eiusdem canonis § 3 apud tribunal Ordinarii loci pertractantur, admitti potest etiam religioni extraneus.

Canon 1658 in paragraph four points out those who are to be, or who may be, appointed judicial advocates and procurators in trials involving religious and determines the source of their approbation. Under certain circumstances these processes are conducted exclusively by and for religious, as, for example, controversies involving exempt clerical religious, or different provinces, of the same exempt clerical institute.[159] In such trials conducted before religious tribunals advocates and procurators must be selected from among qualified members of the religious institute in question.

Before assuming their respective judicial duties they, too, must be approved. Their approbation must derive from the one who acts as judge in the particular case. Consequently, approval must be forthcoming from the provincial superior or from the local abbot in trials concerning members of the same exempt clerical institute or members of a particular monastery. Should the litigation involve different provinces of exempt clerical religious or autonomous monasteries, the judges granting approbation will be respectively the supreme moderator, or delegate, of the religious institute or monastic congregation.[160]

In other cases affecting religious, the litigation is conducted before the tribunal of the ordinary. For example, trials involving physical or moral religious persons of different religious institutes, trials concerning non-exempt or lay religious of the same institute, and cases

158. Canon 1607, § 1; cf. canons 1655; 1657.
159. Canon 1579, §§ 1, 2.
160. Canon 1579, §§ 1, 2.

between religious and the secular clergy or laity. In these processes legal assistants may be admitted who have no connection with any religious institute. They may be religious of the particular institute, clerical, or lay, provided that they are qualified. In these circumstances approbation is obtained from the ordinary.[161]

161. Canon 1658, § 2; cf. canon 1657, § 3.

CHAPTER VI

THE AUTHORIZATION OF JUDICIAL ADVOCATES AND PROCURATORS

THE MANDATE OF THE JUDICIAL PROCURATOR

CANON 1659. — § 1. Procurator ne prius a iudice admittatur quam speciale mandatum ad lites scriptum, etiam in calce ipsius citationis, mandantis subscriptione munitum, et locum, diem, mensem et annum referens, apud tribunal deposuerit.

Canon Law has not failed to recognize the dangers and difficulties inherent in unrestricted power of attorney. As a result, in order to safeguard litigants from exploitation the Church's procedural law has surrounded the judicial relationship of principal and procurator with a precautionary guarantee whereby the agent must demonstrate his authentic, legal right to represent a client before an ecclesiastical court. This guarantee consists of a document which, together with its essential legal requirements, provides the subject matter of canon 1659.

Before a judge can admit a procurator to represent a client in his tribunal, the procurator must have been furnished with a special mandate authorizing him precisely to act in judicial matters. Lacking such authorization from the client, the agent must be barred by the judge or presiding judge.[1]

The extreme importance of the responsibility which rests upon the judge in this connection lies in the fact that such judicial activity in the absence of a legitimate mandate is invalid and results in a sentence that is vitiated by irremediable nullity.[2]

---

1. Cf. art. 49, § 1, *Instructio*. The regulations of the Holy Roman Rota indicate that it is the duty of the *Ponens* to certify the mandate's authenticity — art. 19, § 2, *Normae*.
2. Canon 1892, n. 3. Cf. Hanssens, "De Sanctione Nullitatis in Processu Canonico" — *Apollinaris*, XI (1938), 259; Lega-Bartoccetti, *Commentarius in Iudicia Ecclesiastica*, I, 341; Capello, *Summa Iuris Canonici*, III, 145; Roberti, *De Processibus*, I, 379.

This testimony of authorization is by law very clearly determined in character. First of all, the mandate must have been granted by the client with a view to judicial proceedings. In the old law a general mandate bestowing powers of attorney for any and all negotiations empowered the procurator to represent his principal in litigation.[3] However, the present legislation, recognizing the added gravity and complexity of judicial acts, considers them as exceeding the limits of ordinary administration. As a result, the general mandate for all transactions is no longer sufficient for judicial matters.[4] Just as in extrajudicial affairs a procurator must have a special mandate in order to perform certain acts for his principal,[5] so when there is question of litigation a specific commission must be forthcoming. Coronata points out that a general authorization, provided that it contained express mention of appointment for judicial matters as well, would comply with the legal requirement of a special mandate.[6]

Specification of the mandate doesn't imply that it must necessarily be determined with reference to a particular process. The judicial mandate may be special for one, for several, or for all cases. In other words, the special *mandatum ad lites* may be general, relatively speaking, in distinction to the absolutely special mandate of canon 1662.[7] Confirmation of this common view is found in the fact that the canon, while demanding several details in the mandate, makes no mention of issuance for a specific case but rather indicates the contrary.[8] Normally, of course, a procurator is commissioned for a particular suit before a diocesan tribunal. However, it might be noted, with

3. Cf. Reiffenstuel, *Ius Canonicum Universum*, Lib. I, tit. 38, n. 86.

4. Roberti, *De Processibus*, I, 330; Coronata, *Institutiones Iuris Canonici*, III, 92; Noval, *De Iudiciis*, p. 180; Cappello, *Summa Iuris Canonici*, III, 145; Cocchi, *Commentarium in Codicem I. C.*, Lib. IV, 134.

5. Cf. canons 186; 1089, § 1; 1445.

6. *Op. cit.*, III, 92.

7. Lega-Bartoccetti, *Commentarius in Iudicia Ecclesiastica*, I, 341; Blat, *De Processibus*, p. 167; Muñiz, *Procedimientos Eclesiásticos*, III, 48; Roberti, *De Processibus*, I, 330; Augustine, *A Commentary on Canon Law*, VII, 114; Noval, *De Iudiciis*, p. 180.

8. The omission of *"ad singulas lites"* appears to have been intentional from a study of the Code's preparatory *schemata* — Cf. Roberti, *Codicis I. C. Schemata*, Lib. IV, *De Processibus*, p. 155. The Rota, on the contrary, requires a special mandate for each case before its tribunal — art. 62, § 2, *Normae*.

Roberti, that there is nothing to prevent a party from designating an agent for certain or even for a single processual act.[9]

A second requisite of the legitimate judicial mandate is that it be granted in writing in order that *"ex tenore ipsius instrumenti liquido cognoscatur intentio constituentis."*[10] Here again there is a departure from the old law. Formerly, it is true, a written mandate was desired and recommended, although any deputation demonstrable in court sufficed.[11] Furthermore, tacit or presumed authorization was countenanced in certain circumstances such as the assuming of representation for relatives, for absent defendants, or for anyone who knowingly failed to contradict such representation.[12] The present legislation, it would seem, absolutely abolishes the further possibility of representation by means of oral, tacit, or presumed authorization. To be valid, the judicial mandate must be written.[13] Only when in conformity with the requirements of canon 1659 is authorization lawful. Consequently, in view of the law, an unwritten mandate is illegitimate. And such a mandate is sufficient to render a sentence irrevocably null.[14]

The written judicial mandate may be drawn up as a distinct document introduced into court separately, or it may be embodied in or attached to the libellus.[15] In this connection, the writer agrees

9. *De Processibus,* I, 327.

10. C. 9, X, *de procuratoribus,* I, 38.

11. Cc. 1, 9, X, *de procuratoribus,* I, 38; c. 1, *de procuratoribus,* I, 10, in Clem.; cf. Reiffenstuel, *Ius Canonicum Universum,* Lib. I, tit. 38, n. 74.

12. C. 34, X, *de officio iudicis delegati,* I, 29. Cf. Reiffenstuel, *ibid.,* nn. 75-79; Bouix, *Tractatus de Iudiciis Ecclesiasticis,* I, 214, 215.

13. Cf. Hanssens, "De Sanctione Nullitatis in Processu Canonico" — *Apollinaris,* XI (1938), 260; Roberti, *De Processibus,* I, 332; Cappello, *Summa Iuris Canonici,* III, 145; Noval, *De Iudiciis,* p. 180. From a study of the Code's preparatory *schemata* on this point, Roberti points to this absolute necessity as an innovation — *Schemata C. I. C.,* Lib. IV, *De Processibus,* pp. 144, 146, 152.

14. Canon 1892, n. 3; cf. canons 1680, § 1; 11. As a result, it appears that Coronata, who seems to stand alone in hesitating to require the written form for validity, fails to justify his position — *Institutiones Iuris Canonici,* III, 92, note 6.

15. Wernz-Vidal, *Ius Canonicum, VI,* 208; Roberti, *De Processibus,* I, 332; Art. 49, § 1, *Instructio.*

with Roberti when he contends that: *"Codex non satis intelligitur ubi dicit mandatum procuratorium esse adiungendum in calce citationis...."*[16] As the canon stands, one may be inclined to believe that the citation proceeds from the *mandans,* whereas, as a matter of fact, it derives from the judge. A lack of precision, it appears, arises from the absence of a link referring the mandate to the citation, with the result that the clause would be clarified were it changed to read: ... *notatum etiam in calce ipsius citationis,* or, *etiam in calce ipsius citationis rei adnotandum.* Sufficient inclusion of the mandate in the official summons of the defendant would obtain provided that mention is made of the fact that the plaintiff proposes to act through a particular procurator.[17] As a result, the canon indicates that the mandate should be granted before the *pars conventa* is summoned since upon completion of that element of procedure the process has been legally set in motion.[18]

Since the judge must have a guarantee of the mandate's unquestioned authenticity,[19] the law demands, in the third place, that the document be fortified with the personally executed signature of the principal. Consequently, even if the mandate is drawn by the hand of another it must be signed personally by the one granting the power of attorney.[20] Some authors, while admitting that official authentication of the signature publicly executed is not of absolute legal necessity, yet recommend it.[21] However, it is precisely with regard to this point that the Matrimonial Instruction of 1936 supplements the Code. Article 49, § 1, demands that the signature of the principal be certified by the pastor or by the curia. This certification, at least with reference to matrimonial procedure, seems to be required for the legitimacy of

---

16. *Op. cit.,* I, 332, note 5.

17. Cf. Coronata, *Institutiones,* III, 92, note 1. Since the executed mandate is not affected by the question of its notification in the citation, it does not appear that failure to make such notification would render the mandate illegitimate in the invalidating sense of canon 1892, n. 3.

18. Canon 1716; Augustine, *Commentary,* VII, 114.

19. Art. 19, § 2, a, *Normae.*

20. Noval, *De Iudiciis,* p. 180.

21. Roberti, *De Processibus,* I, 332; Coronata, *Institutiones,* III, 92.

the mandate with such rigor that its absence would provide another basis for invoking canon 1892, n. 3. While this added precaution against the intrusion of false procurators must be observed in all matrimonial cases, a particular necessity for such authentication might be noted in those processes involving persons who are not known personally and in trials conducted before courts of quasi-domicile. In the event that the document is executed in the diocesan tribunal, the litigant's signature may be certified by the curia itself. At the same time, it may be authenticated by any pastor who performs this act of official recognition within the confines of his parochial jurisdiction. Such certification on his part would be performed after the manner of the ecclesiastical notary who may act in his official capacity only within the territory of the local ordinary who appointed him.[22]

In view of the Code's stringent insistence upon this element of personal authorization, which flows from the very nature of the power of attorney, it seems that issue may be taken with the teaching of Lega-Bartoccetti to the effect that a single exception is possible in this regard. After emphasizing the principle: *"Mandatum autem dandum esse ab eo cuius persona agenda est in iudicio a mandatario, explorati iuris est,"* it is maintained that an express mandate is not required of the litigant who, owing to gratuitous patronage, is favored with *"advocatum seu procuratorem"* designated by the court. Tacit acquiescence with the court's choice is deemed sufficient.[23] However, this assimilation of advocates and procurators with reference to canon 1916 appears to be unwarranted. Furthermore, it should be stated as a general principle that even when the procurator is deemed necessary by the court,[24] his power must derive solely and expressly from the litigant concerned. Needless to say, in cases which require judicial representation refusal of the party to commission an agent would by that very fact deprive him of the right to stand in judgment.[25] On the other hand, refusal of a party to designate a procurator deemed necessary by the judge

22. Canon 374, § 2. Cf. S. C. C., March 28, 1908 — *ASS*, XLI (1908), 288.
23. *Commentarius in Iudicia Ecclesiastica*, II, 1021.
24. Cf. canon 1655, § 3.
25. Cf. canons 1648, § 3; 1649; 1654, § 1.

would give rise to an incidental question that would require immediate solution.[26]

A fourth essential requirement for the legitimate mandate consists in the definite specification of the details of place and time with regard to its execution. The document must contain at least the name of the city wherein it is signed. Then, too, it must clearly indicate the day, month and year which witnessed the signature of the principal. All of these details involve the validity or invalidity of the mandate.[27] Hence the need of particular attention in the fashioning of the mandate to these elements which may appear to be of secondary importance.

Finally, since the judge may admit the procurator only by virtue of the judicial mandate, the document must be made available to the court. In accordance with Canon Law, it must be deposited either in its original form or as an authenticated copy in the chancery of the tribunal in which the suit is to be adjudicated.[28]

---

26. In order to obviate possible confusion with reference to the authorization of other legal representatives mentioned in canons 1648, 1650, and 1651, it might be noted that: "Differt procurator a curatore et tutore qui negotia agunt nomine alieno, non de mandato domini, sed vel de mandato iuris aut alius tertiae personae, e. g., iudicis." — Coronata, *Institutiones*, III, 86. A tutor is designated for the protection of a person who is incapable of defending himself by reason of age. On the other hand, a guardian is given to a person who is unable to defend himself because of some mental condition. A mandate given to such assistants must conform to canonical requirements and its absence is penalized by legal sanction: (Canons 1659; 1892, n. 3). Although in many instances a tutor or guardian is for all practical purposes a procurator, still the distinction must be clearly retained which points to the procurator receiving his mandate directly from the litigant whereas the tutor and guardian may be commissioned by legal authority.

27. Blat, *De Processibus*, p. 167. Cf. canon 1892, n. 3.

28. Canon 1819. Cf. Noval, *De Iudiciis*, p. 180. Formularies of the judicial mandate, together with the advocate's commission (cf. canon 1660), may be found for the ordinary contentious case in Cappello, *Praxis Processualis*, p. 13; for the matrimonial process in Doheny, *Practical Manual for Marriage Cases*, pp. 140, 141 (the date must be added); Labouré-Byrnes, *Procedure in the Diocesan Matrimonial Courts of First Instance*, pp. 130, 157; and for criminal trials in Cappello, *op. cit.*, p. 187; likewise in Muñiz, *Procedimientos Eclesiásticos*, III, 50-52. For examples embodied in various types of the bill of complaint, see Kealy, *The Introductory Libellus*, appendix I, pp. 85-97. Formularies to be employed in the tribunal designation of legal assistance may be found in Cappello, *op. cit.*, pp. 91, 92.

CANON 1659. — § 2. Quod si mandans scribere nesciat, hoc ipsum ex scriptura constet necesse est, et parochus vel notarius Curiae vel duo testes, loco mandantis, mandatum subsignent.

So important in the eyes of the law is the principal's signature upon the commission of a judicial procurator that special provision is made for those cases in which a party is unable to affix his name. Explicitly, canon 1659, § 2 states the procedure to be followed when one is intellectually incapable of writing, yet this procedure must be extended, it seems, to embrace instances of physical incapacity as well.

In the first place, the written document, evidently formulated by the hand of another, must contain, in addition to the details of paragraph one, an announcement of the fact that the principal is incapacitated with regard to the affixing of a personal signature. Secondly, in order to lessen the possibility of forgery and subterfuge the law requires an additional guarantee of the mandate's genuineness. This guarantee may consist of the pastor's signature or in the signature of an ecclesiastical notary of the diocesan curia. The signature of either would give the document official legal value.[29] In the absence of signatures on the part of pastor or notary, such a mandate must be signed by two witnesses endowed, as Blat cautions, with the natural faculties of authenticating the fact to which they bear testimony.[30] The testimony of two such witnesses is considered sufficient proof of authenticity in this matter.[31]

Nevertheless, the Matrimonial Instruction of 1936 must be kept in mind again at this point. In order that a mandate signed by two witnesses in place of the principal be accepted in cases of matrimonial procedure, the signatures of the witnesses must be certified by a pastor or by the diocesan curia just as the personal signature of the party requires such authentication.[32]

29. Canons 373; 374, § 2.
30. *De Processibus,* p. 168.
31. Canon 1791.
32. Art. 49, § 2, *Instructio.*

Before proceeding to a consideration of the mandate's specific limitations, it should be noted that the juridical relationship existing between principal and procurator based on the legitimate mandate is a strictly contractual relationship.[33] As such, it must look to the civil legal systems of respective nations as to a supplementary source of law in its regard.[34] Provided that the canonical norms surrounding this relationship are diligently observed, however, there will not only be no conflict with the civil law but rather legal support and confirmation.

On the one hand, therefore, the procurator must act strictly within the limits of his commission,[35] while, on the other, the party must abide by the acts performed in accordance with that mandate.[36] And since powers of attorney are determined precisely by the wording of the mandate expressing the client's will, tribunals should prudently adopt, when possible, definite procuratorial formulas. In this manner, no room is left to misinterpretation or doubt of just what power has been given and received.

With reference to fraudulent, deceitful, or neglectful conduct on the part of the procurator, several distinctions are necessary. In the event that an agent manifestly exceeds his power of attorney, his acts, the invalid acts of a false procurator, in no way jeopardize or alienate rights of the client who may, therefore, disclaim all responsibility.[37]

---

33. Cf. Wernz-Vidal, *Ius Canonicum*, VI, pars I, 209, 210; Lega-Bartoccetti, *Commentarius in Iudicia Ecclesiastica*, I, 346, 347; Blat, *ibid.*, p. 158; Noval, *De Iudiciis*, p. 170; Coronata, *Institutiones Iuris Canonici*, III, 87.

34. Canon 1529: Quae ius civile in territorio statuit de contractibus tam in genere, quam in specie, sive nominatis sive innominatis, et de solutionibus, eadem iure canonico in materia ecclesiastica iisdem cum effectibus serventur, nisi iuri divino contraria sint aut aliud iure canonico caveatur.

35. Canon 203, § 1: Delegatus qui sive circa res sive circa personas mandati sui fines excedit, nihil agit.

36. *Qui facit per alium est perinde ac si faciat per seipsum* — Reg. 72, R. J., in VI°.

37. Cf. cc. 3, 4, 13, X, *de procuratoribus*, I, 38; c. 33, X, *de rescriptis*, I, 3; Reiffenstuel, *Ius Canonicum Universum*, Lib. I, tit. 38, nn. 107, 120; Bouix, *Tractatus de Iudiciis Ecclesiasticis*, I, 216; canons 203, § 1; 1625, §§1, 3; 1681; 1892, n. 3; Lega-Bartoccetti, *Commentarius in Iudicia Ecclesiastica*, I, 346.

In like manner, should deceit or fraud on the part of the procurator constitute a delict, punishment would affect solely the procurator, provided, of course, that such conduct was not countenanced, even tacitly, by the principal.[38]

On the other hand, while a litigant is not forced to persevere with a delinquent procurator,[39] still he must bear the consequences of neglect provided that the agent acts validly within the specifications of his mandate.[40] His freedom of choice involves that risk. Nevertheless, the client through an *actio mandati directa* may seek redress for injurious effects occasioned by the procurator's delinquency.[41] At the same time, the agent is protected by the *actio mandati contraria*. In such a suit against his client he may seek reimbursement for all expenses legitimately incurred in the faithful pursuance of his duty. And in like manner, he may institute proceedings to obtain the honorarium prescribed by law.[42]

It has been pointed out that Canon Law sanctions the absence of a legitimate judicial mandate by declaring the sentence irremediably null.[43] Should a procurator lack power of attorney in conformity with canon 1659 and, in matrimonial procedure, in conformity with article 49 of the 1936 Instruction, not only would his own acts be null, but likewise would the acts performed against or with him by the judge or opposing party be invalid. Once the sentence is pronounced in such a process the court is absolutely incapable of validating the sentence, nor can the passage of time in any way effect its convalidation.[44]

---

38. *Non debet aliquis alterius odio praegravari* — Reg. 22, R. J., in VI°.

39. Cf. canons 1663; 1666.

40. Reiffenstuel, *op. cit., Lib.* I, tit. 38, n. 121; Pirhing, *Ius Canonicum,* Lib. I, tit. 38, n. 80; Bouix, *op. cit.,* I, 219, 220.

41. Lega-Bartoccetti, *op. cit.,* I, 347; Coronata, *Institutiones Iuris Canonici,* III, 95; Cocchi, *Commentarium in Codicem I. C.,* Lib. IV, 136; Reiffenstuel, *op. cit.,* Lib. I, tit. 38, nn. 110, 111, 121, 125, 128; Bouix, *op. cit.,* I, 221.

42. Canon 1664, § 1; cf. Reiffenstuel, *op. cit.,* Lib. I, tit. 38, nn. 113, 114; Bouix, *op. cit.,* I, 221; Coronata, *op. cit.,* III, 95; Cocchi, *op. cit.,* p. 136.

43. Canon 1892, n. 3.

44. Cf. canons 1667; 1893; 1897; art. 208, *Instructio.*

However, since none of the commentators of the Code appear to have eliminated the possibility of ratification in this matter prior to the sentence, Lega-Bartoccetti seem to be justified in maintaining that there should be no departure from the old law.[45] Ratification, they argue, would not imply a presumed mandate, but would establish rather a legal fiction whereby the mandate would be considered to have existed from the start. The author fails to see that the law prohibits the possibility of a principal's convalidating by ratification the invalid acts of an illegitimate procurator. Such ratification should follow the requirements of canon 1659, and must be forthcoming prior to the pronouncement of sentence. Against the public act of sentence ratification on the part of a private individual would be valueless. The sole remedy at this juncture appears to lie in recourse to the Supreme Apostolic Signatura with a view to petitioning sanation of the sentence.

ARTICLE 2

LIMITATIONS OF THE PROCURATOR'S MANDATE

CANON 1662. Nisi speciale mandatum habuerit, procurator non potest renuntiare actioni, instantiae vel actis iudicialibus, nec transigere, pacisci, compromittere in arbitros, deferre aut referre iusiurandum, et generatim ea agere pro quibus ius requirit mandatum speciale.[46]

In receiving a judicial mandate to represent another in a lawsuit, the procurator is empowered to perform those judicial acts which are necessary for the execution of his commission. From the inception of the process to its termination he may posit acts in the name of his principal which are connected with that end provided that the acts

---

45. *Commentarius in Iudicia Ecclesiastica*, I, 346. Cf. Reg. 10, R. J., in VI°: *Ratihabitionem retrotrahi, et mandato non est dubium retrotrahi;* canon 6, n. 4.

46. Cf. art. 50, *Instructio.*

are not prohibited by express provision of law. Canon Law does restrain the agent from performing certain judicial acts. Despite possession of the *mandatum ad lites*,[47] he is legally incapable of taking
certain steps which would alienate or jeopardize the rights of his
client unless an additional authorization is forthcoming in the form
of a special mandate. This distinct commission, then, is special in
that it has reference to a particular legal act specified by law. With
regard to form, details and deposition it must conform with canon
1659. Thus the law affords litigants an opportunity of pondering the
consequences of certain judicial acts at greater length before permitting
the procurator to proceed validly.[48] *"In generali concessione non veniunt ea quae quis verosimiliter non esset in specie concessurus."*[49]
Canon 1662 proceeds to list not an exhaustive enumeration of acts
demanding this particularly special designation, but rather a series of
examples by way of demonstration.[50]

First, the procurator lacking a specifically special mandate cannot
validly renounce or relinquish the action, an instance, or any judicial
acts legally connected with the process.[51] He is commissioned to represent his client in an action. Consequently, without special authorization he cannot alienate this right itself of his client to petition before
a tribunal the vindication of a right. Similarly, in the absence of
specific permission he is powerless to forego the exercise of this action
which he is commissioned to conduct. The instance embraces all the
judicial acts which have a bearing upon the instruction of the process
and which are intended to result in the declaration of a definitive
sentence.[52] In like manner, the procurator without special authority
is incapable of renouncing all or any of the judicial acts which refer

47. Canon 1659.

48. Canon 1892, n. 3.

49. Reg. 81, R. J., in VI°.

50. Lega-Bartoccetti — *Commentarius in Iudicia Ecclesiastica*, I, 343, note 1,
345; Roberti, *De Processibus*, I, 331; Coronata, *Institutiones* III, 93.

51. Cf. canon 1740; art. 87-91, *Normae*. In art. 88, § 2, the Rota decrees that
the opposing procurator cannot accept or reject the other's renunciation without
a special mandate.

52. Cf. canon 1732.

to the merits of the case or which pertain to the form of procedure according to norms prescribed by law.[53]

Secondly, an agent cannot validly negotiate a transaction without definite authorization.[54] In the strict sense, a transaction is a contract between the parties wherein a supposed or doubtful legal claim is settled by peaceful agreement for a mutual consideration, thereby ending the lawsuit pending or obviating a process about to be instituted.[55] Here, again, the law takes the view that a litigant can't reasonably be expected or presumed to have granted his procurator such extensive power. If granted, it must be proved.

In the third place, the procurator is declared incapable of entering into agreements with the opposing party whereby a lawsuit involving a clear, certain claim is terminated or avoided through an amicable remittance of the claim as a donation out of pure liberality.[56]

Fourthly, unsupported by a special mandate the procurator is not in a position validly to effect a settlement of his client's claim by a compromise through arbitration.[57] This is true, whether, with the other party, he attempts to submit the controversy to arbiters who strive to effect reconciliation according to strict rules of law, or to arbitrators who proceed according to principles of canonical equity.[58]

A fifth judicial element requiring a special mandate in the procurator restrains the agent from giving or requiring of the other party

53. Canon 1642, § 1. Note, then, that the canon refers to formal, explicit renunciation and not that which is legally presumed as, for example, in canons 1788, 1628. For such renunciation a special mandate is not required: Cf. Lega-Bartoccetti, *op. cit.*, I, 344.

54. Cf. canons 1925-1928.

55. Cf. Wernz-Vidal, *Ius Canonicum* VI, pars II, 611; Noval, *De Iudiciis*, p. 468; Muñiz, *Procedimientos Eclesiásticos*, III, n. 85; Blat, *De Processibus*, p. 169; Coronata, *Institutiones*, III, 366.

56. This distinction between *"transigere"* and *"pacisci"* is that of Ulpian, D (2, 15) 1. Cf. c. 4, *de procuratoribus*, I, 19, in VI°; Reiffenstuel, *Ius Canonicum Universum*, Lib. I, tit. 38, n. 100.

57. Cf. canons 1929-1931; c. 9, X, *de arbitris*, I, 43; Reiffenstuel, *ibid.*, n. 101.

58. Cf. Muñiz, *ibid.*, p. 68; Noval, *ibid.*, p. 475; Wernz-Vidal, *ibid.*, p. 624; Coronata, *ibid.*, p. 369.

judicial oaths.[59] This provision refers to the probatory oaths which a procurator when duly authorized may give and demand. Consequently, there is here question of the supplementary oath,[60] of the estimatory oath,[61] and of the decisory oath.[62] It might be noted that the procurator should swear in these matters according to a formula drawn up by his client. Moreover, since circumstances rendering these oaths expedient can't always be foreseen, the court should prohibit the agent from taking them unless the formula is adaptable to the point under discussion.[63]

After enumerating concrete examples of judicial acts removed by law from the procurator's ordinary power, canon 1662 in a general manner includes all those acts for which the law is accustomed to require special authorization. To what law precisely does the canon refer? And what are the acts ordinarily so prohibited? As Lega-Bartoccetti point out, the question is of no little importance since there is always the sanction of nullity to be considered in the event of an illegitimate or non-existent mandate.[64]

Obviously, the *"ius"* of canon 1662 embraces first of all the law of the Code.[65] Furthermore, owing to the fact that canon 1662 emphasizes examples taken from the old law, it is safe to assume that judicial acts so prohibited in pre-Code legislation would be included.[66] As a result, there appears to be no dissenting voice among authors to the effect that the procurator needs special permission to petition a restoration to pre-trial status, required by implication in the old law.[67]

59. Cf. canons 1316, § 2; 1746.

60. Cf. canons 1829-1831; Moriarty, *Oaths in Ecclesiastical Courts,* p. 66.

61. Cf. canons 1832, 1833; Moriarty, *op. cit.,* p. 80.

62. Cf. canons 1834-1836; Moriarty, *op. cit.,* p. 85.

63. Cf. Noval, *De Iudiciis,* p. 380; Moriarty, *op. cit.,* p. 70.

64. *Commentarius in Iudicia Ecclesiastica,* I, 344; canon 1892, n. 3.

65. Cf. for example, canon 1656, § 1.

66. C. 9, X, *de arbitris,* I, 43; cc. 4, 5, *de procuratoribus,* I, 19, in VI°; canon 6, n. 2.

67. Cf. canons 1905-1907; c. 7, X, *de in integrum restitutione,* I, 41; glossa in c. 4, *de procuratoribus,* I, 19, in VI°; Reiffenstuel, Lib. I, tit. 38, n. 103; Lega-Bartoccetti, *op. cit.,* I, 345; Coronata, *Institutiones,* III, 346; Noval, *De Iudiciis,* p. 182; Doheny, *Canonical Procedure in Matrimonial Cases,* p. 114.

In fact, Noval, in adding his view that the *"ius"* of canon 1662 may likewise refer to elements implicitly contained in the present legislation, cites, with justification, petition for the *restitutio in integrum*.[68]

Blat, moreover, maintains that the canon embraces any particular written law in this regard.[69] His opinion appears to find support in the most recent regulations of the Holy Roman Rota.[70] In addition, some commentators hold that a particular or general custom would be sufficient to induce the obligation of a special mandate for certain acts.[71] Again, there seems to be no canonical reason for taking exception to that interpretation. And finally, it must be noted that the civil law of a particular region could likewise make a special mandate compulsory for the positing of certain judicial acts.[72]

In this connection one judicial act has occasioned no little controversy among authors, namely, the power of the procurator to interpose the *querela nullitatis*.[73] Noval,[74] supported by Roberti,[75] argues from canon 1664, § 2, that a special mandate is implicitly required. Others, however, incline to the view that special authorization is unnecessary provided that the original judicial mandate has not been revoked.[76] This opinion seems preferable. The writer feels that a procurator who has been commissioned for the conduct of an entire process not only has the right but also the obligation of inter-

68. *Op. cit.*, p. 182; cf. canon 1664, § 2.

69. *De Processibus*, p. 169.

70. Art. 99, § 1, *Normae*. However, the legal reason underlying this canon should be kept in mind. Otherwise, special authority demanded for ordinary acts would make for an increasing and unnecessary exposure of the sentence to the sanction of nullity.

71. Blat, *op. cit.*, p. 169; Noval, *op. cit.*, p. 182; Cocchi, *Commentarium in Codicem I. C.*, Lib. IV, 134.

72. Canon 1529; cf. Noval, *op cit.*, p. 182.

73. Canon 1897.

74. *Op. cit.*, p. 182.

75. *De Processibus*, II, 234.

76. Coronata, *Institutiones*, III, 339; Wernz-Vidal, *Ius Canonicum*, VI, pars I, 569; Muñiz, *Procedimientos Eclesiásticos*, III, 479. Doheny, while appearing to require a special mandate at one point, must be grouped with those who consider it unnecessary since he argues for this view — *Canonical Procedure in Matrimonial Cases*, cf. pp. 114 and 347.

posing such a plea when legally possible. His authorization, unless revoked, continues to the point when all the judicial acts pertaining to the process have been performed, not exclusive of the execution of the sentence. This position will be supported by subsequent argumentation with reference to remedies against the sentence in Chapter IX, article 4.

It has been emphasized that the special mandate demanded by canon 1662 is a distinct authorization with reference to a particular act specified by law. Consequently, a judicial mandate granting permission for such acts in general terms would not suffice. *"In generali concessione non veniunt ea quae quis verosimiliter non esset in specie concessurus."*[77] None of the commentators on the present legislation take issue with that conclusion which obtained in the old law.[78] On the other hand, should a judicial mandate contain an added express authorization with reference to a specific act for which special permission is required, such a mandate, obviously, would fulfill the demands of canons 1659 and 1662.

A final question, however, suggests itself at this point. In the old law, provided that a mandate contained express authorization for some act requiring special permission, it could be assumed that the mandate extended to embrace other such acts not expressly mentioned.[79] This provision was interpreted as referring to acts of equal or of lesser moment than the act explicitly authorized, not to those of greater importance.[80] Few authors have attempted to reconcile this with the Code. Blat maintains that this interpretation of the old law may still be considered effective.[81] The present writer, on the contrary, agrees with Lega-Bartoccetti that it can no longer be followed.[82] To retain the old law in this particular would be to retain the possibility of the presumed mandate which the Code has obviously eliminated entirely.

77. Reg. 81, R. J., in VI°.

78. C. 4, *de procuratoribus*, I, 19, in VI°; cf. Lega-Bartoccetti, *op. cit.*, I, 345.

79. C. 4, *de procuratoribus*, I, 19, in VI°.

80. Cf. Reiffenstuel, *Ius Canonicum Universum*, Lib. I, tit. 38, nn. 91-93.

81. *De Processibus*, p. 169.

82. *Op. cit.*, I, 345.

ARTICLE 3

CUSTODY OF THE PROCURATOR'S MANDATE

CANON 1660. Mandatum procurationis asservari debet in actis causae.

A further indication of the importance attached to the judicial mandate by Canon Law is evidenced by the fact that a distinct canon is devoted to the regulation of its custody. This document must be preserved with the judicial acts of the trial *"quae meritum quaestionis respiciunt."*[83]

The prescription of canon 1660 is not surprising when one considers the precautions surrounding the mandate in canons 1659 and 1662. In the designation of a judicial procurator an extremely important grant of power has occurred. Beyond the mandate itself there is no juridical proof that such power of attorney was bestowed nor that the one claiming it is to be recognized. Doheny points to the particular difficulty that would confront a court of second or third instance should the document not appear in the acts. Such courts would lack means of ascertaining the legal value of an alleged mandate.[84]

It is noteworthy that the regulations of the Holy Roman Rota place the responsibility of conserving the procuratorial mandate upon the Notary.[85]

ARTICLE 4

COMMISSION OF THE JUDICIAL ADVOCATE

CANON 1661. Advocatus, ut causae patrocinium suscipiat, habeat necesse est a parte vel a iudice commissionem ad instar mandati procuratorii, de qua in actis constare debet.[86]

---

83. Cf. canon 1642, § I; art. 49, § 3, *Instructio;* Blat, *De Processibus,* p. 168.
84. *Canonical Procedure in Matrimonial Cases,* p. 114.
85. Art. 62, § 1, *Normae.*
86. Cf. art. 49, § 4, *Instructio.*

Before undertaking the pleading of any case, whether for plaintiff or defendant, the advocate must be granted legitimate authorization. Unlike the procurator's mandate, his commission may derive from the party concerned or from the judge before whom the controversy is to be investigated. In form, this commission of the lawyer is to be modelled after that of the procuratorial mandate. Consequently, the litigant who wishes to avail himself of an advocate's legal assistance should state so in writing.[87] Similarly, if through necessity of law the court deems it expedient to appoint or to augment counsel a decree should be issued to that effect.[88] Moreover, the written commission, in conformity with canon 1659, must contain the further details of time and place. And finally, in order that the acts might bear evident proof of this authorization, the document of appointment is to be filed in and preserved with the acts of the case.[89]

It is of interest to note that Roman tribunal regulations with reference to the advocate's commission are couched in terms practically identical with those concerning the procuratorial mandate.[90]

Blat is of the opinion that preservation of the document itself in the acts isn't essential provided that after being shown to the tribunal notification of its contents is duly recorded in the acts by the Notary.[91] In fact, Wernz-Vidal[92] and Muñiz[93] point to the possibility of even oral appointment provided, again, that such authorization is authenticated in the acts of the trial. In such cases, together with those in which a litigant would leave selection of counsel to the court's discretion, care should be taken to obtain the party's signature to that effect. This would appear to satisfy the requirement of the canon that the advocate's commission resemble that of the procurator's mandate.

87. Roberti, *De Processibus*, I, 340; Coronata, *Institutiones*, III, 92; Cocchi, *Commentarium in Codicem I. C.*, Lib. IV, p. 135.

88. Cf. canon 1655.

89. Cf. canon 1660.

90. Cf. *Lex Propria S. R. Rotae et Signaturae Apostolicae*, 29 June, 1908, can. 18, § 1 — *AAS*, I (1909), 20; *Regulae Servandae in Iudiciis apud S. R. Rotae Tribunal*, 4 Aug., 1910, art. 4, n. 1 — *AAS*, II (1910), 783.

91. *De Processibus*, p. 168.

92. *Ius Canonicum*, VI, pars I, 202.

93. *Procedimientos Eclesiásticos*, III, 45.

At this point, however, a possible exception may be noted with reference to those occasions which demand appointment of defense counsel by the court.[94] Owing to the freedom which the litigant enjoys of accepting or rejecting the lawyer thus assigned, tacit authorization is considered to be granted in the absence of an exception to the contrary. Express authorization of the party in these circumstances is, therefore, unnecessary and tribunal designation suffices.[95]

A question may be raised in this connection with regard to a procurator's power to appoint an advocate for the client whom he represents. Some of the commentators who consider this point feel that he may do so on condition that he has been granted a specific mandate to this effect.[96] Roberti, on the contrary, mentions this possibility without any reference to an additional grant of power.[97] In view of the fact that legal assistance is for the most part expedient, not to say necessary, and considering, too, that the advocate selected must be canonically qualified and approved,[98] it is difficult to conceive in what manner the procurator could jeopardize or alienate the rights of his client in commissioning an advocate on his own initiative. As a result, unless a party has reserved such appointment to himself or has actually appointed or announced his intention of appointing an advocate, the present writer is of the opinion that such designation is not beyond the scope of a procurator's office.

Furthermore, one might inquire whether or not the legitimately commissioned procurator can personally assume the rôle of pleading the case without having recourse to authorization as provided for in canon 1661. In practice, one and the same person may and usually does occupy both offices by specific appointment in a particular lawsuit.[99] However, while the advocate can't presume to designate a procurator nor to join that official's duties to his own, it doesn't appear that one must hold a converse position with regard to the judicial agent. Pro-

---

94. Cf. canons 1655, 1916.

95. Lega-Bartoccetti, *Commentarius*, II, 1021.

96. Wernz-Vidal, *ibid.*, p. 202; Muñiz, *ibid.*, p. 45; Coronata, *Institutiones*, III, 92; Noval, *De Iudiciis*, p. 181.

97. *De Processibus*, I, 337.

98. Cf. canons 1657; 1658, § 2.

99. Cf. canon 1656, § 4.

vided that the client has not appointed two distinct officials, in which case the procurator must content himself with representation, the procurator may assume also the office of advocate, particularly if the selection of counsel has been left to his judgment. Needless to say, he must be in possession of the legal qualifications required and meet with the ordinary's approval in that capacity.[100]

100. Cf. canons 1657; 1658, § 2; Lega-Bartoccetti, *Commentarius in Iudicia Ecclesiastica*, I, 346. In the old law, a procurator who failed to defend his client's interests when necessary could be rejected — Cf. Pirhing, *Ius Canonicum*, Lib. I, tit. 38, n. 56; Bouix, *Tractatus de Iudiciis Ecclesiasticis*, I, 216.

CHAPTER VII

THE REJECTION AND REMOVAL
OF JUDICIAL ADVOCATES AND PROCURATORS

ARTICLE 1

POWER OF THE JUDGE TO REJECT ADVOCATES AND PROCURATORS

CANON 1663. Tum procurator tum advocatus possunt a iudice, dato decreto, repelli sive ex officio sive ad instantiam partis, iusta tamen de causa.[1]

Since the judge has the right to supervise the instruction of the process over which he presides, he may decide, within legal limitations, the persons who may or may not participate in the lawsuit.[2] Canon Law expressly empowers the judge or collegiate tribunal to reject advocates and procurators from practice in ecclesiastical courts. This rejection may occur at the very outset of a process, or it may prove to be a necessary measure during the course of the trial.[3] Needless to say, an official lacking authorization, approbation, or canonical qualifications not only can but must be rejected by the court.[4]

The judge's power of rejection cannot be exercised arbitrarily. In order to expel these officials the court must base its action on a just cause, a cause that will be proportionate to the rejection in the prudent and considered judgment of the court.[5] The Matrimonial Instruction of 1936 indicates more clearly than the Code that rejection is a serious matter casting reflection on the officials concerned. In adding *"et gravi de causa,"* the Instruction emphasizes that the debarment is occasioned by a deficiency or delinquency of considerable importance.[6] For example, should an official prove incapable from a technical point of

1. Cf. art. 51, *Instructio.*
2. Cf. canons 1640; 1757; 1796.
3. Cf. Blat, *De Processibus,* p. 169.
4. Cf. canons 1657; 1658; 1659.
5. Cf. Grabowski, "Adwokatura" — *Ateneum Kaplanskie,* XXXV (1935), 245; Noval, *De Iudiciis,* p. 182.
6. Art. 51, *Instructio.*

view,[7] lacking in proper respect and obedience to the court,[8] unworthy by reason of shameful legal practice,[9] or unfitted by moral standing,[10] the judge would be perfectly within his rights in banishing that official from the tribunal.[11]

In objecting to the tribunal activity of advocates and procurators the judge must issue an official pronouncement stating the fact of their rejection.[12] In it the court may outline the motives dictating this measure although there doesn't appear to be any legal necessity for explanation. The Code is generally specific when an exposition of reason is required.[13]

The law provides a twofold source of repudiation. The advocate and procurator may be barred on the initiative of the court itself or at the instigation of the adverse party. Particularly in those cases in which the court has provided legal assistance would it be the right and duty of the judge to intervene. Cases are rare in which a client would request the court for a decree of debarment owing to the fact that simple revocation of authorization would satisfy a desire to dispense with a particular aid.[14] Consequently, when exception is taken to these officials by a party it will generally proceed from the opposing litigant as a legal measure of defense.

In the event that an advocate or procurator considers himself unjustly banished from the ecclesiastical tribunal, he retains full liberty of recourse to the bishop in which he may petition a review of his

7. Cf. canons 1657; 1619.

8. Canon 1640, § 2.

9. Canons 1665; 1666.

10. Canons 2263; 2294.

11. Wernz-Vidal, *Ius Canonicum*, VI, Pars I, 204; Coronata, *Institutiones*, III, 93; Augustine, *A Commentary on Canon Law*, VII, 116; art. 21, 57, *Normae*.

12. Cf. canon 1868, § 2.

13. Cf. canons 1709; 1840, § 3; 2225; Blat, *De Processibus*, p. 169; Noval, *De Iudiciis*, p. 182. Whereas the signatures of the presiding judge and of the notary suffice for the admission of an advocate and procurator, the authority of the entire tribunal, expressed by a majority vote if a difference of opinion exists, is necessary to reject the legal assistant. Hence, the decree of rejection must contain the signatures of all the judges. A formulary of such a decree may be found in Cappello, *Praxis Processualis*, p. 90.

14. Cf. canon 1664, § 1.

plight.[15] Commenting on the obvious impossibility of such recourse should the bishop have presided himself, Doheny recommends recourse to the Roman Congregation or Tribunal concerned, depending upon the type of case and official.[16]

Provided that the advocate or procurator does not labor under the penalty of infamy and provided that his rejection does not deprive him of the right to exercise the office, dismissal from one tribunal will not disqualify him from pleading in another, or, for that matter, in the same tribunal in another case if he was debarred for reasons peculiar to that case.[17]

Canon Law makes a specific provision that must be noted here, namely, for cases in which the procurator ceases to exercise his office, whether because of rejection, removal, renunciation, or death. A vacancy arising in his post causes an interruption of the instance until such time as the party concerned designates another or announces his intention of conducting the suit personally.[18] The norms of the Holy Roman Rota oblige a client in these circumstances to commission another procurator as quickly as possible. Should the Tribunal deem it necessary, or the adverse party petition, a peremptory period of time may be granted the client in which to comply. Furthermore, the Rota decrees that a procurator's cessation from office after the conclusion of the case does not interrupt the instance, and the Ponens after citing the parties may proceed to the remaining stages of the process.[19] Since this last regulation of the Rota appears to run counter to the Code which makes no distinction with regard to stage of the trial and interruption, it might be remarked that the discrepancy lies in terminology peculiar to the Rota. According to the Code, a case is said to be concluded when the litigants have nothing more to adduce

15. Cf. art. 51, *Instructio.*

16. *Canonical Procedure in Matrimonial Cases,* p. 116. From the preparatory schemata of the Code, it appears that several canonists denied the possibility of any recourse. Others held that recourse could be lodged with the superior tribunal for administrative examination — Roberti, *Codicis I. C. Schemata,* Lib. IV, *De Processibus,* 156, 157.

17. Cf. Grabowski, "Adwokatura" — *Ateneum Kaplanskie,* XXXV (1935), 245.

18. Canon 1735.

19. Art. 80, *Normae.*

by way of proof, whereas in the style of the Rota a case is concluded only after the briefs and responses have been considered.[20]

Unlike the provision of law regarding the departing procurator, cessation from office on the part of the advocate does not interrupt the instance. The parties and the court retain the faculty of designating others.[21]

ARTICLE 2

POWER OF THE LITIGANTS TO REMOVE ADVOCATES AND PROCURATORS

> **CANON 1664. — § 1. Advocati et procuratores possunt ab eo a quo constituti sunt, removeri, salva obligatione solvendi honoraria ipsis debita; verum ut remotio effectum sortiatur, necesse est ut ipsis intimetur, et, si lis iam contestata fuerit, iudex et adversa pars certiores facti sint de remotione.**

A second means of terminating the commission granted to judicial advocates and procurators consists in the freedom which the litigants enjoy of revoking that commission. *"Omnis res, per quascumque causas nascitur, per easdem dissolvitur."*[22] In the old law a client could not dismiss his procurator after the joinder of issue except for a serious reason.[23] That distinction, it appears, is abolished by the present legislation. As a result, removal may be effected at any stage of the process.[24] And it may be effected precisely by those who are in a position to judge the advisability of such a course of action, namely, by those who authorized the officials. Consequently, not only the parties but even a procurator may revoke this commission provided he is the one

---

20. Canon 1860; art. 121, *Normae.*

21. Cf. Roberti, *De Processibus,* I, 340.

22. Reg. 1, R. J., in VI°.

23. C. 2, *de procuratoribus,* I, 19, in VI°; cf. Reiffenstuel, *Ius Canonicum Universum,* Lib. I, tit. 38, nn. 136, 139, 156.

24. Blat, *De Processibus,* p. 170; Roberti, *De Processibus,* I, 333; Wernz-Vidal, *Ius Canonicum,* VI, pars I, 204; Coronata, *Institutiones,* III, 94, note 6. Augustine appears to retain the position of the old law — *A Commentary on Canon Law,* VII, 116.

who designated them according to law.[25] While these officials normally are authorized to act for the duration of a lawsuit, the parties may regard their employment as resting on a day to day basis that may be terminated at any time.

At the same time, it doesn't appear that such freedom would permit unreasonable discharging, at least not the type of removal which, proceeding from no legitimate motive at all, would occasion material or moral detriment to the legal assistant. It is true that the Code requires no reasons for removal, that no explanation need be tendered the official, court, or adverse party, and that the court and opposing party seem unable to intervene.[26] Nevertheless, the natural law reflected in the legal principle *"Mutare consilium quis non potest in alterius detrimentum"* cannot be disregarded.[27] Therefore, Noval is justified in maintaining that should an extreme case arise, for example, one in which unjustifiable removal would cast a blemish on the good name or legal reputation of an official, the judge would be within his rights in opposing that revocation.[28]

Notification of removal is made not by a decree of the court but by an express pronouncement of the party taking this action. Tacit revocation, permissible in the old law, is no longer countenanced.[29]

Should a litigant feel constrained to remove his advocate or procurator before the issue in pleading is determined,[30] it is sufficient that he serve express notification of the dismissal to the official concerned. It must be noted, however, that such revocation has no juridical effect until the official has received the notice of his discharge. As a consequence, acts performed prior to authentic notification of removal are valid.[31]

25. Cf. Noval, *De Iudiciis*, p. 183.

26. Noval, *op. cit.*, p. 183; Wernz-Vidal, *op. cit.*, VI, pars I, 204; Grabowski, "Adwokatura" — *Ateneum Kaplanskie*, XXXV (1935), 244.

27. Reg. 33, R. J., in VI°.

28. *Op. cit.*, p. 183; cf. canon 1678.

29. C. 8, *de procuratoribus*, I, 19, in VI°; Roberti, *op. cit.*, I, 333; Blat, *op. cit.* pp. 170, 171; Coronata, *op. cit.*, III, 94; Noval, *op. cit.*, p. 183.

30. Canon 1726.

31. Cf. c. 2, *de procuratoribus*, I, 19, in VI°; Reiffenstuel, *Ius Canonicum*, Lib. I, tit. 38, n. 156.

In the event that a party sees fit to discharge a legal assistant after the *litis contestatio,* additional notification is necessary. The removal remains legally ineffective until the fact has been made known not only to the officials directly involved but likewise to the judge, or presiding judge, and to the adverse party.[32] Formerly, it sufficed, in these circumstances, to notify either the judge or opposing party.[33] In the present legislation, until authentic information has been received by the official, judge and adverse party, all acts of the official, and of the court with the official, remain valid just as though the revocation had not occurred.[34] This would remain true even if the party decided upon conducting his case personally or actually commissioned another legal assistant. After the process has been duly inaugurated, it is of considerable importance to the court, and to the opposing parties, to realize with whom they are treating in the matter of legal counsel and representation. In order to obviate confusion on this score, the law requires that a party inform both the court and opposing party in order that removal of his advocate or procurator become effective, since up to that point they are presumed to be unaware of the revocation.

The Code prescribes no standard form to be followed with reference to this removal. Any manner of notification that will stand in the acts of the case as a legitimate proof of the fact will suffice. For example, a declaration of the party in court before the judge, official, and opposing party, entered in the acts by the notary, would satisfy the requirements of the Code. However, in stating that parties should make known such revocation in writing, just as the authorization, Roberti indicates a principle that should be adhered to as a sound general rule.[35]

In declaring that litigants are free to discharge advocates and procurators, canon 1664, § 1, emphasizes an obligation that must be borne in mind in exercising that power, namely, the obligation of remunera-

---

32. Cf. art. 52, § 1, *Instructio.* A formulary of such notification may be found in Cappello, *Praxis Processualis,* p. 90.

33. Cc. 3, 4, X, *de procuratoribus,* I, 38.

34. Reiffenstuel, *ibid.,* n. 161; Noval, *op. cit.,* p. 183; Coronata, *op. cit.,* III, 94.

35. *De Processibus,* I, 333.

tion. Since a subsequent article will be devoted to the question of judicial expenses with reference to these officials, it will suffice at this point merely to indicate that the fees established in the tribunal concerned must be honored by the client.[36] Even should the advocate and procurator be removed owing to inefficiency and incapability they have a right to receive the fees corresponding to the work performed to the point of dismissal.[37] Similarly, they must be reimbursed for expenses incurred.[38] In a disagreement with regard to fees, the matter is to be placed before the judge who tries the case since this would be a dispute arising in connection with it.

Since canons 1663 and 1664, § 1 have outlined methods by which the authorization of judicial advocates and procurators may be terminated, it will not be out of place to note several further methods of so doing aside from the death of the officials already indicated.[39]

Needless to say, an advocate or procurator and the client may mutually agree to sever their relationship. In these circumstances, notification must be forwarded to the judge and opposite party after the pleading in issue as in the case of removal.[40] Again, authorization would automatically be withdrawn in the event that a party renounced that for which it had been granted.[41] In addition, the official himself, in the absence of fraud or deceit, may resign for a just motive.[42] The commission will cease to exist, however, only upon acceptance of the resignation by the client together with notification to court and adverse party if after the *litis contestatio*.[43] In connection with resignation, moreover, it must be noted that in matrimonial procedure, once the process has been instituted, these officials cannot renounce their commissions without a just cause which must meet with the

36. Cf. canon 1909, § 1.

37. Cf. Wernz-Vidal, *Ius Canonicum*, VI, pars I, 204.

38. Coronata, *Institutiones*, III, 94; Reiffenstuel, *ibid.*, n. 113.

39. Cf. canon 1735; art. 80, *Normae;* Eichmann, *Das Prozessrecht des C. I. C.,* p. 98; Lega, *De Iudiciis Eccles. Civil.,* p. 130.

40. Cf. Schmalzgrueber, *Ius Canonicum Universum*, Lib. I, tit. 38, n. 39; Bouix, *Tractatus de Iudiciis,* I, 222.

41. Cf. canon 1740; Eichmann, *op. cit.,* p. 98; Coronata, *op. cit.,* III, 95.

42. Cf. Bouix, *op. cit.,* I, 223.

43. Cf. Reiffenstuel, *op. cit.,* Lib. I, tit. 38, n. 144; Coronata, *op. cit.,* III, 95; Roberti, *De Processibus,* I, 333.

approval of the presiding judge.[44] Furthermore, authorization would cease with the death of one's principal provided that death occurred before the pleading in issue.[45] Finally, with the completion of the instance by pronouncement of a definitive sentence, authorization is considered at an end, at least with reference to the case terminated. Nevertheless, the procurator still retains the right to appeal.[46]

44. Art. 54, n. 3, *Instructio*.

45. Reiffenstuel, *op. cit.*, Lib. I, tit. 38, n. 132. Cf. canons 1732; 1733; Roberti, *De Processibus*, I, 333. In the light of the canons cited, Coronata appears to confuse interruption with extinction of power — *op. cit.*, III, 95.

46. Cf. canon 1664, § 2; art. 52, § 2, *Instructio;* Roberti, *op. cit.*, I, 333; Coronata, *op. cit.*, III, 95.

CHAPTER VIII

PENAL SANCTIONS AFFECTING ADVOCATES AND PROCURATORS

ARTICLE 1

SPECIFICALLY PROHIBITED TRANSACTIONS

CANON 1665. — § I. Vetatur uterque emere litem, aut sibi de immodico emolumento vel rei litigiosae parte vindicata pacisci.

§ 2. Quae si fecerint, nulla est pactio, et a iudice vel ab Ordinario poterunt poena pecuniaria mulctari; advocatus praeterea tum ab officio suspendi, tum etiam, si recidivus sit, destitui et titulo privari.

In her zeal that ecclesiastical tribunals stand as seats of just judgment the Church does everything in her power to prevent anything savoring of injustice from entering her courts. As a result, some transactions of a particularly repugnant nature by which falsehood and deceit might be occasioned on the part of legal assistants are expressly interdicted.

First, the advocate and procurator are prohibited from the purchase of lawsuits, " . . . *ne actionis iudicialis turpe fiat commercium.*"[1] In other words, they are forbidden to obtain or to assume for a consideration things or rights belonging to others which are already the subject of litigation or which possess judicial possibilities. A real danger would otherwise exist of skilled lawyers being tempted to seek all types of weak, perhaps abandoned, cases for practically no consideration in the hope of reaping rich rewards by prosecuting them successfully. Obviously, were such conduct countenanced, considerable disturbance would result owing to the raising of undesired cases, suits which the parties would in all probability prefer to remain untouched

---

1. Lega-Bartoccetti, *Commentarius in Iudicia Ecclesiastica*, I, 353. Cf. art. 45, § 3; 46, *Lex Propria S. R. Rotae et Sign. Apostolicae*, 29 June, 1908 — *AAS*, I (1909), 20.

or to otherwise settle.[2] This prohibition regarding purchase of lawsuits does not include the ceding of cases by reason of other legitimate title, for example, by testament or because of acknowledged indebtedness or out of pure liberality.[3]

In the second place, the canon restrains advocates and procurators from entering into any agreement resulting in the demand for or reception of excessive fees.[4] Consequently, it is strictly forbidden to contract for the payment of an exorbitant sum by way of reward or bonus in the event of a favorable prosecution.[5] Such a prohibition eliminates the danger of any possible tendency to employ fraudulent, deceitful, or other illegitimate means in an attempt to gain lucrative decisions. Moreover, it obviates possible deception whereby in stressing the hopelessness of a client's suit the advocate forms an unjust bargain with the client. Furthermore, the law has in mind that, despite the granting of gratuitous patronage, there are people of moderate circumstances who, faced with a condition which this canon seeks to avoid, would forego necessary legal assistance. Abuse in this connection is to be measured according to financial standards that have been established by law.[6]

A third restriction prevents the advocate or procurator from contracting for part of the disputed thing which is the object of the litigation. They must refrain from entering into a *pactum de quota litis* by the terms of which the party is obliged to surrender to the legal assistant a portion of the thing restored or coming to him by favorable sentence. Included in this provision, therefore, is the situation in

2. Cf. Reiffenstuel, *Ius Canonicum Universum*, Lib. I, tit. 37, n. 46; Lega-Bartoccetti, *op. cit.*, I, 353; Vermeersch-Creusen, *Epitome*, III, 41; Roberti, *De Processibus*, I, 338; Noval, *De Iudiciis*, p. 184.

3. Reiffenstuel, *ibid.*, n. 49; Lega-Bartoccetti, *op. cit.*, I, 353; Noval, *op. cit.*, p. 184; Blat, *De Processibus*, p. 172.

4. Cf. art. 54, n. I, *Instructio;* art. 58, *Normae;* Schmalzgrueber, *Ius Ecclesiasticum Universum*, Lib. I, tit. 37, n. 12.

5. Cf. S. R. Rotae, *S. Angeli de Lombardis* — *AAS*, XII (1920), 85-91. In this decision the Rota referred to canon 1665 as invalidating a contract by which an advocate was to receive fifty percent of the amount recovered.

6. Cf. canons 1909, § 1; 1507, § 2; 2408; chapter IX, article 5, A, of this dissertation.

which a successful lawyer receives a great deal and the unsuccessful expert nothing. As a consequence, it restrains those who with that in mind would possibly resort to any means to attain the successful issue of a lawsuit.[7]

The penal character of canon 1665 appears in paragraph two. The first sanction placed upon the foregoing agreements is automatic nullification of the pacts negotiated. By invalidating these transactions the law primarily safeguards the public good. As a result of this sanction, parties to such agreements are not bound in conscience to honor them. Either may petition a declaration of the pact's invalidity, and either may oppose an exception of nullity.[8]

Descending to punishment of a more personal nature, the law provides for the possible imposition of fines. Should a transgression of this kind occur during or be connected with a particular lawsuit, the judge presiding at that trial could inflict a fine in proportion to the gravity of the offense. Upon completion of the instance, or even during the course of the trial if the erring official is denounced to him, the ordinary may impose the fine.[9] It should be noted that payment of a fine in no way releases the official from the obligation of restoring that which has been illegitimately gained.[10] Moreover, it is absolutely forbidden for the advocate or procurator to compute fines with expenses to be asked of the client.[11]

With regard to judicial advocates who have been commissioned in that capacity in a stable manner, further punitive steps may be taken. In addition to the nullification of the agreement and imposition of fines, they may be suspended from the office either for a fixed period or indefinitely according to the gravity of the guilt.[12] Lega-Bartoccetti maintain that such suspension could affect either office or both when

7. Cf. Reiffenstuel, *ibid.*, n. 44; Schmalzgrueber, *ibid.*, n. 13; Roberti, *De Processibus*, I, 339; Coronata, *Institutiones*, III, 94.

8. Cf. canons 1679; 1682; 1667; Blat, *De Processibus*, p. 172; Lega-Bartoccetti, *Commentarius in Iudicia Ecclesiastica*, I, 353; Noval, *De Iudiciis*, p. 185; Grabowski, "Adwokatura" — *Ateneum Kaplanskie*, XXXV (1935), 358.

9. Cf. canons 2291, n. 12; 2297; 2408; 198; 94, § 1; Lega-Bartoccetti, *op. cit.*, I, 353.

10. Canon 2408.

11. Art. 21, *Normae*.

12. Cf. canons 2291, n. 10; 2408.

combined in an individual.[13] Should a lawyer already proven guilty in this regard persist in entering into such prohibited transactions, he may be deprived of his title of ecclesiastical advocate and enjoined from ever again exercising the office.[14] This suspension and deprivation of office may be inflicted either by the judge or by the ordinary.[15]

ARTICLE 2

Sanctions Regarding Betrayal of Office in General

CANON 1666. Advocati ac procuratores qui ob dona aut pollicitationes aut quamlibet aliam rationem suum officium prodiderint, ab officio repellantur, et, praeter damnorum refectionem, mulcta pecuniaria aliisve congruis poenis plectantur.[16]

Upon entering the office of ecclesiastical advocate or procurator, or before assuming the rôle in a particular case, the officials solemnly swear to exercise the functions of their office with all possible diligence and with utmost fidelity.[17] The law demands of advocates and procurators absolute integrity of character and a love for truth and justice. They are to regard their office and treat their work with the same scrupulous faithfulness, honesty and fairness which they expect to find in the judge in reaching his decision. In permitting them to participate in the administration of justice between individuals, public authority has honored them and has vested in them a sacred trust that cannot be betrayed by misrepresentation, deceit, or falsehood. Prompt and severe reprisal on the part of court authority is demanded by law for the dishonoring of the profession. Canon 1666 provides for actual violation of one's oath of office.

Betrayal of the legal assistant's trust may be effected in diverse ways. First of all, it is possible to dishonor the office through culpable sins

13. *Op. cit.*, I, 354.
14. Cf. canons 2208, § 1; 2408.
15. Cf. canons 1640, § 2; 1625, § 3.
16. Cf. art. 54, n. 2, *Instructio*.
17. Canon 1621, § 1. For examples of such oath, cf. Doheny, *Practical Manual for Marriage Cases*, pp. 129, 141.

of omission, through blameworthy ignorance or neglect which jeopardizes the position of the client and enhances the legal prospects of the opposing party. On the other hand, the advocate and procurator might be moved to deliberate illegal action. It may be that his mode of conduct is intended to further the interests of his client, or, as Lega-Bartoccetti view the canon, it may be directed maliciously toward a favoring of his adversary, thus betraying his office and his client as well.[18]

Abuse of the office is possible in the very assumption of a lawsuit, for one cannot engage in a case which he clearly perceives to be unjust. If, moreover, during the progress of a trial undertaken in good faith its unjust foundation becomes apparent, the legal assistant must relinquish its prosecution and strive to induce his client to act in like manner.[19]

This moral principle, however, admits an exception in favor of the defendant in criminal proceedings. It is always lawful, in fact prescribed, to defend an accused person despite knowledge of his guilt. Until convicted the accused is never obliged to suffer punishment, and the present law requires that he be assisted in seeking to escape conviction.[20]

It is not necessary for the legal assistant to have certitude with regard to the justice of a case. Should the claim have good, probable reasons in its favor it may be undertaken. In extremely doubtful matters, there should be some reasonable hope of successful issue, and if such hope is slight, in comparison with the position of the adversary, the client should be made fully aware of the situation.[21]

In the actual conducting of the process by pleading for and representing the client, the advocate and procurator must be guided by this

18. *Commentarius in Iudicia Ecclesiastica*, I, 354.

19. St. Thomas, *Summa Theologica*, IIa, IIae, Q. 71, art. 3; Vermeersch, *Theologia Moralis*, II, 504, 505; Reiffenstuel, *Ius Canonicum Universum*, Lib. I, tit. 38, nn. 28, 29, 30; Grabowski, "Adwokatura" — *Ateneum Kaplanskie*, XXXV (1935), 250, 251.

20. Cf. canon 1655, § 1; Grabowski, *ibid.*, pp. 251, 252.

21. Schmalzgrueber, *Ius Ecclesiasticum Universum*, Lib. I, tit. 37, nn. 15, 16; Grabowski, *ibid.*, pp. 250, 251.

general principle: They are permitted to do everything, and only those things, which the client could legitimately do in his own behalf.[22] Consequently, there must be, for example, no recourse to fraudulent and fictitious delays.[23] All forms of lying, deceit and misrepresentation are to be avoided.[24] Again, the office would be profoundly dishonored by the corruption of witnesses or by the employment of false witnesses,[25] as it would be by the fabrication and falsification of documents or the use of such documents.[26] In addition, it need hardly be mentioned that no violation of the court's dignity by way of disobedience or lack of respect will be countenanced;[27] nor will infractions of particular tribunal regulations be tolerated.[28] Grave abuse, furthermore, would likewise consist in wilful exceeding of the procurator's mandate,[29] in malicious withholding of cogent proofs, in all forms of collusion with the opposite party, and in permitting the *fatalia legis* to lapse.[30] Advocates and procurators, moreover, are bound to observe the oath of secrecy whenever it is imposed by law or the court,[31] just as they must refrain from harmful violation of the professional secrecy which should characterize relations with the client.[32] Then too, they are not free to trifle with the conducting of gratuitous cases assigned to them.[33] In like manner, abuse must be considered to exist in the event that an advocate or procurator would attempt to occupy other judicial offices, such as that of judge or notary, in the same case in

22. Cf. Blat, *De Processibus*, p. 173; Coronata, *Institutiones*, III, 96; Noval, *De Iudiciis*, p. 185; Muñiz, *Procedimientos Eclesiásticos*, III, 46; Doheny, *Canonical Procedure in Matrimonial Cases*, p. 121.

23. Cf. canon 1749; art. 95, *Instructio*.

24. Cf. Reiffenstuel, *op. cit.*, Lib. I, tit. 37, n. 33; Office of St. Andrew Avellino, *Lectio IV*, Nov. 10.

25. Cf. canon 1755, § 3; art. 121, § 3, *Instructio*.

26. Cf. canons 2362; 2406.

27. Cf. canon 1640, § 2.

28. Cf. art. 21, 49, 56, § 1, 57, *Normae*.

29. Canon 1892, n. 3.

30. Cf. canons 1634; 1736; 1881; 1883; 1886.

31. Cf. canons 1623; 1625, §§ 2, 3; art. 130, § 1, *Instructio*; art. 9, *Normae*.

32. Cf. canon 1755, § 2, n. 1.

33. Cf. canon 1916, § 1; art. 240, § 1, *Instructio*.

which their services have already been enlisted in the rôle of legal assistant.[34]

These and similar violations of one's oath of office must be punished regardless of the reason underlying such abuse. Specifically, the canon mentions two motivating influences which may lead to a miscarriage of justice, namely, the bestowal of gifts and the acceptance of promises designed to pervert a faithful execution of one's official duty. In speaking of gifts, the law does not intend to banish marks of gratitude or the granting of trivial things out of courtesy and friendship. Such manifestations should not be presumed to exert undue influence. If it is asserted that they have done so in a particular case the contention must be proven.[35] Rather is the law directed toward grants which are intended and received as bribes, since it is not unusual for clients or adverse parties to attempt by means of gifts and promised favors to cause the advocate or procurator to act unjustly.

While canon 1666 refers in a particular manner to gifts and promises, it immediately proceeds to add: " ... *aut quamlibet aliam rationem.*" In other words, abuse of one's office for any reason whatsoever other than bribery still remains abuse and will be punished as such. For example, it is possible to conceive circumstances in which an official would be moved to dishonor his station from motives of spitefulness or revenge against his client or the opposing party, from sympathy for the adverse party, or, again, perhaps from the hope of being in a position to profit from a client or adversary at a later date.

Canon Law prescribes that the advocate or procurator found guilty of betraying his trust be ejected from office. If approved for all cases he must be deprived of his title. Should he have been commissioned for a particular case he must be prohibited from again assuming that

34. Canon 1613. Cf. Toso, "An Notarii et Advocati Munera Incompatibilia Sint in Causis Ecclesiasticis" — *Ius Pontificium*, XVIII (1938), 81-84. With regard to the recently constituted regional matrimonial tribunals in Italy, it is provided that the office of judge cannot be held by one who actually exercises the rôle of advocate or procurator in an altogether different case even before a different tribunal — S. C. S., 10 July, 1940, art. 8 — *AAS*, XXXII (1940), 305.

35. Noval, *De Iudiciis*, p. 185; Cocchi, *Commentarium*, Lib. IV, 137; Blat, *De Processibus*, p. 173.

rôle.[36] Furthermore, besides the obligation of restitution for all damage occasioned,[37] the law prescribes the imposition of fines or of other appropriate penalties.[38] Consequently, the judge or the ordinary may inflict other punishments or censures provided by law, taking into consideration the quality of the one guilty and the type of wrong committed together with its circumstances.[39]

Against advocates and procurators who have thus forfeited the right to exercise their functions in ecclesiastical courts, the judge, collegiate tribunal, or the ordinary may proceed in an administrative manner provided that a criminal suit is not intended.[40]

It is worthy of note, in this connection, that the law likewise provides for those who induce or would attempt to induce these officials to perform or to omit some act contrary to the duty of their office.[41]

36. Cf. canons 1625, § 3; 2291, n. 8.

37. Cf. canons 1737; 2210; Cocchi, *op. cit.*, Lib. IV, 136.

38. Cf. canons 2291, n. 12; 2223, § 3.

39. Cf. Lega-Bartoccetti, *Commentarius in Iudicia Ecclesiastica*, I, 354; canons 2196; 2199; 2203; 2207. From regulations of the Rota it might be noted that disciplinary measures against delinquent advocates and procurators follow a graduated pattern: note of reprehension, admonition, fines, privation of case assumed, suspension from office, and ejection from the official register — Cf. art. 21, 57, 131, 183, 184, *Normae*.

40. Wernz-Vidal, *Ius Canonicum*, VI, pars I, 205; Muñiz, *Procedimientos Eclesiásticos*, III, 46.

41. Canon 2407: Qui Curiae officiales seu administros quosvis ecclesiasticos, iudices, advocatos vel procuratores donis aut pollicitationibus ad actionem vel omissionem officio suo contrariam inducere tentaverit, congrua poena plectatur et ad reparanda damna, si qua illata sint, compellatur.

CHAPTER IX

THE RIGHTS AND DUTIES OF THE ADVOCATE AND PROCURATOR AT VARIOUS STAGES OF THE CANONICAL PROCESS

ARTICLE 1

THE ADVOCATE AND PROCURATOR IN THE INTRODUCTORY PERIOD

A. *Assistance in formulation of the libellus*

It is in formulating the introductory bill of complaint that the prospective litigant is actively assisted by the judicial advocate and procurator for the first time. An official attitude which discountenances or prohibits such aid is opposed to the stand of the Sacred Rota and, from the nature of the case, appears to be entirely unwarranted. Counsel, direction and active assistance to the client in this connection is in no manner disapproved in law,[1] nor is there any legal restriction preventing these experts from recasting a *libellus* which lacks clarity and precision, provided that there is no distortion of the facts adduced.[2] On the contrary, the technical character of the *libellus,* its essential juridical form and content, seem to demand legal assistance in its formation.[3] Recourse to such aid consequently lessens the possibility of the bill's rejection owing to technical defect.[4]

The *libellus* may be formulated in the vernacular as proceeding from the client, and it may be presented personally or by mail to the Bishop, Vicar General, Officialis or Diocesan Tribunal.[5] Since the *libellus* will vary in form and content with the specific case, the legal adviser must

---

1. Cf. art. 44, § 2, *Instructio.*

2. Cf. Doheny, *Canonical Procedure in Matrimonial Cases,* p. 127.

3. Cf. canons 1706; 1708; art. 55; 57, *Instructio;* Doheny, *op. cit.,* p. 132; Kealy, *The Introductory Libellus in Church Court Procedure,* pp. 33-36, 37-47.

4. Cf. canon 1709; art. 62, *Instructio.*

5. Coronata, *Institutiones,* III, 144; Roberti, *De Processibus,* I, 279.

be capable of adapting and applying the requirements of law to the particular suit.[6]

Although the plaintiff may be assisted in drawing up the bill of complaint, care must be given to the legal requirement of the signature. Preferably, the bill should be signed by the client. However, the procurator, properly authorized, has the right in law to sign the *libellus* as representing the genuine petition of his principal.[7] The advocate, on the contrary, possesses no such right.[8]

In addition to observing the fundamental legal requirements for the *libellus*,[9] an alert advocate and procurator may render valuable assistance to the court by joining to the bill documents which are deemed necessary. For example, besides authentic documents pertaining to the facts of the petition such as probatory letters and certificates of baptism, marriage, divorce, and death, proceedings would be facilitated by affixing properly certified documents of their own authorization and of petition for approbation when this is lacking.[10] It may happen that the advocate and procurator is to be assigned by the court at a preliminary hearing. This, however, would not prevent the party from requesting in the bill of complaint the appointment of a particular assistant.[11] In like manner, information might be included establishing the identity of the party according to law and in keeping with possible diocesan or tribunal regulations.[12] Similarly, besides affording sufficient detail with reference to the person and location of witnesses and suggesting points upon which they are particularly fitted to testify,[13] the lawyer in matrimonial procedure might forward testimony with a view to establishing the religious character, probity, and credibility of the

6. For diverse examples, cf. Kealy, *op. cit.*, Appendix I, 85-97; Doheny *Practical Manual for Marriage Cases*, p. 130 sq.

7. Canon 1708, § 3.

8. Cf. S. R. Rota, *Neo-Ebor.*, Decis. XLIV, 29 Dec., 1911 — III (1911), 516; Doheny, *Canonical Procedure in Matrimonial Cases*, p. 127.

9. Canon 1708; art. 57, *Instructio*.

10. Cf. canons 1659; 1661; 1658, § 2; art. 48, § 4; 49, § 1; 60, *Instructio;* art. 62; 65, *Normae;* Kealy, *The Introductory Libellus*, pp. 44, 64.

11. Cf. canons 1655, §§ 1, 2, 3; 1916; art. 43; 46; 237, *Instructio;* art. 54; 183, Normae; S. R. Rota, *Regulae Servandae in Liquandis Procuratorum et Advocatorum Proventibus*, 26 May, 1939 — *AAS*, XXXI (1939), 624.

12. Cf. art. 58, *Instructio*.

13. Cf. canon 1761, § 1; art. 59; 125, *Instructio*.

witnesses.[14] Furthermore, documentary justification should likewise be submitted at this point to sustain a plea for gratuitous patronage.[15]

In compiling documents for introduction with the *libellus*, the advocate and procurator must file only original documents or fully authenticated copies as required by law, obtaining them, whenever possible, from ecclesiastical records.[16]

The advocate and procurator may continue to assist the plaintiff with regard to the *libellus* in the event that it is rejected by the court.[17] If, in his judgment, it has been refused illegitimately, recourse may be had within an equitable period of ten days to the superior court of second instance or directly to the Tribunal of the Sacred Rota.[18] Such recourse is effected by means of a further *libellus* to which must be attached the rejected bill of complaint together with the decree of rejection.[19] While the finding of the superior court is entirely decisive,[20] there nevertheless seems to be no legal objection to the appearance of another *libellus* in the tribunal of first instance with regard to the same matter.[21] Moreover, Kealy points out that a legal adviser

14. Art. 138, § 1. *Instructio.*

15. Cf. canons 1914; 1915; 1910, § 2; art. 237; 238, § 1, *Instructio;* art. 176; 177, *Normae;* S. R. Rota, *Regulae Servandae*, 26 May, 1939 — *AAS,* XXXI (1939), 624. Doheny indicates several practical means of complying with this law — *Canonical Procedure in Matrimonial Cases,* p. 383. A form for the petition of gratuitous patronage may be found in Cappello, *Praxis Processualis,* pp. 90, 91.

16. Cf. canons 1819; 1820; art. 157; 158; 159; 160; 163; 168, *Instructio;* Grabowski, "Adwokatura" — *Ateneum Kaplanskie,* XXXV (1935), 253.

17. Canon 1709, §§ 1, 2; art. 44, § 2, *Instructio.*

18. Canons 1709, § 3; 34, § 3, n. 3; 35; art. 66, § 1, *Instructio;* Kealy, *op. cit.,* pp. 72, 73; Doheny, *op. cit.,* p. 139. Since the recourse of canon 1709, § 3, is in the nature and has the effect of an appeal, it may be introduced in the tribunal *a quo.* However, there can be no doubt that the complaint may be filed immediately with the higher court *ad quem.* Cf. Kealy, *op., cit.,* pp. 73-75; Cappello, *Praxis Processualis,* p. 14; Roberti, "An recursus ad superius tribunal ob rejectionem libelli proponendus sit coram iudice a quo" — *Apollinaris,* I (1928), 73, 74.

19. Coronata, *Institutiones,* III, 146; Muñiz, *Procedimientos Eclesiásticos,* III, n. 123. For a model form, cf. Cappello, *Praxis Processualis,* p. 14.

20. Cf. canon 1880, n. 7; art. 66, § 1, *Instructio;* Kealy, *op. cit.,* p. 76.

21. Roberti, *De Processibus,* I, 432; Kealy, *op. cit.,* p. 76.

may attempt to convince the court of what is felt to be erroneous rejection, thus perhaps effecting its readmittance.[22]

The need for legal direction will likewise be experienced by the prospective litigant whose *libellus* meets with no response. In the absence of a decree admitting or rejecting the bill of complaint within a continuous month, the advocate and procurator may insist upon action from the tribunal. Preferably this will be lodged in writing.[23] Five days after the filing of this plea, should it continue to be ignored, recourse may be had to the ordinary, provided that he is not the judge, or to the superior court, requesting that the inferior tribunal be compelled to consider the bill or that substitute judges be designated. "It is more in conformity with ecclesiastical discipline and the hierarchical organization of the Church to direct the recourse to the ordinary."[24]

Should the negligent judge be the ordinary himself, Noval maintains that recourse must be directed specifically to the tribunal of the Roman Pontiff.[25] Roberti [26] and Wernz-Vidal[27] hold that it may be lodged with the court of second instance provided that the recourse involves no criminal proceeding against the allegedly delinquent bishop. Recourse to either tribunal seems permissible. The superior court has authority to designate a substitute judge, whereas the Holy See is in a position to compel the ordinary to a fulfillment of his duty.[28]

In having recourse to obtain action on the *libellus* it is sufficient to present a copy of the unheeded bill together with the date of its introduction and date of petition for recognition. In addition, there will be the request for compulsory action or for the appointment of new judges.

When recourse against this tribunal negligence is made to the ordinary fruitlessly, Kealy is justified in recommending complaint not to the court of second instance but to the Sacred Consistorial Con-

---

22. *Op. cit.*, p. 68.

23. Cf. Coronata, *Institutiones*, III, 146.

24. Kealy, *The Introductory Libellus*, p. 78; cf. canons 1710; 34, § 3, nn. 1, 3; 35; art. 67, *Instructio*.

25. *De Iudiciis*, pp. 282, 283; cf. canons 1625, § 1; 1557, § 1, n. 3.

26. *De Processibus*, I, n. 286.

27. *Ius Canonicum*, VI, pars I, 325.

28. Cf. canons 1615, § 3; 1625, § 1; 1710.

gregation.[29] Complaint against unavailing recourse made to the superior court would be patterned after the procedure outlined in canon 1710.

B. *The formal summons*

Upon receiving a formal citation to appear in court for the contesting of a lawsuit,[30] the defendant's first step should be concerned with the designation of a judicial advocate and procurator. In the event that a procurator has already been commissioned by the *actor* and by the *pars conventa*, the summons may be directed to these officials who may respond in the names of their clients, representing them before the tribunal according to the terms of the citation.[31] Realizing, however, that the offices of advocate and procurator are not always combined in one person, the Matrimonial Instruction of 1936 has introduced a legal change of considerable practical importance. In this process a summons may be presented to a duly authorized advocate who thereby is enabled to substitute for the procurator in responding.[32] It is to be noted, furthermore, that legal representatives may appear in court of their own accord, thereby affording the tribunal an opportunity of disclosing the allegations of the plaintiff and of hearing both parties, in which circumstances the citation becomes unnecessary.[33] In matrimonial cases introduced by the promotor of justice owing to the inability of the parties to challenge the validity of their marriage, it appears that the consorts may be cited and may respond through the representatives permitted them by law provided that the tribunal issues no decree to the contrary.[34]

---

29. *The Introductory Libellus*, p. 78; cf. canon 248, § 3.

30. Canon 1711, § 1; art. 71, § 1, *Instructio*.

31. Cf. canons 1712, §§ 2, 3; 1647; art. 74, § 3; 44, § 2, *Instructio*. In some cases this representation will be necessary: cf. canons 1648, § 3; 1649; 1654, § 1; 1655, § 4; 1713.

32. Art. 74, § 4, *Instructio;* cf. canon 1661; Doheny, *Canonical Procedure in Matrimonial Cases*, p. 159.

33. Canons 1711, § 2; 1647; art. 74, § 2; 44, § 2, *Instructio*.

34. Cf. art. 46; 35, § 1, n. 2; 38; 39; 41, § 4; 45; 74, § 4; canon 1647; Doheny, *op. cit.*, p. 159.

It is the advocate and procurator who must scrutinize the summons delivered to the client or to himself since he alone, in ordinary circumstances, can be expected to appraise it juridically. Consequently, he must be in a position to do so in accordance with the legal requirements for its validity since the rights of both plaintiff and defendant may require safeguarding at this point.[35]

A further consideration to be borne in mind by the advocate and procurator with reference to the summons is that of contumacy.[36] Provided that a declaration of contumacy is legally possible, the procurator of the opposite party may request the judge to issue a decree declaring the contumaciousness of the delinquent litigant or procurator according to law.[37] Upon the insistence of the opposing procurator a delinquent plaintiff, as well as a defendant, may be declared contumacious, in which event the plaintiff is deprived of his right to prosecute the case.[38] Moreover, the defendant could then demand that the case be dropped and the acts considered void, or, despite the plaintiff's absence, he might seek to have the suit carried through to completion.[39]

C. *The contestatio litis*

In order to determine the object of the controversy clearly and precisely by the formulation of the issue in pleading, the parties once again may and should have recourse to the assistance of the advocate and procurator.[40] In accordance with the terms indicated by the cita-

35. Cf. canons 1715; 1723; 1894, n. 1; art. 76; 84; 209, n. 1; 16, § 1, *Instructio.*

36. Contumacy in the judicial sense is defined by Coronata as: . . . *inobedientia commissa erga iudicem ab eo qui legitime in iudicium citatus, nulla iusta causa impeditus, nec per se nec per procuratorem, comparet sive initio sive decursu iudicii, qua inobedientia extante, contumax absens proprio iure renuntiare consetur.* — *Institutiones,* III, 279. Cf. canons 1842; 1848; art. 89, §§ 1, 2, *Instructio.*

37. Canons 1843; 1844, § 1; cf. art. 70, § 2, *Normae.*

38. Canons 1842; 1849; 1850, § 1. Cf. art. 91, § 1, *Instructio;* art. 74, *Normae.*

39. Canon 1850, § 3. Cf. canon 1850, § 2; art. 91, § 2, *Instructio.*

40. Cf. canon 1726.

tion,[41] the issue may be joined by any person who has a right to be a party in the suit. As a result, legally authorized procurators may appear before the tribunal to effect this element of procedure.[42] It does not seem necessary for both procurators to appear in court simultaneously since some authors point to the possibility of their positions being presented in writing or in any manner which establishes a petition and its contradiction.[43] Doheny makes specific mention of the fact that an advocate may be present at the joinder of issue in addition to the procurator.[44] Such a course is advisable owing to the possibility of his gaining thereby an early insight into the general character of the case, together with clues which the exchange of views might suggest.

In the event that the terms of the controversy are not clearly defined or admit of some misunderstanding, the procurator of either party may call upon the judge to provide for precise formulation of the doubt.[45] The *contestatio litis,* embodying the specific grounds upon which a contention is based and disputed, is the cornerstone of the process.[46] At the very outset, therefore, the legal adviser must have a sufficient grasp of the facts under discussion and of the law involved to establish a formula of doubt which actually embraces the particular difficulty to be adjudicated. He will be mindful of solemn processual principles which forbid the court to deviate from the petition and which demand that the sentence be conformable to the bill of complaint.[47] Consequently, should error, new evidence or some other grave reason indicate the desirability, or perhaps the necessity, of a change, one's legal representative may so petition the court. At the

41. Cf. canons 1712, § 3; 1715, § 1.

42. Cf. canon 1727; art. 65; 66, *Normae;* Noval, *De Iudiciis,* p. 293; Wernz-Vidal, *Ius Canonicum,* VI, pars I, 342; Cappello, *Praxis Processualis,* p. 19. In addition to the authorization required for acting at this stage, the official not yet approved must petition and obtain such approbation: cf. canon 1658, § 2; art. 48, § 4, *Instructio.*

43. Wernz-Vidal, *op. cit.,* VI, pars I, 341; Coronata, *Institutiones,* III, 158; Muñiz, *Procedimientos Eclesiásticos,* III, 240.

44. *Canonical Procedure in Matrimonial Cases,* p. 172.

45. Cf. canons 1728; 1729, § 3; art. 88, *Instructio;* art. 77, § 2, *Normae.*

46. Noval, *op. cit.,* p. 291; Eichmann, *Das Prozessrecht des C. I. C.,* p. 125.

47. Canon 1873, § 1, n. 1; art. 77, § 1, *Normae.* Cf. *Appollinaris,* II (1929), 76-78.

same time, however, in these circumstances the opposing procurator should be alert in safeguarding the rights of his own client.[48]

Before the issue in pleading is formulated, the advocate and procurator will reflect upon his right and consider what is perhaps his duty with regard to proposing possible exceptions.[49] Ordinarily, exceptions are to be lodged before the *contestatio litis,* as, for example, the exception of relative incompetency of the court[50] or the exception of suspicion against ministers of the tribunal because of their undue interest, influence, or connection in the case.[51]

A further incidental matter which may require adjustment prior to the joining of issue concerns possible disagreement with regard to judicial expenses and the granting or rejection of gratuitous patronage already requested.[52]

Once again, too, at the *contestatio litis,* legal representatives must be mindful of their rights and obligations with reference to the question of contumacy.[53]

Occasionally, moreover, the advocate and procurator may find it practical at this stage to invoke canon 1730 should he foresee that some element of proof now available will be difficult or impossible to adduce at a later date. For any just cause, as outlined in the canon, the court may be requested to receive testimony or alleged proofs immediately.

48. Canons 1729, § 4; 1731, n. 1; cf. art. 76, § 3, *Normae.*

49. Cf. Grabowski, "Adwokatura" — *Ateneum Kaplanskie,* XXXV (1935), 253.

50. Cf. canons 1628, § 1; 1559-1568; 1610; 1964; 1558; 1628, § 2; 1892, n. 1; 1893; art. 3, *Instructio.*

51. Cf. canons 1628, § 1; 1613-1617; 1837; art. 187, *Instructio.* Counsel should note that the reasons advanced in can. 1613 appear to be demonstrative, not taxative. Furthermore, while can. 1613 restrains certain officials specifically, in similar circumstances it may be extended to others as, for example, the notary, experts, advocates and procurators — Cf. Coronata, *Institutiones,* III, 54; Roberti, *De Processibus,* I, 156; Doheny, *Canonical Procedure in Matrimonial Cases,* pp. 313, 314; Muñiz, *Procedimientos,* III, 112, note 3, 146, note 4, 147. A form for the lodging of such exceptions may be found in Cappello, *Praxis Processualis,* p. 80.

52. Canon 1631.

53. Canon 1729, § 1; art. 115, *Instructio.*

With the issue in pleading established, the judge grants to the contending parties a period of time deemed adequate for the marshalling and presentation of proof. Here again, in like manner, counsel might foresee that, owing to peculiar circumstances, the allotted time is insufficient. Provided that his reasons are just and that no attempt is made to delay the process unduly, he may petition the court for an extension of time.[54]

ARTICLE 2

THE ADVOCATE AND PROCURATOR IN THE PROBATORY STAGE

A. *Interrogation and judicial confession of the parties*

In order to expedite instruction of the process in the probatory stage, the parties are permitted to indicate matters for investigation to be proposed to each other and to suggest points upon which the respective parties should be interrogated.[55] As a result, the advocate and procurator with a view to strengthening his case may request permission of the judge to present a list of points to be explored or topics to be proposed to and answered by the other party.[56] Granted this permission, he has no legal right, as Muñiz points out, to oppose the judge who inspects, modifies, or even rejects his proposals.[57] It is noteworthy that the Rota in granting this power to procurators requires a special mandate.[58] In commenting upon this regulation, however, Bernardini notes that since the questionnaire of a legal representative in no way prejudices the position of his client, canon 1745, § 1, is to be preferred which makes no mention of additional authorization.[59]

---

54. Cf. canons 1731, n. 2; 1620; 1634, §§ 2, 3.
55. Canons 1742; 1745, § 1; art. 110; 113; 114; 117, *Instructio.*
56. Cf. Cappello, *Praxis Processualis*, p. 50.
57. *Procedimientos*, III, 272; cf. Noval, *De Iudiciis*, p. 304; Doheny, *Canonical Procedure in Matrimonial Cases*, p. 243.
58. Art. 99, §§ 1, 2, *Normae.*
59. "Normae S. R. Rotae Tribunalis" — *Apollinaris*, VII (1934), 429-478, ad 99.

Unlike the period before the Code in which authors admitted the possibility of a client's responding through a procurator in possession of a special mandate, the present legislation requires that response to interrogation must proceed from the litigants directly. Needless to say, they are in the best position to render adequate replies. Then, too, there is the added element of judicial evaluation which attaches to one's manner of responding.[60]

While the Code does not explicitly exclude the parties and their legal advisers from attending the interrogation of the adverse party, some authors maintain that ordinarily they are not to be admitted.[61] This position will be discussed briefly in the following treatment with regard to the hearing of witnesses.

With reference to the judicial confession of a litigant,[62] the sole practical point which suggests itself concerns the possibility of such confession proceeding from a legal representative. There can be no doubt that the law inclines to exclude the procurator in this element of procedure.[63] Nevertheless, in the absence of an invalidating clause to the contrary, together with the broader attitude of the old law, several commentators maintain that a judicial confession may proceed from a procurator who pursues this course with the knowledge of his client.[64] Provided that no particular law or tribunal regulation decrees otherwise, it isn't clear that confession made in such fashion can be declared invalid.[65] However, Roberti is to be commended in opposing such procedure.[66] And while it is legally sound to follow those authors who permit indirect confession only by virtue of express

60. Canon 1746. Cf. Reiffenstuel, *Ius Canonicum Universum*, Lib. II, tit. 18, n. 245; Noval, *op. cit.*, p. 305; *Reg. Serv. in Iudiciis apud S. R. Rotae Tribunal*, 4 Aug., 1910, § 146, n. 2 — *AAS*, II (1910), 783.

61. Wernz-Vidal, *Ius Canonicum*, VI, pars I, 372; Coronata, *Institutiones*, III, 174. Cf. canon 1771; *Reg. Serv. S. R. R.*, art. 146, n. 3 — *AAS*, II (1910), 783; art. 101; 128, *Instructio*.

62. Canon 1750.

63. Cf. canons 1746; 1743, § 1; 1647; 1662.

64. Coronata, *op. cit.*, III, 184; Muñiz, *Procedimientos*, III, 228, note 2; Augustine, *A Commentary on Canon Law*, VII, 198.

65. Cf. canons 15; 1662. Hanssens is of the opinion that such confession is invalid — *Apollinaris*, XII (1939), 206.

66. *De Processibus*, II, 330.

special authorization,[67] tribunals would act more in conformity with the spirit of the law in requiring that the parties themselves be directly responsible for an act of such a nature and of such consequences.[68]

B. *The testimony of witnesses and experts*

In consulting his client with a view to the marshalling of witnesses, an advocate and procurator will aid his case considerably and, at the same time, render no little service to the court by regarding the legal prescriptions affecting those unfit, suspect, and debarred with reference to testimony.[69] At the same time, moreover, in order to safeguard the rights of his client, the legal assistant might feel justified, owing to peculiar circumstances of a case, in petitioning the judge to summon witnesses *ex officio*.[70] Similarly, counsel will be mindful that recourse to the assistance of experts, beyond that demanded by law, may be occasioned at his instigation.[71] Consequently, if expert opinion is deemed helpful or necessary, a request for such aid may be presented to the tribunal together with proposed questions or points for particular attention.[72]

Furthermore, the advocate and procurator should be mindful of his right to petition the court for a re-summoning of a witness or expert for subsequent deposition regarding facts which he feels must be further elucidated in the interests of truth and justice.[73]

Not only does Canon Law permit the litigants to summon witnesses,[74] but it grants them the right to challenge the admittance of certain others as well. Motivated by a just cause, for example, owing

---

67. Noval, *De Iudiciis,* p. 318; Vermeersch-Creusen, *Epitome,* III, 76; Wernz-Vidal, *op. cit.,* VI, pars I, 388.

68. Cf. canons 1751; 1752; 1662.

69. Cf. canons 1757; 1758; 1974; art. 119; 120; 122, *Instructio.* Cf. also canon 1761, § 1; art. 59; 97; 125; 138, of the same Instruction.

70. Cf. canons 1619; 1759, § 3; art. 123, *Instructio.*

71. Cf. canons 1792; 1793; art. 140, § 2, *Instructio.* Cf. also canons 1976; 1982; art. 139 of the same Instruction.

72. Canon 1799, § 1; art. 147, § 3, *Instructio;* art. 98, *Normae.*

73. Canons 1781; 1786; art. 107; 135, *Instructio.*

74. Canons 1759, § 1; 1754; art. 123; 125, *Instructio.*

to the fact that the law designates one as unfit, suspect, or debarred,[75] the advocate and procurator may request the court to exclude the person or the testimony of the undesirable witness.[76] The foundation for such a plea of rejection must be proved, particularly if it is filed for a reason not specified in law.

In order to provide an opportunity for lodging such a petition of reprobation, the law ordains that the names of witnesses summoned be communicated to the respective clients.[77] In this connection the lawyer will note that he has but a peremptory period of three days equitable time dating from this notification in which to file an exception of disapproval.[78] Obviously, therefore, he must not only be fully aware of legal requirements,[79] but must at once consult his client with a view to obtaining information upon which to base possible exception.

The right of the advocate and procurator with reference to exceptions lodged against witnesses is in like manner applicable to the possible exceptions taken to experts.[80]

These officials, too, should regard their client's right to notification in the event that following publication of the testimony new witnesses are admitted or previous witnesses are recalled for examination on points already investigated.[81]

The title of this dissertation seems to justify at this point brief mention of advocates and procurators specifically in the rôle of witness. Canon Law considers these officials entirely unqualified to appear as a witness in the discussion of a case in which they have exercised their

75. Canons 1757; 1758.

76. Canon 1764, § 2. Cf. can. 1783, § 2; 1764, § 5; 1785; 1783; 1858; 1859; art. 131, §§ 2, 3, *Instructio;* Coronata, *Institutiones,* III, 205; Roberti, *De Processibus,* II, 53; Vermeersch-Creusen, *Epitome,* III, 68. A form may be found in Cappello, *Praxis Processualis,* p. 85.

77. Canon 1763. Note particularly art. 126, *Instructio.*

78. Canon 1764, § 4; art. 131, § 1, *Instructio.* Cf. canons 1634; 34, § 3, n. 4; 35; Lega-Bartoccetti, *Commentarius,* II, 690.

79. Canon 1757; art. 119, *Instructio.*

80. Canons 1795; 1796; 1978; 1979; 1982; art. 142; 143; 145, *Instructio.*

81. Canon 1786; art. 135, *Instructio.*

office.[82] However, one who assisted a litigant merely by direction in the capacity of counsellor, either before or during the process, without actually and officially engaging in the trial, may be summoned and admitted as a witness.[83] At the same time, an advocate who has acted as legal adviser, owing to confidences made to him, may be bound by the seal of professional secrecy. With permission of his client he may testify, but, on the other hand, the law empowers him to plead exemption from the obligation of so doing.[84]

In addition to the right of summoning and of challenging witnesses, the advocate and procurator has a right to be present as witnesses and experts take the required oaths.[85] While no obligation of attending results from notification of this element of procedure, Doheny points out that: "Their presence at this ceremony would help to confirm their confidence in the experts [and witnesses] and at the same time should duly impress the experts [and witnesses] with the serious and sacred nature of their duty."[86] Contrary to the old law, moreover, it doesn't appear that a procurator could oppose the testimony of a witness or expert who has taken the oath legally in his absence, even though the absence be involuntary.[87]

A further consideration affecting the advocate and procurator concerns possible prescriptions of secrecy with reference to deposition in matrimonial cases. Should the necessity of obviating grave dissension demand it, he may be placed under a special oath of secrecy which restrains him from communicating the information revealed, and its source, not only to outsiders but to his client as well.[88] This regulation, therefore, is not only an exception to canon 1763 but an extension of the exception provided for in that canon which

82. Canon 1757, § 3, n. 1; art. 119, § 3, n. 1, *Instructio.* Lega-Bartoccetti discuss the possibility and conditions for permitting their testimony as a basis for *indicia* — *Commentarius,* II, 674.

83. Coronata, *Institutiones,* III, 195; Doheny, *Canonical Procedure in Matrimonial Cases,* p. 229. Cf. Lega-Bartoccetti, *op. cit.,* I, 334.

84. Canon 1755, § 2, n. 1; art. 121, *Instructio.*

85. Canons 1767, § 2; 1797, § 2; art. 146, *Instructio.*

86. *Op. cit.,* p. 265. Cf. Lega-Bartoccetti, *op. cit.,* II, 696.

87. Coronata, *Institutiones,* III, 209; Augustine, *A Commentary on Canon Law,* VII, 219. Cf. Reiffenstuel, *Ius Canonicum,* Lib. II, tit. 20, 496.

88. Art. 130, §§ 1, 2, *Instructio.* Cf. canons 1625, § 3; 1782; art. 134; 184, *Instructio;* Torre, *Epitome,* p. 51.

empowers the court to defer notification of the names of witnesses as a means of avoiding difficult and embarrassing situations. In these cases in which the court sees fit to withhold names even temporarily, a practical point might be raised by the lawyer aware of such procedure. There doesn't appear to be any reason preventing him from the filing of a request that the names be submitted under oath of secrecy not to his client but to himself. Success in this direction would enable him to proceed with adequate defense measures and with investigation intended to establish the legal status of the witness.

A question of considerable practical importance with reference to witnesses derives from canon 1771. This law prohibits the parties from assisting at hearings of witnesses save where the judge deems that they should be admitted.[89] Commentators have not extended this law to include barring of advocates and procurators. However, the Matrimonial Instruction of 1936 is explicit in excluding not only the litigants but legal assistants as well. This general regulation may prudently be waived only by way of exception should circumstances appear to warrant it.[90] Consequently, it is clear that no general permission may be extended to lawyers permitting them to assist at the depositions of witnesses in all matrimonial processes.

Nevertheless, in view of the fact that relaxation of this general law is legally possible, the present writer recommends the lodging of a petition for admittance to all hearings of a particular trial. From a consideration of the importance of the defense rôle, which may be aided considerably by such an attendance, it should not be difficult to adduce motives sufficient to influence the tribunal. Personal contact would undoubtedly make for a more intelligent evaluation of testimony in the lawyer's brief. It would place him in a more favorable position with regard to the lodging of possible exceptions and to the formulation of subsequent questions. In fact, his presence at times would obviate the necessity of recalling witnesses for further testimony since clarifying questions could be proposed at once. Furthermore, attendance of the legal adviser is the most practical manner of fulfilling

---

89. The reasons for this exclusion are well outlined by Lega-Bartoccetti, *Commentarius*, II, 703-705; cf. Coronata, *Institutiones*, III, 212; Noval, *De Iudiciis*, p. 341.

90. Art. 128; cf. art. 96, § 1, *Instructio*.

what at times might prove an obligation, namely, that of safeguarding
his client's rights with regard to precise court reporting.[91] In addition,
noting the right and the duty of the *defensor vinculi* to be present at
all hearings,[92] one might ask if the lawyer, who likewise enters the
trial in the interests of truth and justice, should not be afforded an
equal opportunity of informing himself not only of facts but of the
personal reactions of those testifying and of insisting that significant
reactions be recorded.[93] If precautions are considered necessary, the
oath of secrecy may always be imposed. Finally, the need for experienced tribunal officials might well be considered. By admitting advocates and procurators to these hearings an added practical manner
presents itself of acquainting them with the rights, duties, and problems of other court ministers. In accordance, therefore, with the practice of many efficient tribunals, which, it might be remarked, find the
custom most satisfactory, it is again suggested that the advocate and
procurator enter a plea, founded upon sound reasons, at the beginning
of each matrimonial process for admittance to all hearings as permitted by law.[94]

Not only may the advocate and procurator present to the court a
list of points for interrogation of witnesses and experts,[95] but also,
when admitted to hearings, he may propose questions to the examining
judge who will then, as he sees fit, interrogate the witness accordingly.[96]
In so doing, the lawyer must be mindful of the legal requirements

91. Cf. canons 1777-1780; 1801; art. 103, § 2, *Instructio;* Doheny, *Canonical
Procedure in Matrimonial Cases,* p. 196; Lega-Bartoccetti, *Commentarius,* II, 716.

92. Canons 1773; 1968, n. 1; art. 70, § 1, *Instructio.*

93. Canon 1779.

94. Art. 128, *Instructio.* It might be noted that these assistants are permitted
to attend confrontations: canon 1772, § 2; art. 133, *Instructio.* Moreover, according to canon 1797, § 2: Partes non solum interesse possunt iurisiurandi praesta-
tioni sed etiam exsecutioni muneris perito demandati, nisi aliud rei natura vel
honestas exigat aut lex vel iudex statuat. While canon 1809 may prohibit advocates and procurators from assisting at the judicial *accessus,* the Rota explicitly
mentions their right of attending and of proposing animadversions — art. 101,
§ 1, *Normae.*

95. Canons 1745, § 1; 1799, § 1; art. 114; 147, § 3, *Instructio;* cf. Cappello, *Praxis Processualis,* p. 50.

96. Canon 1773; art. 101, *Instructio.*

governing judicial interrogation.[97] Questioning on his part will at times be necessary. Such necessity would arise, for example, if the judge should be delinquent in the matter of *ex officio* questions. At all times there is the possibility that his questions will prove helpful. The lawyer who recognizes here an important and perhaps decisive judicial factor will, by the same token, be conscious of a twofold essential need. First, a firm grasp of the canonical principles involved. Second, a thorough and conscientious study of the case facts. Only by diligent preparation, with no reliance on set formulas or questionnaires previously used, can clear, pertinent questions be fashioned. Furthermore, in order to formulate adaptable queries, there should be an attempt made to investigate something of the background of those testifying.

In the event that canon 1775 is violated to such an extent that apparent injustice results to his client or witness, what course may the lawyer pursue? While admitting the impossibility of filing immediate objections with the auditor, Doheny recommends what appears to be the most practical remedy, written complaint to the tribunal or to the bishop. Should this point of procedural law suffer continued disregard at the hands of a particular official, the matter should be brought to the attention of the *promotor iustitiae* as provided for by law expressly in matrimonial trials.[98]

A final consideration with reference to those about to testify consists in the question of their preparation for judicial examination. The parties, witnesses, and experts are never to be forwarned of questions to be proposed to them.[99] Failure to observe this prescription of procedural law would defeat the purpose of judicial hearings, while, on the other hand, the manner of court questioning makes previous preparation unnecessary. As a result, the advocate and procurator may do nothing more than indicate the broad, general outline which he feels the interrogation may follow, explaining technical terms likely to be encountered. There must be absolutely no attempt made to induce

97. Canons 1774; 1775; art. 99; 100; 102, *Instructio.*

98. *Canonical Procedure in Matrimonial Cases,* p. 194. Cf. art. 16, § 1, *Instructio.*

99. Canon 1776; art. 103, § 1, a, *Instructio.*

or to influence specific replies, to say nothing of other forms of collusion.[100] At the same time, the lawyer would be entirely within his rights in explaining to his client or witness the extent of one's obligation to respond to questioning.[1]

In this connection, it appears that the advocate and procurator must refrain entirely from attempting to interview the opposing party and witnesses summoned by that party for the purpose of securing information. In adhering to this principle he will avoid the danger and escape the suspicion of having exerted undue influence. Furthermore, by presenting his questions to the court, whose duty it is to investigate, the lawyer possesses adequate means of deriving desired information.[2]

C. *Documents*

With regard to documentary evidence deposited and preserved in the tribunal chancery, it is sufficient to note that even prior to the publication of the process,[3] the advocate and procurator may consult the documents with permission of the judge. Such inspection, needless to say, is fully in accord with his office of safeguarding the rights of his client. For example, the lawyer on occasion may find it necessary to challenge the authenticity of such evidence.[4] Again, in discovering documentary excerpts adduced as evidence, he may feel it his duty to petition the court for summoning of the complete original or copy.[5] Furthermore, noting the absence of pertinent documentary evidence known or believed to be in the possession of the opposition, he may again petition the tribunal with a view to effecting production of these instruments.[6]

---

100. Canon 1755, § 3; art. 121, § 3, *Instructio*.

1. Cf. canons 1743, § 1; 1755; art. 111; 121, *Instructio;* Lega-Bartoccetti, *Commentarius,* II, 714; Doheny, *Canonical Procedure,* pp. 206, 232.

2. Doheny, *Canonical Procedure,* p. 122.

3. Canon 1858; art. 175, *Instructio*.

4. Canons 1815; 1820; 1821. Cf. canons 1813; 1814; 1819; art. 160; 161; 162, *Instructio*.

5. Cf. art. 166, *Instructio*.

6. Cf. art. 167, *Instructio;* canons 1822; 1824.

ARTICLE 3

THE ADVOCATE AND PROCURATOR IN THE DEFINITIVE PERIOD

A. *Publication of the process*

After all the proofs have been adduced and recorded, the court proceeds to the publication of the process whereby all the evidence, including that which to the present has remained secret, is made available to interested officials and litigants. With the authorization of this publication by judicial decree, the advocate and procurator receives the right to examine all the evidence and to request a copy of the processual acts.[7]

At this point, a twofold regulation of the 1936 Matrimonial Instruction must command the attention of the legal assistant. First, in the same decree by which he authorizes publication, the presiding judge establishes an equitable period of time within which the proofs submitted may be strengthened, clarified, and completed by the presentation of additional arguments. Secondly, provided that proper precautions are taken, and provided that the opposition and tribunal officials are consulted, it is declared legally permissible still to introduce new witnesses.[8]

It need scarcely be pointed out that the advocate and procurator should avail himself of the information essential to his pleading at the earliest opportunity. In like manner, sincere appreciation of his responsibility in matrimonial litigation should urge him to seize upon the limited opportunity afforded him of possibly improving his case. Should he perceive that the accumulation of hoped for evidence is impossible within the time allotted, he may petition the court for an extension.[9]

Mention has been made of the lawyer's right to inspect the acts and to procure a copy of them. Must this *"facultas"* of canon 1859 be regarded as a strict right or rather as a practical concession to be

---

7. Canons 1858; 1859; art. 175, §§ 1, 2; 134, *Instructio;* art. 120, *Normae.*
8. Art. 175, §§ 3, 4, *Instructio.* Cf. art. 135, *Instructio;* canons 1786; 1983; 35.
9. Canon 1634, § 2.

ordinarily granted but possibly denied? Cappello indicates the practical aspect of this question in connection with a matrimonial case in which the defendant expressed his firm determination to divulge all the acts submitted to him.[10]

Fundamentally the litigant has a right to defend himself. His defense measures, however, will prove adequate only in proportion to his knowledge of the total evidence compiled against him. Canon 1859 takes into consideration that such defense results not from momentary inspection of the acts, but rather from continued study and reference to them. Consequently, in granting this twofold "faculty," the Legislator intended not merely a right to petition, but a right to inspect and possess the acts, a right which, *per se,* cannot be denied. At the same time, should the judge prudently fear that publication of the acts will result in serious harm to a litigant or to the Church, he would be justified at any time during the progress of the trial in binding all concerned to secrecy.[11] On the other hand, provided that one refused this oath, or provided that the court distrusted an oath in these circumstances, the party would not be in a position to invoke canon 1859 in his favor. In intending to abuse a right established only as a means of defense, such a person must be considered as having forfeited that right.[12]

B. *Conclusion of the case*

With the termination of the equitable period providing for the introduction of new proof, the tribunal proceeds to the conclusion of the trial. This judicial decree may be issued prior to the expiration of that time limit only in the event that the parties and *defensor vinculi,* if engaged, have officially rested their cases.[13]

Since the *conclusio in causa* is a formal declaration to the effect that the evidence is exhausted, the furnishing of further proof is ordinarily prohibited. Nevertheless, under certain circumstances, additional support for one's contention may yet be adduced. In order to do so, the

10. Cappello, "Quaestio Canonica" — *Periodica,* XIX (1930), 71-73.
11. Cf. canon 1623, § 3.
12. Cf. Cappello — Periodica, XIX (1930), 71-73.
13. Canon 1860; art. 176; 177, § 1, *Instructio;* art. 121, *Normae.*

process must involve a dispute which can never become *res iudicata*,[14] or there must be a question of pertinent documents now made available for the first time, or witnesses, previously impeded lawfully from testifying, must now be in a position to appear.[15] At times the advocate and procurator will discover his most cogent elements of proof only after the conclusion of the case. As a result, he must be mindful of this opportunity which the law affords him. Should his efforts to introduce new evidence at this point meet with a decree of rejection from the presiding judge, recourse may be had to the collegiate tribunal which will express its opinion according to majority vote.[16]

On the other hand, counsel must look to the safeguarding of his client's right in the event that new evidence adduced by the other party or by the *defensor* is admitted. He has a right to notification and a right to time sufficient for due cognizance of the added proof and for the preparation of adequate defense. Failure on the part of the court to abide by this notification would invalidate the process.[17]

C. *The discussion of the suit — the brief*

Discussion of the evidence adduced, in the light of the legal principles involved, follows the issuance of a decree concluding the case. To this end the lawyer is directed by the court to submit his brief within a suitable period of time. For any reasonable cause the advocate may petition the court for an extension or for an abbreviation of the time specified for the filing of his defense. Such a plea should be made ten days before the period lapses.[18] This principal mode of

14. Cf. canons 1902; 1903.

15. Canon 1861, § 1; art. 178, § 1; 175, § 3, *Instructio.* Cf. Ciprotti, "De novis probationibus post conclusionem in causa" — *Apollinaris*, XII (1939), 110-113.

16. Art. 178, § 2, *Instructio;* cf. canon 1577, § 1.

17. Canon 1861, § 2; art. 178, § 3, *Instructio;* art. 121, *Normae.* Since the invalidating clause is intended to guarantee equal judicial protection, Doheny seems justified in arguing *a pari* from canon 1587 that the trial would be valid in which the parties, legally uninformed of new proof, yet examined it and had the opportunity of refuting it — *Canonical Procedure in Matrimonial Cases*, pp. 303, 304.

18. Canon 1862. Cf. canon 1634, §§ 2, 3; art. 179, § 1; 181, *Instructio:* art. 40, d; 129, §§ 1, 2, *Normae.*

pleading and of presenting one's defense must be filed in writing,[19] and while it may be drawn up either by the litigant himself or by the legal assistant,[20] the Rota regulation should be observed which prohibits the party and lawyer from submitting separate pleadings.[21] Nevertheless, counsel for the defendant in a matrimonial process may file his own defense supplementing that of the *defensor vinculi* if it is deemed necessary. Moreover, the advocate should write his brief in Latin, whereas the party, it appears, may write in the vernacular or in any language known to the court.[22] A further requirement stipulates that the defense be drawn up in multiple copy according to the nature and necessity of the case. Copies must be available for each judge constituting the tribunal, for the *defensor vinculi* and *promotor iustitiae* if they participate, and for the opposing party. It is advisable to submit in addition a copy solely for purposes of inclusion in the case records.[23] The Matrimonial Instruction of 1936 requires that the brief, signed by the advocate, be submitted to the presiding judge who gives his approval for the execution of the necessary copies by affixing his signature to the foot of the text.[24]

The presiding judge may order that the lawyer's argumentation be printed together with a summary of the statements and important pertinent documents bound in brochure. Before the advocate can proceed to have his defense printed, however, the brief must be presented in manuscript and approved for publication. Furthermore, in order that strictest secrecy be maintained, the work is then committed only to approved printers.[25] While printing of the brief is practically necessary for the Rota owing to the requirements of the Tribunal and of the *Studium*, it doesn't appear that diocesan courts experience this need. Typed copies are sufficient and afford greater assurance of the secrecy demanded by law. In this connection, both advocate and procurator must be mindful of their obligation, particularly at this stage,

---

19. Canon 1863, § 1; art. 179, § 2, *Instructio:* art. 122, *Normae.*
20. Canon 1862, § 1.
21. Art. 123, *Normae.*
22. Cf. art. 122; 123, *Normae.*
23. Canon 1863, §§ 1, 2; art. 179, § 2, *Instructio;* art. 126, § 1, *Normae.*
24. Art. 179, § 2, *Instructio.*
25. Canon 1863, §§ 3, 4; art. 179, § 3, *Instructio;* art. 122, 125, § 1, *Normae.*

to prevent such judicial matter from falling into the hands of others.[26] In like manner, although the advocate is permitted to submit with his brief a copy of those acts which serve to illustrate and to strengthen his argumentation,[27] it is not customary, nor is it necessary, in diocesan tribunals to include the *summarium* of documents prescribed by the Rota which usually contains all of the *acta causae* and *acta processus*. Such acts are readily available in the original to members of the tribunal.

With regard to the extent of one's pleading, the advocate must be guided by particular tribunal regulations or, in their absence, by limitations imposed by the presiding judge.[28] For example, the Rota restricts the brief to twenty pages while the rebuttal is not to exceed ten pages. An extension may be granted by the court for a just reason.[29] It is noteworthy that in matrimonial procedure this regulation of the Rota has been adopted as the ordinary norm.[30]

The advocate's brief, with reference to actual content and construction, consists of a heading, three main divisions or sections, and a conclusion. The lawyer begins by indicating the diocese, type of case, the names of the litigants, and then addresses his pleading to the court.[31]

The first principal section of the defense outlines a brief history of the case, the *species facti*. In a matrimonial process, for example, the lawyer recounts the names, ages, religion, and domiciles of the parties concerned, together with the salient facts of their courtship, marriage,

---

26. Cf. art. 184, *Instructio*.

27. Canon 1863, § 3; art. 179, § 4, *Instructio*.

28. Canon 1864.

29. Art. 124, *Normae*. Note that an extension cannot be in excess of 40 and 20 pages, and that if granted to one party it is automatically permitted to the other. Doheny provides a form for the requesting of an extension — *Practical Manual for Marriage Cases*, p. 198.

30. Art. 182, *Instructio*.

31. For example:
   Mediolanensis
   Nullitatis Matrimonii
   Pro Domina Elvira M., actrice, adversus Dominum Iacobum., reum conventum.
   Restrictus Iuris et Facti.
   Iudicibus H. S. T. Rev. . . .

disagreements and separation. He then notes the time and the occasion whereat the party decided to institute action, indicating the contention upon which the suit is based.

Secondly, in the section *in iure, ad ius quod attinet*, he expounds clearly and succinctly the principles of law involved. Needless to say, therefore, the advocate must be thoroughly conversant with the substantive law on the matter in hand. He will cite at this point the pertinent canons of the Code together with other possible sources of present-day Canon Law. Moreover, in striving to emphasize certain distinctions and aspects of the law under discussion, he may refer to the doctrine of approved authors as well as to the decisions of higher tribunals in like cases. In the interests of precision and facility in this regard, nothing could be recommended more profitably than constant study of the patterns afforded by the decisions of the Sacred Rota.

The third section of the advocate's brief, *in facto, ad factum quod attinet*, is devoted to a consideration of the case facts. Here the lawyer endeavors to prove that the facts as demonstrated by testimony, documents, expert opinion, presumptions, and by other proofs correspond to the law requiring a favorable decision. The twofold responsibility here confronting him need hardly be stressed. First, he must investigate the case with utmost thoroughness. Realizing that preparation is the foundation of success in advocacy, he must not be content with obtaining a knowledge of the facts in outline. They must be known in their breadth and in their depth, in their relation to each other and to the ruling principles of law. Secondly, he must possess adequate knowledge of the law of evidence.[32] For example, he will first of all be cognizant of what must be proved and of where the burden of proof lies.[33] There must be the knowledge of what constitutes adminicular proof, indication of proof, corroboratory evidence, and knowledge of the confidence to be reposed in such proof. Similarly, he must appreciate the canonical probative force of judicial and extra-judicial depositions, of sworn and non-sworn testimony.[34] Furthermore, the

32. Cf. for example, Wanenmacher, *Canonical Evidence in Marriage Cases* (Philadelphia: The Dolphin Press, 1935), pp. 75-381.

33. Cf. canons 1747; 1748; art. 94, 117, *Instructio*.

34. Cf. canons 1750-1753; art. 96; 116; 117, *Instructio*.

advocate must be in a position to evaluate juridically the testimony of witnesses,[35] and likewise to discuss the findings of experts in the light of canonical requirements.[36]   Again, he must be aware of what to demand of documents intended as evidence in order to weigh precisely their judicial value.[37]   In addition, he will be mindful of legal presumptions and of their correct evaluation.[38]

In his evaluation of evidence in canonical procedure the skilled advocate will not alone strive for flawless argumentation in behalf of his client, but will likewise note the possibility of attacking on similar grounds faulty evidence advanced by the opposing party, the *defensor vinculi,* or the *promotor iustitiae* which appears to jeopardize the interests of his client.

Moreover, he should in general attempt to foresee the line of pleading and the possible objections and exceptions of the opposition. In refuting their argumentation beforehand, he will deprive it of much of its effectiveness.[39]

Finally, with regard to this section of his brief, the advocate must bear in mind that his defense rests upon the arguments which he puts into writing, not upon what he has in mind.[40]   As a result, he should strive to plead in such a manner that the judges will readily perceive the law, the facts, the interpretations and the applications as he intends. Should the brief lack clarity and force in this regard, it may possibly occasion more harm than good. At the same time, the pleading is to be marked by rigid intellectual honesty, with nothing in the way of strained interpretations and of far-fetched application.

---

35. Cf. canons 1757; 1758; 1774; 1789-1791; 1974; art. 100; 118-120; 122; 136; 138, *Instructio.*

36. Cf. canon 1804; art. 154, *Instructio.*

37. Cf. canons 1813-1820; art. 156; 157; 159; 160; 163; 164; 165; 169, *Instructio.*

38. Cf. canons 1825-1828; 1014; 1015, § 2; 1086, § 1; 1814; art. 171-174, *Instructio.*

39. *Egli è come un soldato, che porta lo sconvolgimento nel campo nemico; ha diritto ad una azione energica, non passiva e negativa, ma anche attiva; quindi non si limiti a difendere il cliente dagli attachi, ma attachi egli stesso gli avversari* — Boriero, *Manuale Teorico-Pratico per Processo Canonico*, p. 271.

40. Cf. canon 1869, § 2.

In a brief conclusion, the lawyer points to the fitness of a favorable sentence with regard to his client's contention as established in the joining of issue. The brief is then signed by the advocate and dated.[41]

A further point to be considered by the advocate and procurator in connection with the brief is the possibility of replying, within the specified time and extent, to the argumentation of the opposing party following interchange of the briefs. This written rebuttal, regulated like the pleading, is generally permitted but once, although for a grave reason the court may allow a *triplicatio*.[42] In the Rota, this response is limited to one half the length of the original brief and must be filed within twenty days.[43] It is to be noted, however, that in the matrimonial process the advocate must reply to the animadversions of the *defensor vinculi* within a period of ten days.[44]

For a time, owing to the absence of an express reference in canon 1865, it was controverted whether or not the briefs of the *defensor vinculi* and *promotor iustitiae* had to be communicated to the parties. Ciprotti,[45] Lega-Bartoccetti,[46] Dolan,[47] and Labouré-Byrnes[48] maintained that these officials were strictly bound by canon 1865. This view, opposed by Muñiz[49] and, seemingly, by Wernz-Vidal,[50] is in accord with Rota practice, appears to be confirmed by canon 1984, and seems to be demanded by the necessity of safeguarding the rights of the parties. Explicit confirmation of this position with regard to

41. *Qui in defensionibus consignandis neglegentes deprehendantur, pecuniaria poena a Ponente mulctentur. Si in neglegentia perseverent, pars moneatur, cuius consensu advocatus neglegens potest a Turno privari suscepto patrocinio aliusque a parte, vel in causis publicis ex officio, legitime electus substitui . . .* — art. 131, *Normae.*

42. Cf. canon 1865; art. 128; 129, *Normae.*

43. Art. 124, § 1; 126, § 4, *Normae.* Cf. *Reg. Servandae apud S. R. Rotae Tribunal,* § 58 — *AAS,* II (1910), 803. Note that a second response granted to one party is thereby conceded to the other: Canon 1865, § 2; art. 128, § 2; 129, *Normae.*

44. Art. 180, §§ 2, 4, *Instructio.*

45. *Apollinaris,* IX (1936), 309, 310.

46. *Commentarius in Iudicia Ecclesiastica,* II, 915.

47. *The Defensor Vinculi,* pp. 87, 88.

48. *Procedure in the Diocesan Matrimonial Courts of First Instance,* p. 96.

49. *Procedimientos Eclesiásticos,* III, 356.

50. *Ius Canonicum,* VI, pars I, 531.

the *defensor vinculi* was forthcoming in the Matrimonial Instruction of 1936.[51]   Doubt may still arise with reference to cases in which the *promotor iustitiae* intervenes in the interests of the common good with both parties already standing in court.   Some authors feel that since he is then not even analogically a party, serving merely to illumine the court, there is no necessity for communicating his observations to the parties.[52] A strict obligation, it is true, does not appear to exist since the official here is not *ex officio* against either party.   However, as Ciprotti points out, it is desirable to afford all concerned the opportunity of possible reply.   In so doing the practice of the Rota is followed and the public good itself is promoted.[53]

In concluding the consideration of actual defense measures, it is to be noted that the advocate and procurator has a right in law to petition the court for permission to engage in the moderate oral discussion provided for in law. Should such procedure be deemed advisable, counsel must abide by the regulations governing this extraordinary phase.[54]

ARTICLE 4

THE ADVOCATE AND PROCURATOR AND REMEDIES AGAINST THE SENTENCE

A. *The procurator's right and duty to appeal*

CANON 1664. — § 2. Lata definitiva sententia, ius et officium appellandi, si mandans non renuat, procuratori manet.

Canon Law enforces the right and emphasizes the duty of the procurator to appeal an adverse definitive sentence.[55]   Provided that

51. Art. 180, *Instructio.*

52. Muñiz, *op. cit.,* III, 354; Wernz-Vidal, *op. cit.,* VI, pars I, 531.

53. *Apollinaris,* IX (1936), 309, 310.

54. Cf. canon 1866; art. 186, *Instructio;* art. 132-134, *Normae.* A form for petitioning oral discussion may be found in Doheny, *Practical Manual for Marriage Cases,* p. 200.

55. Cf. canons 1868, § 1; 1879; art. 212, § 1, *Instructio;* Lemieux, *The Sentence in Ecclesiastical Procedure,* p. 5; Connolly, *Appeals,* p. 64.

this plea for redress to a superior court is possible,[56] the procurator of either plaintiff or defendant may lodge an appeal against the definitive sentence of any inferior instance.

In declaring that the procurator has a right to appeal, the Code indicates that this official, commissioned to place any and all legitimate judicial acts conducive to the best interests of his client, can employ this legal means of safeguarding those rights to the ultimate stages provided by law. Furthermore, states the Code, he has a duty to do this. So intimately is the legal remedy of appeal associated with the sentence that negligence in this regard would be no less serious than delinquency during the course of the trial. Lega-Bartoccetti point out that he who neglects to apply a remedy to a legal set-back sustained is at fault in equal measure with the one who culpably failed to prevent the reverse.[57]

A client, needless to say, may refuse to permit his procurator to carry the lawsuit to a superior tribunal. In such circumstances the right and obligation of the legal representative in this respect ceases, just as it would if the party expressly renounced his right to appeal.[58] Whenever possible, therefore, it would be prudent for the procurator to consult his client in order to ascertain his attitude on this point. For it may be that, owing to close personal following of the case, a client, appreciating a well founded decision, would discourage appeal. On the other hand, however, it is frequently impossible for the party to decide the merits of a case which the attorney may be forced to ponder for days. Moreover, at times there is the problem of distance separating litigant and agent. In situations of this kind, rather than risk loss of the period allotted for filing the appeal, the procurator should proceed with this element of procedure. In this manner, the client's rights are not placed in jeopardy, whereas renunciation is still open to the client.

Considerable difference of opinion is to be found among commentators with regard to the extension of the procurator's right and duty

---

56. Cf. canons 1880; 1903; 1989; art. 214; 217, *Instructio;* Connolly, *op. cit.,* pp. 72-88.

57. *Commentarius in Iudicia Ecclesiastica,* I, 348.

58. Cf. canon 1880, n. 9; 1662.

in this connection. Unquestionably, he is free, barring restraint on the part of his client, to file the appeal.[59] However, does canon 1664, § 2 permit the procurator to represent his client before the superior court trying the case in the second instance? Some authors maintain that a special mandate is essential for prosecuting the case in the appellate court. Their position is based upon the nature of each instance in an ecclesiastical court as an entirely independent juridical unit. Consequently, it is claimed, authorization for a trial is valid for that trial in only one instance.[60]

To the writer it appears that this attitude lacks a necessary distinction. In the absence of reservation on the part of the client or refusal to the procurator, the canon seems to be concerned not only with the right of interposing an appeal but with the right of prosecuting it as well. If appeal is possible according to law, the procurator's office remains. In the first place, since the Code makes no clear distinction between lodging and prosecution of the appeal, there is nothing to prevent recourse to the old law. Here one finds not only no mention of a special mandate for actually conducting the second instance but rather the contrary.[61] Secondly, the juridical institution of appeal embraces not only the initial phase of its lodging, but of effective lodging or the total instruction of the superior instance. Hence, and here one finds the support of Noval,[62] the wording of the canon substantiates this view. The clause *"si mandans non renuat"* would lack precise signification in any other interpretation. It does not seem to refer to interposition of the appeal alone since this has been shown to be an ordinary defense measure demanded *ex officio*. It is true that the

59. Cf. Coronata, *Institutiones*, III, 95; Cappello, *Summa Iuris Canonici*, III, 146; Cocchi, *Commentarium*, Lib. IV, *De Processibus*, 135.

60. Cf. Hanssens, "De Sanctione Nullitatis in Processu Canonico" — *Apollinaris*, XI (1938), 249, 262; Coronata, *op. cit.*, III, 95; Eichmann, *Das Prozessrecht*, pp. 97, 98.

61. Cf. c. 14, X, *de procuratoribus*, I, 38; Bouix, *De Iudiciis*, I, 223; canon 6, nn. 2, 4. It is noteworthy that only one of the preparatory drafts of the Code excluded this right. While omitted in the law, therefore, the point was considered: Roberti, *C. I. C. Schemata*, Lib. IV, *De Processibus*, 154.

62. *De Iudiciis*, pp. 181, 184.

appellate hearing constitutes a separate juridical unit. But that fact does not necessarily signify that a judicial mandate was granted for a particular judicial instance.[63] It may have been granted for a particular suit regardless of the number of instances, or for trials regardless of the number of suits.[64] As a result, a mandate *ad lites,* which of itself may be valid for several distinct processes, should *a fortiori* be valid for distinct instances of the same case. This is the clear view of Vermeersch-Creusen,[65] and it appears to be the position of Lega-Bartoccetti who require a special mandate only when the procurator has been originally commissioned for a specific instance.[66] Moreover, neither Roberti, who requires confirmation of the original mandate,[67] nor Connolly, who recommends it,[68] seem to require this for the validity of continued action in the appellate court. Consequently, the agent who has received a legitimate mandate that is unrestricted with reference to a particular instance, and who is not restrained by the client, may legally interpose an appeal and conduct that instance in the superior tribunal.[69]

A limitation with regard to this interpretation of canon 1664, § 2, must be observed according to the Matrimonial Instruction of 1936. Here it is expressly provided that the mandate expires upon pronouncement of a definitive sentence in the case. By "case" must be understood "instance" since the procurator is still empowered to interpose an appeal.[70] Therefore, with reference to matrimonial processes which, in the event of a declaration of nullity, must be tried in two instances,

---

63. Hence the Rota seems to feel the necessity of a particular regulation requiring a special mandate for each instance in its tribunal: art. 62, § 2, *Normae.*

64. Lega-Bartoccetti, *Commentarius,* I, 341; Blat, *De Processibus,* p. 167; Roberti, *De Processibus,* I, 330; Augustine, *A Commentary on Canon Law,* VII, 114; Noval, *De Iudiciis,* p. 180; Coronata, *Institutiones,* III, 92.

65. *Epitome,* III, 41.

66. *Commentarius,* I, 349.

67. *Op. cit.,* I, n. 210; II, n. 479.

68. *Appeals,* pp. 154, 155.

69. Note that particular regulations may prohibit this, and that approbation may again be necessary.

70. Art. 52, § 2, *Instructio.*

a procurator must be commissioned specifically for both instances in the original mandate. In the absence of this express authorization, the law confines him to the first instance.

An additional change to be noted in this Instruction consists in the fact that it appears to render both procurator and advocate capable of filing the appeal. The words *"procuratori manet"* of canon 1664, § 2, have been studiously omitted from article 52, § 2, with the result that in these trials, barring refusal, either official is in a position to appeal.[71]

Furthermore, with regard to appeals in matrimonial procedure, attention must be called to those cases in which the parties have forfeited the right to challenge the validity of their marriage.[72] In such cases it is the promoter of justice alone who can appeal a declaration of validity. Should he prudently decide against appealing the case, further redress seems impossible.[73] If, in failing to lodge appeal, the promoter gives evidence of positive neglect, the parties through their legal assistants may attempt to induce him to act, or, failing in that, they themselves could once again denounce their marriage to the ordinary.[74]

Finally, it should be pointed out that owing to the rôle of the *defensor vinculi,* the procurator of a client upholding the validity of the marriage bond isn't compelled to file appeal against a declaration of nullity. The defender's appeal would suffice, although the legal assistant may likewise plead if he chooses to do so.[75]

Given the right[76] and the possibility[77] of filing an appeal, the procurator must be mindful of the *fatalia legis* prescribed for lodging the plea in the tribunal *a quo* and for its prosecution in the superior court *ad quem.*[78] In like manner, he will note in what the appeal consists

71. Doheny, *Canonical Procedure in Matrimonial Cases,* pp. 118, 353.

72. Cf. art. 35, § 1, n. 2; 38; 39, *Instructio.*

73. Art. 46, *Instructio.*

74. Canon 1971, § 2; art. 37, § 4, *Instructio.*

75. Cf. canons 1986; 1887, § 1; art. 212, § 3, *Instructio.*

76. Canon 1664, § 2; Connolly, *Appeals,* p. 64.

77. Canon 1880; Connolly, *op. cit.,* pp. 72-88.

78. Cf. canons 1881; 1883; 1885; 1886; 1887, § 2; 34, § 3, n. 3; 35; 1635; 1639; art. 204, § 4; 215, *Instructio;* Connolly, *op. cit.,* pp. 103-112, 159-166.

technically[79] and that its interposition in oral or written form is dependent upon the manner of publication of the sentence.[80]

In the event that the procurator appeals to the Sacred Rota[81] he should take the necessary steps to effect his own release, provided that he is not a Rotal Procurator and that he does not intend, in this capacity, to conduct the suit before that Tribunal. A formal document of his resignation must be forwarded to the Rota together with the acts in order that one of that Tribunal's approved procurators might immediately be assigned to represent the party.[82]

An appeal cannot be filed prior to the formal publication of the sentence.[83] As a consequence the question may arise whether or not the parties, and in particular their legal assistants, must await that publication in order to receive information relative to its contents. Publication of the sentence, it will be noted, may occur a month after the actual decision has been reached.[84] The question assumes a practical aspect in cases wherein great distance separates client and agent, and in trials which witness continued attempts to adduce additional proof that is felt to exist. At times, even though the procurator exhausts the period allotted for appeal, time might be too short. Following a practice of the Sacred Rota,[85] the Matrimonial Instruction of 1936 makes a provision which, consequently, should be noted. Provided that the tribunal has not ordained secrecy, the court's decision may be made known orally, and even in writing upon request. Such communication of the decision has no bearing upon the time limit set for appeal.[86] Needless to say, the advocate and procurator

79. Cf. canons 1884; 1891, § 2; Connolly, *op. cit.*, pp. 153-159. Forms may be found in Cappello, *Praxis Processualis*, p. 38; Doheny, *Practical Manual*, p. 218.

80. Cf. canons 1877; 1882; 1707; art. 204, *Instructio;* Connolly, *op. cit.*, pp. 112-116.

81. Cf. canons 1599, § 1, n. 1; 247, § 3; art. 12; 216, *Instructio;* S. C. S. Off., 27 Jan., 1928 — *AAS*, XX (1928), 75.

82. Cf. Doheny, *Canonical Procedure*, p. 118. In his *Practical Manual*, pp. 218, 219, Doheny includes a form for effecting this release.

83. Cf. canon 1868; art. 196, *Instructio*.

84. Art. 200, *Instructio*.

85. *Regulae Servandae*, § 179 — *AAS*, II (1910), 835.

86. Art. 199, *Instructio*. Cf. canon 1881.

should at times find this regulation of no little value. If, during the trial, he suspects that the decision may be placed under secrecy until formal publication of the sentence, he might consider proposing a timely request with a view to obtaining the decision himself under oath of secrecy for specified reasons.[87]

B. *The complaint of nullity*

If he is persuaded that the sentence is invalid owing to some extrinsic defect, the advocate and procurator of either plaintiff or defendant should consider it his right, and perhaps his duty, to invoke an extraordinary legal remedy by presenting to the court which issued. the sentence a formal complaint of nullity.[88]

In this connection, the first practical question which suggests itself is that of requisite authorization for addressing this allegation to the tribunal, whether it is lodged as an exception or introduced as an action. As already indicated in the commentary on canon 1662, contrary to the opinion of Noval and Roberti, it appears that the legitimate procurator may proceed with this element of procedure without having recourse to a special mandate. This position is supported by Coronata, Muñiz, Wernz-Vidal and Doheny.[89]

Secondly, in emphasizing that the legal assistant must be mindful of the irregularities and errors which invalidate the sentence irremediably[90] and remediably,[91] a further practical point might be noted with reference to the extension of canons 1892 and 1894. It is maintained by some authors that this enumeration of invalid sentences is exclusive, in the sense that a complaint of nullity cannot be invoked

87. S. R. R., *Regulae Servandae*, § 179, n. 2 — *AAS*, II (1910), 835.

88. Canon 1897, § 1. Cf. Lega-Bartoccetti, *Commentarius*, II, 1031, 1032; Glynn, *The Promoter of Justice*, pp. 311-315; Noval, *De Iudiciis*, p. 438; Coronata, *Institutiones*, III, 339.

89. Noval, *op. cit.*, p. 182; Roberti, *De Processibus*, II, 234, I, 331; Coronata, *op. cit.*, 339; Muñiz, *Procedimientos*, III, 479; Wernz-Vidal, *Ius Canonicum*, VI, 569; Doheny, *Canonical Procedure*, p. 347.

90. Canon 1892. Cf. canons 1556-1558; 1571; 1576, § 1; 1628, § 3; 1651; 1654; 1659, § 1; 1662; S. C. S. Off., 27 Jan. 1928 — *AAS*, XX (1928), 75; art. 207; 13; 49; 78, *Instructio*.

91. Canon 1894. Cf. canons 1711-1725; 1871-1874; art. 209, *Instructio*; Pont. Comm., 14 July, 1922 — *AAS*, XIV (1922), 529.

against sentences which are void because of other processual defects. Arguing merely from the silence of *these* canons regarding other invalidating irregularities, they indicate that recourse must be had to the remedy of appeal or of *restitutio in integrum,* as, for example, in seeking to remedy a violation of canon 1861, § 2.[92] On the contrary, other authorities, headed by Roberti, contend with more reason that this enumeration is not exhaustive and that all sentences void because of some other invalidating processual error, whether of positive or of natural law, may be opposed by the *querela nullitatis.*[93]

In the third place, in observing how, when, and where he can avail himself of the complaint of nullity against a sentence irreparably[94] or reparably void,[95] the advocate and procurator should pay particular attention to the possibility and advisability of entering the complaint in conjunction with the ordinary remedy of appeal. This procedure should be followed when the nullity of the sentence is dubious lest the limited opportunity of appealing be dissipated in the event that the *querela* is not sustained. Furthermore, when there is question of remediable nullity, whether the sentence is sanated or not, the appeal will be directed against the point of grievance which might yet remain.[96] In proposing the complaint of nullity together with an appeal, one must abide by the regulations of law governing appeals.[97] At the same time, a noteworthy observation is made by Lega-Bartoccetti who find no legal barrier preventing introduction of the *querela nullitatis* after the filing of an appeal as an incidental case before the

92. Coronata, *op. cit.,* III, 337; Muñiz, *op. cit.,* III, 430; Wernz-Vidal, *op. cit.,* VI, 573; D'Angelo-*Periodica,* XVIII (1929), 37. Cf. Crnica, *Jus Pontificium,* XV (1935), 145-155.

93. Roberti, *De Processibus,* II, 228-231. The author here lists a number of such invalidating defects to which may be added a similar comment with regard to can. 1873, § 1, n. 1 in *Apollinaris,* II (1929), 76-78. Cf. Lega-Bartoccetti, *Commentarius,* II, 1022, 1025; Cappello, *Summa,* III, 278 (Cappello, however, feels that the enumeration of can. 1894 is exhaustive — p. 281); Hanssens, "De Sanctione Nullitatis" — *Apollinaris,* XII (1939), 238-249.

94. Canon 1893; art. 208, *Instructio.*

95. Canon 1895; art. 210, *Instructio.*

96. Cf. Noval, *De Iudiciis,* p. 438; Blat, *De Processibus,* p. 408.

97. Canons 1881; 1883.

tribunal instructing the appellate process.[98] An additional point of practical importance is emphasized by Lega-Bartoccetti with reference to the conjunction of the complaint of nullity and appeal. They maintain, justifiably, it appears, that the complaint of nullity may be proposed in this manner not only against a sentence reparably invalid, which canon 1893 might indicate at first glance, but also against a sentence vitiated by irreparable nullity.[99]

A final consideration to be borne in mind by the legal assistant at this point concerns the right of taking exception to the judge. If he fears that the tribunal which pronounced the sentence impugned for nullity is prejudiced, and holds that it is suspect, he may demand that other judges be substituted in the same tribunal to hear the complaint of nullity.[100] The law doesn't require that evidence be adduced in support of this suspicion. It suffices that such fear exist. Nevertheless, the doubt should be prudent, in the sense that one should be able to provide some sound reason arising from circumstances giving a degree of probability to the charge.[1]

With regard to the extraordinary remedy against the sentence, *restitutio in integrum,* occasionally, albeit rarely if he has been alert, the advocate and procurator will find it necessary to inform his client of the opportunity of recourse to this procedure.[2] Furthermore, depending upon the decisive or uncertain position of the tribunal with reference to the controverted extension of canons 1892 and 1894, the legal assistant might prudently consider the advisability of employing this remedy alone or in conjunction with the lodging of a complaint of nullity. It has already been noted in the discussion of canon 1662 that the procurator must be empowered with special authorization in order to petition the concession of this remedy.[3]

---

98. *Commentarius,* II, 1030; cf. canons 1567; 1837.

99. *Commentarius,* II, 1024, 1025, 1029.

100. Canon 1896; art. 211, § 4, *Instructio.*

1. Lega-Bartoccetti, *Commentarius,* II, 1031; Noval, *De Iudiciis,* p. 438; Blat, *De Processibus,* p. 408.

2. Canon 1905. Cf. canon 1906.

3. Cf. S. R. Rota, Decisio LII, vol. XXII (1930), 587, n. 5; canon 1662; 6, nn. 3, 4; Roberti, *De Processibus,* II, 266; Coronata, *Institutiones,* III, 346; Noval, *op. cit.,* p. 182; Lega-Bartoccetti, *op. cit.,* I, 345; Doheny, *Canonical Procedure,* p. 114; Hanssens, "De Sanctione Nullitatis" — *Apollinaris,* XII (1939).

ARTICLE 5

THE ADVOCATE AND PROCURATOR WITH REGARD TO
REMUNERATION AND GRATUITOUS PATRONAGE

A. *Remuneration of advocates and procurators*

Canon Law recognizes the right of judicial advocates and procurators to compensation for tribunal services.[4] Moreover, the Code specifies the source from which regulations are to proceed governing the determination of these judicial fees. Every tribunal should have an official register of court expenses, including stipulations pertaining to lawyers, drawn up by a provincial council or by a meeting of bishops.[5] By means of such arrangement the law provides for the observance and for the maintenance of local customs and for varying necessities of time and place.[6] The provisions of this list, needless to mention, must be rigidly observed by advocates and procurators.[7]

The register of fees in question pertains primarily to those advocates and procurators who, having been approved for the assumption of all cases, bear a title to that office. Underlying its drafting will be this principle: no judicial advocate or procurator should be compelled to have recourse to other occupations for material assistance to the detriment of his judicial office. Should officials find it possible to engage in additional compatible occupations, the fees will naturally be modified proportionately. For example, the remuneration of clerical lawyers would be defined after taking into account other sources

4. Cf. canons 1664, § 1; 1909, § 1; art. 233, *Instructio*. This right was expressly mentioned in four of the preparatory schemata of the Code. Cf. Roberti, *C. I. C. Schemata,* Lib. IV, *De Processibus,* pp. 160, 161. For a brief outline of previous legislation on this point, cf. Grabowski, "Adwokatura" — *Ateneum Kaplanskie,* XXXV (1935), 351-358.

5. Cf. canons 283-291; 292, § 1.

6. Cf. canon 1805. It appears that remuneration according to custom with reference to experts may be extended to lawyers.

7. Cf. canons 1665; 1507, § 2; 1909, § 1; 2408; art. 234, § 3, *Instructio;* art. 58, *Normae.*

of ecclesiastical income assured them.[8] The Sacred Congregation of the Sacraments appears to have that in mind when, in demanding lists of fees for the Italian regional tribunals, it speaks of fees for advocates and procurators which " . . . *uti par est, distabunt a procuratorum et advocatorum proventibus in tribunali S. R. Rotae vigentibus."*[9]

Where no such registers of established judicial expenses exist, the specification of fees for ecclesiastical lawyers must be left to the prudent determination of the judge or ordinary in individual cases.[10] It might be noted, furthermore, that this determination of fees for legal assistance doesn't provide for incidental expenditures for which additional reimbursement may be sought.[11]

Some little investigation has disclosed few instances wherein diocesan tribunals have actually established the desired register of judicial expenses, and it has been found practically impossible to set down anything approaching a standard or average agreed upon by tribunals, at least with reference to legal assistants. For the most part, no provisions have been made at all. As a matter of fact, in some cases regulations exist forbidding the remuneration of advocates and procurators. This attitude has been occasioned by the desire to obviate any and all danger of associating ecclesiastical courts with mercenary motives. It is true that some people will stop at no pretext to justify an unwillingness to submit their difficulties to a Church court. However, with proper explanation there should be no hostility toward the question of defraying judicial expenses and of remunerating those who render legal aid. Furthermore, at the very outset the parties have the opportunity of manifesting a possible lack of resources. If after investigation

---

8. S. C. Sacr., *Normae Pro Exsequendis Litteris Apostolicis "Qua Cura"* die 8 Dec., 1938 *Motu Proprio Datis,* art. 17; 18; 10 Julii, 1940 — *AAS,* XXXII (1940), 306.

9. Art. 20, S. C. S., *ibid.*

10. Coronata, *Institutiones,* III, 351; Wernz-Vidal, *Ius Canonicum,* VI, pars I, 594; Roberti, *De Processibus,* II, 538.

11. Muñiz, *Procedimientos,* III, 458; Coronata, *op. cit.,* III, 350; Wernz-Vidal, *op. cit.,* VI, pars I, 590; S. R. Rota, Notanda II, *Procuratorum et Advocatorum Proventus Pro Causis Actis Coram Tribunali S. R. Rotae* — *AAS,* XXXI (1939), 622.

such a claim is found to be justified, no difficulty at all will be experienced in obtaining reduction or exemption from these expenses.[12]

As a result, it has been deemed not unhelpful to summarize the most recent regulations of the Holy Roman Rota on this point, together with its regulations governing advocates and procurators in the handling of judicial expenses. Officials of the Rotal Tribunal alone are affected by these norms; so much so that, should they practice before a diocesan tribunal, they would abide by the financial provisions of that court.[13] Nevertheless, just as all Rotal norms can and do serve as models for inferior courts, so may these provisions stand as examples, *mutatis mutandis,* especially with regard to arrangement. In addition, aside from possible influence on diocesan tribunals, these regulations should be noted since the *Officiales* of inferior courts are enjoined to notify all persons contemplating appeal to the Rota of their content.[14]

Rota Register of Fees for Advocates and Procurators.[15]

	Minimum	Maximum
1. *Pro praevio studio causae et pro examine actorum:*	$10.00	$50.00
2. *Pro introductione instantiae:*	5.00	10.00
3. *Pro instructione:*	5.00	75.00
4. *Pro quaestionibus incidentibus simul sumptis:*	5.00	40.00
5. *Pro defensione, una cum summarii compositione, responsionibus, discussione orali:*	25.00	175.00

Should these amounts appear to be quite substantial, it must be remembered that they have been stipulated for officials who devote much of their time and attention to this work. Furthermore, besides the latitude existing between the amounts designated, the Rota provides that: "... *D. Ponens facultatem habet si graves alicuius causae*

12. Cf. canon 1915; art. 238, *Instructio;* art. 177, *Normae.*

13. S. R. Rota, *Procuratorum et Advocatorum Proventus,* 26 Maii, 1939 — *AAS,* XXXI (1939), 622, notula 1.

14. S. R. Rota, *Regulae Servandae in Liquandis Proventibus,* 26 Maii, 1939 — *AAS,* XXXI (1939), 625.

15. *AAS,* XXXI (1939), 622. The amounts noted are based upon an average exchange rate of 20 lire to the dollar as of May 26, 1939. For previous registers given in greater detail, cf. *AAS,* I (1909), 32-35; *AAS,* II (1910), 843-845; *AAS,* XXVI (1934), 487-491.

circumstantiae id suadeant, summas supra inscriptas minores minuendi, maiores augendi."[16] Moreover, the Rota regulations understand a cumulation of the two offices in one person.[17] Consequently, if for any reason the offices are dissociated, each official receives a portion of the established fee.[18] In like manner, should the client commission a plurality of assistants, the specified sum cannot be augmented by more than one-half for two or more than twofold for any number.[19]

A further noteworthy element sanctioned by the latest Rota regulations is what Roberti terms a *"novum, opportunum principium,"* namely, that of advance guarantee of payment of judicial expenses by the litigant.[20] Not infrequently, with completion of a process, especially in the event of an adverse decision, the question of judicial expenses is utterly ignored by the client. The Rota seeks to eliminate this injustice by guaranteeing sufficient funds to defray tribunal costs including the lawyers' fees.[21] The following arrangement designed by the Rota may be employed as a model, *mutatis mutandis,* by diocesan tribunals.

First, the party is to deposit either with his advocate and procurator or directly with the tribunal treasury funds sufficient to defray all expenses incurred by the litigation.[22] In order not to burden the client unduly, one half of the total, which total is not to exceed $300.00, is to be deposited when the case is introduced, the remainder before the publication of the acts.[23] Should the amount deposited prove insufficient during the course of the trial, it must be augmented with the approbation of the *ponens* who is to be notified of the amount deposited and expended.[24]

Secondly, in presenting his mandate to the tribunal, the advocate and procurator, or the client himself, must deposit the sum of $10.00

16. S. R. Rota, *Regulae Servandae,* Notanda III — *AAS,* XXXI (1939), 622.

17. Cf. canon 1656, § 4; S. R. Rota, *ibid.,* art. I.

18. Roberti, "Adnotationes" — *Apollinaris,* XII (1939), 468.

19. S. R. Rota, *Regulae Servandae,* art. III — *AAS,* XXXI (1939), 624.

20. "Adnotationes" — *Apollinaris,* XII (1939), 468.

21. Cf. canons 1909, § 2; 1788; 1626; art. 78, *Normae;* art. 235, *Instructio.*

22. Cf. art. 235, *Instructio.*

23. Cf. canons 1732; 1725, n. 5; 1837; art. 78, § 1, *Normae.*

24. S. R. Rota, *Regulae Servandae in Liquandis Proventibus Proc. et Advoc.,* art. I, nn. 1-4 — *AAS,* XXXI (1939), 622-625.

with the tribunal treasury. This amount will be increased by the *ponens* in the event that incidental questions are to be disposed of prior to the pleading in issue.[25] Furthermore, if the lawyer holds the $150.00 deposited at the beginning of the instance, he must regularly deposit $50.00 with the treasury, repeating this procedure before publication of the acts. Hence, $100.00 is deemed sufficient for tribunal expenses, while $200.00 is considered ample for printing and remuneration of officials. Should circumstances warrant, the *ponens* may always increase these amounts. The litigants are to be forwarned of this procedure by the chancellor of the tribunal, since, for one thing, failure to observe the regulations may automatically stop the process.[26]

Thirdly, within fifteen days following pronouncement of the sentence the *ponens* must be informed with regard to expenses and fees by documents from the chancellor and advocate. A decree of approval or of modification is then issued and appended to the definitive sentence forwarded to the advocate and procurator. Against this decree, the official who feels himself mistreated has the sole remedy of recourse to the *turnus* concerned. Against the decision of the *turnus* there is no appeal.[27] The advocate and procurator must then within ten days defray all expenses. Should he appeal the definitive sentence he retains the right of seeking financial readjustment in the appellate court.[28] Finally, he must render an account, together with an authentic copy of the court's financial decree, to the client from whom he has received a deposit of money, in order that the party may readily perceive what is the balance yet to be paid or what is due him.[29]

B. *Gratuitous patronage on the part of advocates and procurators*

Nothing has been more pronounced in the history of ecclesiastical processual law than the Church's insistence upon the accordance of gratuitous patronage in her tribunals to those unable to bear the burden

25. Cf. canons 1628, § 1; 1629, § 1.

26. *Reg. Servandae,* art. II, nn. 1-4 — *AAS,* XXXI (1939), 622-625. Cf. can. 1736.

27. Cf. canon 1913, § 1; art. 169, *Normae.*

28. Cf. art. 44, f., *Normae.*

29. Reg. Servandae, art. IV, nn. 1-7 — *AAS,* XXXI (1939), 622-625. Cf. S. C. Sacr., *Normae,* 10 July, 1940, art. 21 — *AAS,* XXXII (1940), 306.

of judicial expenses. Unlike the civil law which, for the most part, regards this as a matter of practical and expedient administration, as a favor, the Canon Law considers it a judicial matter, a strict right.[30] Lest the rights of those who are incapable of meeting court fees be left defenseless, the law gives such persons the right of bringing action after having received a reduction or even exemption from judicial expenses.[31]

If one's modest circumstances do not permit payment for the costs of the tribunal itself, then is that person still less able to compensate an advocate and procurator for pleading his case and for representing him at court. Consequently, the Code prescribes that the judge designate a lawyer from the number of those licensed to practice in his court to assume gratuitously the defense of the poor person's interests.[32]

Should the advocate so designated be unwilling or unable to assume the task, he must submit his reasons to the judge and abide by his decision. In the event that the proffered excuses are considered of not sufficient weight, the lawyer may be compelled to accede under pain of canonical sanctions.[33] And if after accepting the suit he gives evidence of careless performance of duty, the court is authorized to force him to render legal assistance worthy of his office.[34]

It is to be noted that the litigant who has obtained a reduction or exemption from judicial expenses is not in a position to select his own

30. Canon 1914; *Lex Propria S. R. R. et Sign. Apostol.*, 29 June, 1908, App. IV, 1-3 — *AAS*, I (1909), 20; *Reg. Servandae*, 4 Aug., 1910, § 207, 208, 212 — *AAS*, II (1910), 783; D'Angelo, S. — *Apollinaris*, II (1929), 514-516.

31. Canon 1914; art. 176, *Normae*; art. 237, *Instructio*. Note that the Instruction speaks of financial consideration with reference to the defendant only when deemed opportune by the court for very grave reasons. This provision is due to the fact that the defendant's rights are capably upheld by the *defensor vinculi*.

32. Canon 1916, § 1; art. 56, § 2; 183; 184; *Normae;* art. 237; 240, § 1, *Instructio*. Note that in order for an advocate to be compelled by the judge to render freely legal assistance, he must be enrolled in the official register of advocates: cf. art. 53, § 2, *Instructio;* Wernz-Vidal, *Ius Canonicum*, VI, 199. In the Instruction and in the Rotal norm a distinction is made between gratuitous patronage and assistance. The first implies complete assumption of the case, whereas the latter connotes merely counsel to a party defending himself.

33. Canons 1916, § 1; 1663; 1666.

34. Cf. art. 240, § 2, *Instructio*.

advocate. Such assistance is always granted to the client *ex officio* by the court.[35] There is no intention of discrimination in this provision, but rather the intention of assuring sound legal aid. At the same time, there is nothing to prevent a party from requesting the designation of a particular assistant in the petition for gratuitous patronage.

One practical manner of supplying legal aid for those lacking means would be the appointment of one or more lawyers, according to necessity, in every diocese who would function as *advocati pauperum*. Those who have the responsibility of observing the injunction: "Thou shalt not go aside in the poor man's judgment,"[36] will find no particular legislation in this regard more in keeping with the ancient mind and practice of the Church than the following decree of the Council of Rome held in 1725:

> ... *Quocirca Episcopos in Domino adhortamur, ut unum aut plures, si id exposcat necessitas, et vires suppetant, in eorum deputent civitate pauperum procuratores vel advocatos pios, probos, et doctos, qui miserabilium causas personarum tam in criminalibus quam in civilibus gratis defendant. . . .* [37]

To the advocate and procurator commissioned by the court in these circumstances the client need render nothing. On the other hand, such officials are forbidden to demand anything from the client by way of remuneration.[38] At the same time, some attempt, it seems, should be made to compensate these officials for their services, particularly if they are licensed as special lawyers for the poor. Since the Code is silent on this point, diocesan tribunals might consider the custom of the Sacred Rota in this regard: *"Iuxta autem regulam apud S. R. R. vigentem, Exc'mus Decanus advocatis qui gratuitum patrocinium praestant, summam quamdam pro singulis causis erogat."*[39] An exemplary decree touching this question, it will be recalled, appeared in the Council of Fermo held in 1726:

---

35. Canon 1916, § 1; art. 237, *Instructio;* art. 183, *Normae;* S. R. Rota, *Reg. Servandae,* sub N. B. — *AAS,* XXXI (1939), 624.

36. *Exod.,* XXIII, 6. Cf. Deut. I, 17; Ps. LXXXI, 3.

37. Tit. VIII, cap. III — *Coll. Lac.,* I, 358. For a brief summary of legislation on this point, cf. Grabowski, "Adwokatura" — *Ateneum Kaplanskie,* XXXV (1935), 245-249.

38. Cf. S. R. Rota, *Reg. Servandae,* sub N. B. — *AAS,* XXXI (1939), 624.

39. S. R. Rota, *ibid.*

Quoniam vero paternam pauperum curam gerere debemus, ubi procuratores vel advocati pauperum in curiis ecclesiasticis constituti non sunt, constituantur; et, quatenus opus sit, praeter exemptiones et praerogativas, iisdem de iure vel consuetudine indultas, etiam aliquod stipendium arbitrio Episcopi ex proventibus locorum piorum assignetur.[40]

The Code proceeds to indicate the manner of providing gratuitous legal assistance in those circumstances in which a judge finds it impossible to call upon licensed advocates. In the absence of such lawyers, the judge must request the ordinary to designate someone qualified to assume the necessary rôle of defender.[41] Needless to say, the ordinary has authority to appoint a skilled lawyer at the request of the judge. However, a further question may be raised. Has the local ordinary power to demand such service from any of his subjects who are canonically qualified, clerical or lay? An affirmative reply seems to be indicated not only by the nature of the case but by the tenor of canon 1916, § 2 as well. In the first place, complete justice must be secured for the poor in ecclesiastical courts. Should their interests demand the services of an advocate, the ordinary must possess authority to provide the required counsel. Secondly, without reservation or limitation the law empowers the ordinary to designate a person qualified for the task at hand. As a result, Woywood appears to be justified in arguing that "as every citizen may be called upon to serve the courts of his country, for example as juror or witness, even though the court allowance is not sufficient perhaps to compensate for loss of business and professional work, so it seems that the local ordinary has authority to call upon qualified men among the subjects of his diocese to serve the poor even without any compensation. The public welfare must in that case be preferred to private inconvenience or loss."[42]

It has already been indicated in what manner the advocate and procurator can assist the litigant in petitioning the court for gratuitous hearing with regard to the procuring of the proofs and documents nec-

---

40. Tit. IV, pars 3 — *Coll. Lac.*, I, 593.

41. Canon 1916, § 2.

42. "Gratuitous Legal Service" — *The Homiletic and Pastoral Review*, XXXIII (1932-1933), 490-500.

essary for the court's investigation.[43] A final detail, therefore, in which the legal adviser may render aid in this connection would arise in the event of a court decree denying gratuitous patronage. If he is persuaded that a right has been violated, he may have recourse from a decree of the *ponens* to the *turnus,* proposing the matter as an incidental question.[44] From the decree of a single judge or of a collegiate tribunal, recourse may be filed with the ordinary or with a superior court.[45] In fact, arguing from canon 1603, § 1, n. 1, D'Angelo maintains that such recourse may be carried even to the Apostolic Signatura.[46]

43. Canon 1915. Cf. Chap. IX, art. 1, A. The *Libellus.*

44. Cf. art. 181, *Normae.*

45. Coronata, *Institutiones,* III, 356; Wernz-Vidal, *Ius Canonicum,* VI, 601; Roberti, *De Processibus,* II, 543; Eichmann, *Das Prozessrecht,* p. 190.

46. "An a denegato gratuito patrocinio dari possit recursus" — *Apollinaris,* II (1929), 514-516.

CONCLUSIONS

1) Owing to the nature of the institutions and because of early evidence both direct and indirect it may be said that the offices of judicial advocate and procurator in the Church are as old as the ecclesiastical process itself.

2) With regard to the legal development of these institutions it may be stated that:

a) The general influence of Roman processual law upon canonical legislation finds here a striking exemplification. The eminently practical and equitable Roman laws affecting corresponding civil officials have left a deep impression on Canon Law, particularly in regard to qualifications, admission, powers, obligations, remuneration and removal. In turn, the Church's application of these principles has profoundly influenced subsequent civil procedure.

b) Although isolated, varied and widely scattered legislation of the early centuries, together with the accepted Roman norms, affords a broad picture of the ecclesiastical advocate and procurator, of their work and standing, nevertheless it is not until the councils of the twelfth century that one discovers a great deal of legislation directly affecting these officials in their tribunal activity.

c) Canon Law in this connection was elaborated extensively in the Decretals of Gregory IX, Boniface VIII and Clement V. In fact, to such an extent was the law crystallized in these collections that the following centuries manifest practically nothing by way of further substantial legal development.

d) Subsequent Papal Constitutions have sought to eliminate abuses connected with the functions of these officials and to direct their efforts into more efficient channels. At the same time, responses of the Sacred Congregations, regulations of the Roman Tribunals and legislation of particular councils have continued to promote concrete application of the Decretal Law.

3) With reference to the present legislation, a development of legal importance is to be noted in the added rigor of the law regarding express, written authorization of the judicial procurator. In like manner, added emphasis is placed upon the requisite qualification of canonical ability in both advocate and procurator, a point which has been de-

cidedly stressed in the Matrimonial Instruction issued by the Sacred Congregation of the Sacraments in 1936.

4) A study of the Church's procedural law cannot but impress one with the necessity of legal experts in support of the litigant, nor, by the same token, can one escape the conviction that men of outstanding ability serving in this capacity make for a high standard of efficiency in the diocesan tribunal.

5) Perhaps in no better way than by her vigilance over these officials has the Church, from earliest times, manifested more definitely her intense concern for just judgment, and, in particular, her solicitude for the poor and defenseless.

BIBLIOGRAPHY

SOURCES

Acta Apostolicae Sedis, Commentarium Officiale, Romae, 1909 —

Acta et Decreta Concilii Plenarii Baltimorensis Tertii (1884) — Baltimorae, 1886.

Acta et Decreta Sacrorum Conciliorum Recentiorum (*Collectio Lacensis*), 7 vols., Friburgi Brisgoviae, 1870-1890.

Acta Gregorii XVI, 4 vols. Vol. IV, Romae: Typographia Polyglotta S. C. de Prop. Fide, 1904.

Acta Sanctae Sedis, 41 vols., Romae, 1865-1908.

Antiquae Collectiones Decretalium cum notis Antonii Augustini, Lerida, 1576.

Bullarium Romanum, 25 vols., Augustae Taurinorum, 1857-1872.

Canones et Decreta Sacrosancti Oecumenici Concilii Tridentini, Taurini: Marietti, 1913.

Codex Iuris Canonici Pii X Pontificis Maximi iussu digestus Benedicti Papae XV auctoritate promulgatus, Romae: Typis Polyglottis Vaticanis, 1917.

Codex Iuris Canonici Schemata, Lib. IV, *De Processibus;* digessit F. Roberti, Civitate Vaticana: Typis Polyglottis Vaticanis, 1940.

Codex Theodosianus, ed. P. Krueger, T. Mommsen, 3 vols., Berolini, 1905.

Codicis Iuris Canonici Fontes cura Emi Petri Card. Gasparri editi, 9 vols., Romae-Civitate Vaticana: Typis Polyglottis Vaticanis, 1923-1939. (Vols. VII-VIII-IX ed. *cura et studio Emi Iustiniani Card. Serédi.*)

Collectanea S. Congregationis de Propaganda Fide, 2 vols., Romae: Typographia Polyglotta S. C. de Prop. Fide, 1907.

Corpus Iuris Canonici, ed. Lipsiensis 2, Aemilius Richter-Aemilius Friedberg, 2 vols., Lipsiae: Tauchnitz, 1879-1881.

Corpus Iuris Civilis, Vol. I, *Institutiones* — recognovit P. Krueger; *Digesta* — recognovit T. Mommsen, retractavit P. Krueger; Vol. II, *Codex Iustinianus* — recognovit et retractavit P. Krueger; Vol. III, *Novellae Constitutiones* — Recognovit R. Schoell; opus Schoellii morte interceptum absolvit G. Kroll, Berolini, 1928-1929.

Corpus Scriptorum Ecclesiasticorum Latinorum, Vindobonae: Apud C. Geroldi Filium Bibliopolam Academiae, 1866-1887; Hoelder, Pichler, Tempsky, 1888 —

Decretales Gregorii IX, una cum Glossis Restitutae, Rome, 1582.

Harduin, Jean, *Acta Conciliorum et Epistolae Decretales ac Constitutiones Summorum Pontificum,* 12 vols., Parisiis, 1715.

Liber Sextus Decretalium, una cum Clementinis et Extravagantibus earumque glossis restitutis, Rome, 1582.

Mansi, J. D., *Sacrorum Conciliorum Nova et Amplissima Collectio,* 53 vols., Paris, Arnhem, Leipzig, 1901-1927.

Migne, J. P., *Patrologiae Cursus Completus — Series Graeca*, 161 vols., Parisiis, 1857-1866.

———, *Patrologiae Cursus Completus — Series Latina*, 221 vols., Parisiis, 1844-1855.

Monumenta Germaniae Historica, Leges, G. H. Pertz edidit, 5 vols., Hanover, 1875-1889.

Quinta Compilatio Epistolarum Decretalium Honorii III, Pont. Max., studio et industria Innocentii Cironii, Tolosae, 1645.

REFERENCE WORKS

Augustine, Chas., *A Commentary on the New Code of Canon Law*, 8 vols., Vol. VII, *Eccles. Procedure*, St. Louis: Herder, 1921.

Bataillard, *Origines de l'Histoire des Procureurs et des Avoués depuis le Vᵉ siècle Jusqu'au XVᵉ*, Paris, 1868.

Bassibey, R., *Le Mariage devant les Tribunaux Ecclesiastiques: Procédure Matrimoniale Générale*, Paris, 1899.

Benedetti, I., *Ordo Judicialis Processus Canonici Instruendi*, Taurini: Marietti, 1935.

Benedict XIV, *De Synodo Diocesana*, Romae, 1748.

Bergman, F., *Pilii, Tancredi, Gratiae, Libri de Judiciorum Ordine*, Gottingen, 1842.

Bernardini, C., *Leges Processuales Vigentes apud S. R. Rotae Tribunal*, Romae, 1935.

Bertolini, C., *Appunti Didattici di Diritto Romano*, Vol. II, *Il Processo Civile*, Torino, 1914.

Bianchi, *Sull Esercizio delle Professioni di Avvocato e Procuratore*, Torino, 1884.

Blat, A., *Commentarium Textus Codicis Iuris Canonici*, 6 vols., Lib. IV, *De Processibus*, Romae: Ex Typographia Pontificia in Instituto Pii X, 1927.

Boriero, F., *Manuale Teorico-Pratico per il Processo Canonico*, Padova, 1909.

Bouissou, *De la Responsabilité des Mandataires ad Lites*, Paris, 1892.

Bouix, M. D., *Tractatus de Judiciis Ecclesiasticis*, 3 ed., 2 vols., Paris, 1883.

Boyd, W. K., *The Ecclesiastical Edicts of the Theodosian Code*, New York: Columbia University Press, 1905.

Brunini, J. B., *The Clerical Obligations of Canons 139 and 142*. Catholic University of America, Canon Law Studies, n. 103, Washington: Catholic University of America, 1937.

Buckland, W. W., *A Manual of Roman Private Law*, Cambridge: Cambridge University Press, 1925.

Calisse, C., *Diritto Ecclesiastico e Diritto Longobardo*, Roma, 1888.

Cappello, F. M., *Summa Iuris Canonici*, 3 vols., Vol. III, Romae: *Apud Gregorianum*, 1936.

———, *Praxis Processualis*, Torino-Roma: Marietti, 1940.

Cenci, L., *De Procuratoribus*, Florentiae, 1957.

Cerchiari, E., *Capellani Papae et Apostolicae Sedis Auditores Causarum Sacri Palatii Apostolici seu Historia S. R. Rotae*, 4 vols., Romae, 1919-1921.

Checchini, A., *Studi sul Ordinamento Processuale Romano e Germanico*, Padova: Tipographia Seminario, 1925.

Cicognani, A. G., *Canon Law*, 2. ed., authorized English version by J. O'Hara and F. Brennan, Philadelphia: Dolphin Press, 1935.

Cocchi, G., *Commentarium in Codicem Iuris Canonici*, 7 vols., Turin, 1925-1927.

Collinet, P., *La Procédure par Libelle*, Paris: Lib. Recueil Sirey, 1932.

Connolly, T. A., *Appeals*, Canon Law Studies, n. 79, Washington, D. C.: Catholic University of America, 1932.

Conti, O., *Origini, Fasti, e Privilegi degli Avvocati Consistoriali*, Roma, 1898.

Coronata, M., *Institutiones Iuris Canonici*, 5 vols., Taurini: Marietti, 1928-1936, vol. III, *De Processibus*, 1933.

Costa E., *Profilo Storico del Processo Civile Romano*, Roma, 1918.

———, *Cicerone Giureconsulto*, Bologna: Zanichelli, 1927.

Cuq, E., *Institutions Juridiques des Romains*, 2 vols., Paris, 1891-1902.

De Angelis, P., *Praelectiones Juris Canonici*, 9 vols., ed. Gentilini, Romae, 1884-1887.

Debray, *De la Représentation en Justice Par le Cognitor*, Paris, 1892.

Devoti, J., *Ius Canonicum Universum et Privatum*, 3 vols., Romae, 1803.

Doheny, W., *Canonical Procedure in Matrimonial Cases*, Milwaukee: The Bruce Publishing Co., 1938.

———, *Practical Manual for Marriage Cases*, Milwaukee: The Bruce Publishing Co., 1938.

Dolan, J., *Defensor Vinculi*, Canon Law Studies, n. 85, Washington: Catholic University of America, 1934.

Dorigny, *De l'Assistance Judiciaire et des Immunités Accordées aux Indigentes*, Paris, 1851.

Douxchamps, *De la Profession d'Avocat et d'Avoué*, Paris, 1904.

Droste, F.-Messmer, S. G., *Canonical Procedure in Disciplinary and Criminal Causes of Clerics*, New York, 1897.

Dubeux, *Etudes sur l'Institution de l'Avocat des Pauvres*, Paris, 1847.

Dugan, H. F., *The Judiciary Department of the Diocesan Curia*, Catholic University of America, Canon Law Studies, n. 26, Washington, D. C.: The Catholic University of America, 1925.

Durandus, Wm., *Speculum Juris*, 3 vols., Venetiis, 1577.

Eichmann, Ed., *Das Prozessrecht des Codex Iuris Canonici*, Paderborn: Ferdinand Schöningh, 1921.

Eisele, F., *Cognitor und Procurator*, Tübingen, 1881.

Enciclopedia Italiana, 36 vols., Milano-Roma, 1830-1933; Vols. V and XXVIII.

Engelmann, A., *A History of Continental Civil Procedure*, Translated by R. W. Millar, Boston: Little, Brown and Co., 1927; Vol. VII of *The Continental Legal Series*, 10 vols.

Esmein, A., *A History of Continental Criminal Procedure,* translated by J. Simpson, Boston: Little, Brown and Co., 1913; Vol. V of *The Continental Legal Series,* 10 vols.

Fagnanus, P., *Commentaria in Quinque Libros Decretalium,* 3 vols., Venetiis, 1729.

Ferraris, F. L., *Prompta Bibliotheca, Canonica, Juridica, Moralis, Theologica, Necnon Ascetica, Polemica, Rubricistica, Historica,* 9 vols., Romae, 1885-1889.

Ferreres, P. I., *Institutiones Canonicae,* 2 vols., 2 ed., Barcinone: E. Subirana, 1920.

Fournier, P., *Les Officialités au Moyen Age,* Paris, 1880.

Gallade, P., *Dissertatio Historico-Canonica de Advocatis Ecclesiasticis,* Heidelberg, 1768.

Glanvell, V. M., *Die Kanonessammlung des Kardinals Deusdedit:* I, Die Kanonessammlung Selbst, Paderborn, 1905.

Glynn, J. C., *The Promoter of Justice,* Canon Law Studies, n. 101, Washington, D. C.: The Catholic University of America, 1936.

Grandclaude, E., *Jus Canonicum iuxta Ordinem Decretalium,* 3 vols., Parisiis, 1883.

Hefele, C.-Leclercq, H., *Histoires des Conciles,* 10 vols. in 19, Paris: Letouzey et Ane, 1907-1938.

Heiner, F.-Wynen, A., *De Processu Criminali Ecclesiastico,* Ratisbon, 1912.

Hilling, N., *Procedure at the Roman Curia,* New York, 1907.

Hostiensis, Cardinalis (Henricus de Segusio), *Commentaria in Quinque Decretalium Libros,* 5 vols., Venetiis, 1581.

————, *Summa Aurea,* Lugduni, 1568.

Hohenlohe, C., *Das Prozessrecht des Codex Iuris Canonici,* Wien, 1921.

Holdsworth, W. S., *A History of English Law,* 9 vols., Boston: Little, Brown & Co., I, 4 ed., 1931, II, 3 ed., 1927.

Hughes, J. A., *Witnesses in Criminal Trials of Clerics,* The Catholic University of America, Canon Law Studies, n. 106, Washington: The Catholic University of America, 1937.

Jolowicz, H. F., *Historical Introduction to the Study of Roman Law,* Cambridge: Cambridge University Press, 1932.

Karlowa, O., *Romische Rechtsgeschichte,* 2 vols., Leipzig, 1885-1901.

Kealy, J. J., *The Introductory Libellus in Church Court Procedure,* Canon Law Studies, n. 108, Washington, D. C.: The Catholic University of America, 1937.

Labouré-Byrnes, *Procedure in the Diocesan Matrimonial Courts of First Instance,* New York: Benziger, 1928.

Lega, M., *Praelectiones in textum iuris canonici de iudiciis ecclesiasticis,* 4 vols., Romae, 1896-1901.

————, *De Iudiciis Ecclesiasticis Civilibus,* Vol. I, 3. ed., Romae, 1905.

Lega, M.-Bartoccetti, V., *Commentarius in Judicia Ecclesiastica juxta Codicem Juris Canonici,* Vol. I, Romae: Anonima Libraria Cattolica Italiana, 1938; Vol. II, 1939.

Lemieux, D. A., *The Sentence in Ecclesiastical Procedure,* Canon Law Studies, n. 87, Washington: The Catholic University of America, 1934.

Mackenzie, *Roman Law,* London, 1898.

Moriarty, E. J., *Oaths in Ecclesiastical Courts.* The Catholic University of America, Canon Law Studies, n. 110, Washington, D. C.: The Catholic University of America, 1937.

Muirhead, J., *Roman Law,* London, 1899.

Muñiz, T., *Procedimientos Eclesiásticos,* 2. ed., 3 vols., Sevilla: Lib. de Sobrino de Isquierdo, 1926.

Noval, J., *Commentarium Codicis Juris Canonici,* Lib. IV, *De Processibus,* Pars I, *De Iudiciis,* Augustae Taurinorum: Marietti, 1920.

Pacchioni, G., *Corso di Diritto Romano,* 2 vols., Torino, 1918.

Panormitanus (Nicolaus de Tudeschis), *Commentaria in Quinque Libros Decretalium,* 8 vols., Venetiis, 1588.

Peries, G., *Code de la Procédure Canonique dans les Causes Matrimoniales,* Paris, 1894.

————, *La Procédure Canonique Moderne dans les causes Disciplinaires et Criminelles,* Paris, 1898.

Pertile, A., *Storia del Diritto Italiano,* 2. ed., 6 vols., Torino, 1891-1902; Vol. VI, *Storia della Procedura.*

Pierantonelli, P., *Ordo Judiciarius in Praxim Traductus Matrimonii Causarum Speciminibus,* 2 vols., Romae, 1883.

Pirhing, E., *Jus Canonicum in Quinque Libros Decretalium Distributum,* 5 vols., Dilingae, 1674-1678.

Pollock-Maitland, *History of the English Law,* 2 vols., Cambridge, 1895.

Reiffenstuel, A., *Ius Canonicum Universum,* 6 vols., Romae, 1831-1834.

Roberti, F., *De Processibus,* 2 vols., Romae: Apud Aedes Facultatis Juridicae ad S. Apollinaris, Romae, 1926.

Roby, H. J., *An Introduction to the Study of Justinian's Digest,* Cambridge: Cambridge University Press, 1886.

————, *Roman Private Law,* 2 vols., Cambridge: Cambridge University Press, 1902.

Salvioli, G., *Storia del Diritto Italiano,* Torino: Unione Tipografico Editrice Torinese, 1930.

————, *Storia della Procedura Civile e Criminale,* Milano: Hoeppli, 1925.

Scialoja, V., *Studi Giuridici,* Vol. I, *Diritto Romano,* Roma, 1933.

Schäfer, P. T., *De Religiosis,* Munster: Aschendorff, 1931.

Schmalzgrueber, F., *Ius Ecclesiasticum Universum,* 12 vols., Romae, 1843-1845.

Schmidt, A., *Thesaurus Juris Ecclesiastici,* 7 vols., Heidelberg, Bamberg, Wirceburg, 1772-1779.

Schroeder, H. J., *Disciplinary Decrees of the General Councils,* St. Louis: Herder, 1937.

Schulte, J. F., *Die Geschichte der Quellen und Literatur des Canonischen Rechts von Gratian bis auf die Gegenwart*, 3 vols., Stuttgart, 1875-1880.

Sherman, C. P., *Roman Law in the Modern World*, 2. ed., 3 vols., New York: Baker, Voorhis & Co., 1924.

Smith, S. B., *Elements of Ecclesiastical Law*, 3 vols., Vol. II, *Ecclesiastical Trials*, 5. ed., New York, 1887.

————, *New Procedure in Criminal and Disciplinary Causes of Ecclesiastics in the United States*. 3. ed., New York, 1898.

Sohm, R., *The Institutes of Roman Law*, translated by James C. Ledlie. 3. ed., Oxford: Clarendon Press, 1926.

Stephanus, M., *De Officio Judicis*, Francofurti, 1625.

Thaner, F., *Anselmi Collectio Canonum una cum Collectione Minore*, Fasciculus I et II, Oeniponte: Librarie Academicae Wagnerianae, 1906, 1915.

Thomassinus, L., *Vetus et Nova Ecclesiae Disciplina Circa Beneficia Et Beneficiarios*, 9 vols., Magontiaci, 1787.

Torre, J., *Epitome Instructionis Matrimonialis*, Neapoli: M. D'Auria, 1936.

Van Hove, A., *Prolegomena ad Codicem Iuris Canonici*, Commentarium Lovaniense in Codicem Iuris Canonici, Vol. I, Tom. I, Mechliniae et Romae: Dessain, 1928.

Vermeersch, A.-Creusen, J., *Epitome Juris Canonici*, 3 vols., Tom. III, Mechliniae-Romae: 1936.

Villien, A.-Magnen, E., *Dictionnaire de Droit Canonique*, Vol. I, Paris, 1924.

Wahrmund, L., *Quellen zur Geschichte des Romisch-Kanonischen Processes im Mittelalter*, 5 vols., Innsbruck: Universitatsverlag Wagner, 1905-1925; Heidelberg: C. Winters Universitats-Buchhandlung, 1931.

Wanenmacher, F., *Canonical Evidence in Marriage Cases*, Philadelphia: The Dolphin Press, 1935.

Wenger, L., *Institutionen des Romischen Zivilprozessrechts*, Munchen: Verlag der Hochschulbuchhandlung Max Hueber, 1925.

Wernz, F. X., *Ius Decretalium*, 6 vols., 2. ed., Romae et Prati, 1906-1913.

Wernz, F. X.-Vidal, P., *Ius Canonicum*, 7 Tomes in 9 vols., Romae: Apud Aedes Universitatis Gregorianae, 1925-1938; Tom. VI, *De Processibus*, 1928.

Wirbel, C., *Le Cognitor*, Paris, 1911.

Wunderlich, A., *Anecdota Quae ad Processum Civilem Spectant*, Göttingen, 1841.

PERIODICALS

Analecta Iuris Pontificii, 28 vols., Romae, 1852-1868, Paris, 1869-1891.

Apollinaris, Romae, 1928 —

Archiv für katholisches Kirchenrecht, Innsbruck, 1857-1861, Mainz, 1862 —

Ateneum Kaplanskie, Wloclawek, 1914 —

Ephemerides Theologicae Lovaniensis, Louvain, 1924 —

Homiletic and Pastoral Review, The, New York, 1900 —

Il Diritto Ecclesiastico, Roma, 1890 —

Il Monitore Ecclesiastico, Roma, 1876 —

Irish Ecclesiastical Record, The, Dublin, 1864 —
Ius Pontificium, Romae, 1921 —
Le Canoniste, Paris, 1878 —
Perfice Munus, Torino, 1926 —
Periodica de Re Canonica et Morali, Bruges, 1905 —

ARTICLES

Bernardini, C., "Normae S. R. Rotae" — *Apollinaris,* VII (1934), 429-478.

———, "Adnotationes ad Acta Apostolicae Sedis": Instr. S. C. S., 15 Aug., 1936 — *Apollinaris,* IX (1936), 521-585.

Bossowski, F., "Quomodo usu forensi audientiae episcopalis suadente nonnulla praecepta ad instar iuris graeci, hebraici, etc., in iure romano recepta sint" — *Acta Congressus Iuridici Internationalis,* Romae: apud Aedes S. Apoll., I (1935), 359-410.

Ciprotti, P., "De Advocatis et Procuratoribus in Causis de Nullitate Matrimonii" — *Apollinaris,* X (1937), 467-469.

———, "De Communicatione Defensionum" — *Apollinaris,* IX (1936), 309-310.

Couly, A., "L'Officialité: Procureurs et Avocats" — *Le Canoniste,* XLVII (1925), 501-516.

———, "L'Officialité: Les Parties en Cause" — *Le Canoniste,* XLVIII (1926), 347-357, 381-391.

D'Angelo, S., "An a denegato gratuito patrocinio dari possit recursus ad Supremum Sign. Apost. Tribunal" — *Apollinaris,* II (1929), 514-516.

Fiamingo, R., "I Tribunali della S. Rota e della Segnatura Apostolica" — *Diritto Ecclesiastico,* XLIII (1932), 345-361.

Grabowski, I., "Adwokatura w Ustawodawstwie Koscielnem" — *Ateneum Kaplanskie,* XXXIII (1934), 249-262; XXXIV (1934), 147-164; XXXV (1935), 238-262.

Hanssens, A., "De Sanctione Nullitatis in Processu Canonico" — *Apollinaris,* XI (1938), 71-109, 215-263, 381-403; XII (1939), 198-251.

Hilling, N., "Die Heranziehung der Advokaten zu den Kirchlichen Prozessen" — *Archiv für katholisches Kirchenrecht,* CIII (1923), 132-136.

Lardone, F. G., "Il Diritto Romano e I Concilii" — *Acta Congressus Iuridici Internationalis,* Roma, II (1935), 103-122.

Pugliese, A., "Avvocati e Procuratori nelle Cause di Nullità di Matrimonio Presso I Tribunali Ecclesiastici" — *Rivista del Diritto Matrimoniale Italiano,* IV (1937), 606-618.

Riccobono, S., "Lineamenti della Dottrina della Rappresentanza Diretta in Diritto Romano" — *Annali del Seminario Giuridico,* Cortona, XIV (1930) 389-427.

Roberti, F., "Avvocati Rotali e Curie Minori" — *Il Monitore Ecclesiastico,* XLVII (1936), 54-56.

———, "De Condicione Processuali Promotoris Iustitiae, Defensoris Vinculi, et Coniugum in Causis Matrimonialibus" — *Apollinaris,* XI (1938), 575-584.

———, "Procuratorum et Advocatorum Proventus Pro Causis Actis Coram Tribunali S. R. Rotae" — *Apollinaris,* XII (1939), 460-470.

Roberti, M., "Cristianesimo e Collezione Giustinianee" — *Cristianesimo e Diritto Romano,* Milano (1935), 1-64.

Steinwenter, A., "Der Einfluss des Romischen Rechtes Auf Den Antiken Kanonischen Prozess" — *Atti del Congresso Internazionale di Diritto Romano,* Bologna, I (1934), 225-241.

Toso, A., "An Notarii et Advocati Munera Incompatibilia Sint in Causis Ecclesiasticis" — *Ius Pontificium,* XVIII (1938), 81-84.

Woywood, S., "How Legal Ecclesiastical Persons Are to be Represented in Court" — *The Homiletic and Pastoral Review,* XXXI (1930-1931), 503-511.

———, "Procurators, Advocates and Exceptions" — *The Homiletic and Pastoral Review,* XXXI (1930-1931), 607-614.

———, "Gratuitous Legal Service and Reduction of Legal Expenditures" — *The Homiletic and Pastoral Review,* XXXIII (1932-1933), 490-500.

BIOGRAPHICAL NOTE

James J. Hogan was born in Philadelphia, Pa., October 17, 1911. After graduating from the Camden (N. J.) Catholic High School he entered St. Charles' Preparatory Seminary, Catonsville, Md. Upon completion of the philosophy course in St. Mary's Seminary, Baltimore, from which he received an A. B., he was enrolled in the North American College, Rome. Priestly ordination was conferred on December 8, 1937. From the Gregorian University he received an S. T. L. Having entered the School of Canon Law at the Catholic University of America in the fall of 1938, he was awarded the J. C. B. in 1939 and the J. C. L. in 1940.

ALPHABETICAL INDEX